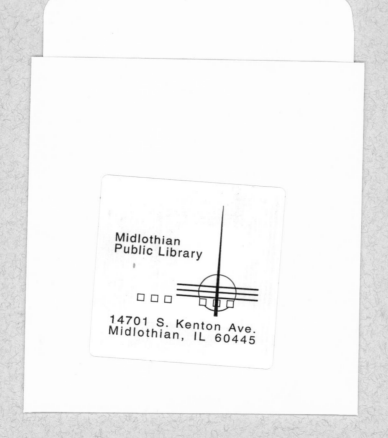

Chicago
CENTER FOR ENTERPRISE

CONTRIBUTING EDITORS
BARBARA MARINACCI AND CAROL V. DAVIS

PICTURE EDITOR
TERI DAVIS GREENBERG

SPONSORED BY THE CHICAGO ASSOCIATION OF COMMERCE AND INDUSTRY

WINDSOR PUBLICATIONS, INC.
WOODLAND HILLS, CALIFORNIA

Chicago

CENTER FOR ENTERPRISE

AN ILLUSTRATED HISTORY
BY KENAN HEISE AND MICHAEL EDGERTON
INTRODUCTION BY EMMETT DEDMON

VOLUME I: THE 19TH CENTURY

Previous page: In 1857 Chicago
lithographer Edward Mendel
depicted an entire block of Lake
Street between Clark and LaSalle as
the grade was being raised four feet.
It was later raised three additional
feet. Prior to raising the grade,
fashionable Lake Street was famous
for its mud. Courtesy, Chicago
Historical Society

Slipcase Illustration: *Boul Mich by the
Elevated Lines* by Navigato/Poster/
1929. Courtesy, Chicago Historical
Society

Windsor Publications
History Books Division
Publisher: John M. Phillips
Editorial Director: Lissa Sanders
Administrative Coordinator: Katherine Cooper
Senior Picture Editor: Teri Davis Greenberg
Senior Corporate History Editor: Karen Story
Production Manager: James Burke
Art Director: Alexander D'Anca
Art Production Manager: Dee Cooper
Composition Manager: E. Beryl Myers

Staff for *Chicago: Center for Enterprise*
Editor: F. Jill Charboneau
Editorial Assistants:
    Todd Ackerman, Susan Block
    Phyllis Gray, Karen Holroyd,
    Mary Mohr, Susan Wells
Compositors:
    Shannon Mellies, Barbara Neiman
Proofreaders:
    Clareen Arnold, Doris Richter Malkin
Designer: Alexander D'Anca
Layout Artist: Cheryl Mendenhall
Production Artists:
    Beth Bowman, Ellen Hazeltine,
    Shannon Strull

First Edition

Library of Congress Cataloging in Publication Data
Heise, Kenan
    Chicago, center for enterprise.
    Bibliography: p. 556
    Includes index.
    Contents: v. 1. The 19th century—v.2. The 20th
century.
    1. Chicago (Ill.)—History. 2. Chicago (Ill.)—
Description. 3. Chicago (Ill.)—Industries.
I. Edgerton,Michael, 1949-   . II. Title.
F548.3.H93 1982   977.3'11   82-50771
ISBN 0-89781-041-4 (set)

CONTENTS

Jevne and Almini, Chicago's Currier and Ives, attempted to portray a hustling, bustling city in the mid-1860s. This scene depicting the corner of Clark and South Water is typical of their style. Note the clean streets and orderly traffic. Courtesy, Chicago Historical Society

Chicago's reputation has many facets, but there is one which has gone unchallenged from the day the first fur trader beached his canoe at the mouth of the Chicago River: Chicago is a good place to do business.

Chicago: Center For Enterprise reflects the fact that a business history is a most appropriate way to tell the story of Chicago. The city's business development has been at the core of its greatness. The honored names in the history of Chicago are the businessmen who built strong commercial enterprises such as Marshall Field, Philip Armour, Gustavus Swift, Cyrus McCormick, Richard Sears, and A. Montgomery Ward. All were giants in commerce as well as builders of their city.

In these two volumes Kenan Heise and Michael Edgerton carry this tradition down to the present day and give recognition to the commercial enterprises that contribute to the vitality and heartbeat of Chicago. The dimensions of this history, as the authors have written it, are broad. Their narrative style is suited to the pace of a city whose rate of growth has been the fastest of any American city.

A look back across the eons of prehistory focuses on the geological forces that created the waterways, the rich farmlands, and the natural resources that have played a pivotal role in the creation of Chicago. "Trade begot Chicago" begins the story of the early explorers, traders and trappers whose barter represented Chicago's first commercial exchange. From these crude beginnings, the authors carry the reader in a spirited fashion through a decade-by-decade documentation of the growth of a city and the business enterprises it spawned.

By 1850 the leaders of Chicago were firm in their belief that "Chicago would be an American hub city—the center of Midwestern commerce and, ultimately, of the whole continent." This prophecy was to be quickly fulfilled. In the very next decade, Chicago evolved from a minor city of small industries and modest commerce into a major trade and manufacturing center. "Zestful and youthful Chicago gained national fame for its astoundingly successful commercialism," they tell us, and "people everywhere wanted its formula."

By the end of the Civil War, Chicago was challenging Pittsburgh as a major iron- and steel-making center. Its stockyards were the largest in the nation and world-famous for their efficiency. Yet the decade of the 1870s was hardly underway when Chicago was devastated by the Great Fire of 1871. Chicago's reaction to the Fire, which destroyed the entire central business district of the city, has never been better described than by Joseph Medill in an editorial which appeared in *The Chicago Tribune* the following day: "All is not lost. Though four hundred million dollars worth of property has been destroyed, Chicago still exists ... . We have lost money, but we have saved life, health, vigor and industry ... . Let the watchword henceforth be: Chicago Shall Rise Again."

After the Fire land value in the central business area or "Loop" grew geometrically; owners sought out architects to maximize the number of offices that could be erected on their piece of land. The result—the world's first skyscraper, the Home Insurance Building, was designed by LeBaron Jenney in 1884. The Chicago School of Architecture, with its distinctive styling, was quickly recognized as the most innovative in the world. By the 1890s Chicago was ready to celebrate and proclaim its success to the world. The occasion was the World's Columbian Exposition, which Chicago wrested away from Eastern competitors to celebrate the 400th anniversary of the discovery of America by Christopher Columbus. "The White City," as the classic buildings of the Fair were known, established Chicago as a cosmopolitan center with a world view and no longer a rugged, unfinished frontier town.

The mood of Chicago as the 20th Century began was expressed by her architects who played, as they had after the Great Fire, a leading role in the shaping of this new Chicago. It was an architect, Daniel Burnham, designer of the "Grand Plan for Chicago," who articulated as well as anyone has done the essential genius of Chicago: "The plan frankly takes into consideration the fact that the American city, and Chicago pre-eminently, is a center of industry and traffic."

For two decades there seemed to be no limit to the ebullience of Chicago business. World War I only accelerated the growth of companies supplying material for the war effort. Chicago believed like the rest of America that there was no limit to material prosperity, and like America, Chicago abruptly found itself facing an uncertain future with the crash in 1929. The "I Will" spirit, which had been born in the Columbian Exposition of 1893, came to the fore, however, as the city went stolidly ahead.

With the end of World War II, transportation again became the dominant theme in Chicago's expansion and business activities. In the earlier days it had been shipping on the Great Lakes waterways, railroads, and trucking. In the 1950s with the opening of O'Hare airport, Chicago made itself the aviation center not only of the United States but of the world.

Meanwhile, the city was having problems. The expressways of which it was so proud only expedited the flight of citizens to the suburbs. The tax base was eroding. But on April 5, 1955, the voters chose Richard Joseph Daley to be their mayor and a new era in cooperation between the business community and the politicians at City Hall had begun. Under Daley Chicago became known as "The City That Works" as a series of new skyscrapers changed the profile of the city's skylines and revitalized the downtown area.

As this history rightfully points out: "The years of Chicago's easy growth were over. The need for stewardship by both the business community and the government was greater and adjustments to changes difficult." Heise and Edgerton conclude, however, that "the strengths of Chicago are its old strengths. In the past its geography, its skilled people, its vast commercial and industrial structure,

its efficient and all-encompassing transportation network have all been repeatedly surprised and challenged by change. Now they are prepared to direct it, to keep Chicago the center for enterprise."

In the true spirit of enterprise this book has been largely underwritten by the 100 or so companies whose histories appear in these volumes. These profiles and sketches of the Chicago businesses of today provide the base for the city's optimism. These companies have provided not only a history which is very readable today but also a resource document for years to come.

In 1884-1886, A.T. Andreas published his classic three-volume *History of Chicago*. It included biographies of leading Chicago businessmen as well as descriptions of the leading cultural, educational and other institutions in the city. *Chicago: Center for Enterprise* is the first publication of comparable scope to appear since that time.

These volumes are a worthy addition to the library of anyone with an interest in Chicago and in particular of the great enterprises which have led to its growth as one of the world's great cities.

Emmett Dedmon

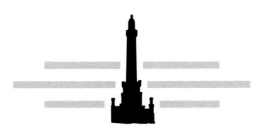

CHAPTER ONE

THE FIRST 500 MILLION YEARS

A PROLOGUE

Facing page: Over 250 million years ago a great Silurian sea rose and covered the swampy shoreline 50 miles south of Chicago. In the process trees, ferns, and other nonflowering plants that stood 80 feet tall were deprived of air and subjected to great pressures. The decaying flora were thereby transformed into bituminous coal deposits. This coal was to later provide immeasurable benefit to Chicago's growth. Painting by Charles R. Knight. Copyright Field Museum of Natural History

Between 1830 and 1900—one human lifetime—Chicago's population exploded from 50 people to almost 2 million. A town—founded on a swamp fronted by a lake—evolved into a major center of commerce on the North American continent.

Chicago grew so quickly and so distinctively that it affected the rest of the nation and the world beyond it. This rapid and dramatic transformation was made possible by people. People of enterprising spirit propelled by visions of what might be done at this place. Motivated not only by personal ambitions but also by the larger needs and opportunities of American society, such people came by the thousands, generation after generation, to take part in the building of Chicago.

Chicago's rapid commercial and industrial development began in long-gone epochs. The reasons for the city's prosperity are literally buried in the earth. With the thousands of books and articles written about the city's history, few pondered Chicago's early geological and anthropological history and sought the key to the city's existence.

Chicago is in the middle of a geologic period rather than at the end. Even land features unaffected by civilization's intrusion are still changing due to such natural forces as lake erosion. The history of the land on which the city was built begins more than 500 million years ago, when the great central plains of the United States were formed. A deep tropical sea extended across the northern part of what is now the United States; the deepest part of the sea is now Lake Superior. Stretching south was a large body of water that geologists refer to as Michigan Bay. These geographic forms were the first vestiges of the Great Lakes.

The Chicago region was under a great sea for so long that thousands of generations of shelled sea animals lived and died there. As time passed, their almost indestructible exoskeletons accumulated on the sea floor, to form limestone beds hundreds of feet thick. These quarries would be integral to Chicago's growth millions of years later. The cement-hard rocks that later were placed along Lake Michigan to stop the tidal erosion of the modern city likewise contained these seashell fossils. This limestone bedrock firmly supports the city's cumulative weight.

Chicago's success as a center for commerce, industry, and transportation began with the geological forces that created a pivotal site with access to major waterways, and close to the richest of land and vital limestone, coal, iron, copper, and lead deposits. The resources created and stored up over a period beginning hundreds of millions of years ago have been conveniently exploited in the course of constructing the metropolis.

The bituminous coal deposits formed by decaying prehistoric trees and plants were near the surface where they could eventually be stripmined. In the late 19th century this accessible coal combined with a new source of iron ore through an efficient transportation system, to put Chicago at the forefront of America's industrialization which depended on the production of iron and steel machinery.

The great explosion of Chicago's population starting in the 1870s occurred almost simultaneously with the opening of the Lake Superior iron fields. In 1860 the United States produced very little iron. The vast iron fields of northern Minnesota and the Upper Peninsula of Michigan were opened in 1884, and within 40 years the United States was producing half the world's iron. Chicago was a hub of this iron and steel making. Its large firms grew swiftly along the southern rim of Lake Michigan, where iron ore could be shipped in by scows and freighters, while coal was easily transported by canal and railroad.

Another vital fossil-fuel source was located in southern Illinois and Indiana when rich petroleum beds were discovered in the 1860s. These beds were formed when thick deposits of plant and animal remains decomposed by bacteria were compressed beneath layers of rock and water, and converted slowly through the millenia into crude oil and natural gas.

At first the natural gas coming from early oil wells was more highly prized than the crude oil itself, which was used mainly as pitch or asphalt, or processed into kerosene and lubricating or medicinal oils. Intensive research later improved refining techniques so as to use as much of the crude oil as possible. And in the meantime, new technologies developed around these products, the most notable ones, of course, being gasoline and diesel fuel for internal-combustion engines, which transformed many aspects of Chicago's transportation as well as its cityscape. In 1889 Standard Oil Company located a major refinery on Lake Michigan, at the town of Whiting, Indiana, close to Chicago. Inevita-

The limestone found in quarries that contributed to Chicago's commercial development formed from the accumulation of the exoskeletons of Niagaran fauna. These marine creatures included shelled animals related to the squid and octopus called cephalopods (previous page); bivalve-shelled animals called brachiopods (facing page, top); extinct animals related to the crab, crayfish, lobster, and shrimp called trilobites (facing page, middle); and corals (facing page, bottom). From Bretz, *Geology of the Chicago Region,* 1939, 1953

bly, the growing industrial activity spread westward across the Illinois border, to become a significant factor in Chicago's economy.

The end of the swamps-and-dinosaurs era was followed by the recent Pleistocene epoch during which time four major massive ice sheets pushed gradually yet powerfully, one after the other, across the Chicago area, sculpting its landscape and enriching it immeasurably. The last of the glaciers, the Wisconsin, which began receding about 13,500 years ago, had the greatest impact on the Chicago area. The Wisconsin seized much of Canada's best top soil and deposited it in the Mississippi River Valley, thereby creating some of the richest farm land in the world. During this time the Great Lakes as we now know them were formed. The overflowing lakes—almost 70 feet higher than now—drained into the ocean eastward through the St. Lawrence River passage, and also across what is now the state of New York toward the Hudson River—where silt deposits helped to form Manhattan Island. Thousands of years later, men would recarve the Mohawk Pass across western New York as a waterway and call it the Erie Canal. Lake Chicago—Lake Michigan's geologic name—had a western outlet at Summit, Illinois, only a few miles west of Chicago—the intersection now of the Stevenson Expressway and Harlem Avenue. There lake water cascaded southwest toward the Mississippi River, mainly using channels that would become the Des Plaines and Illinois rivers.

At Chicago's back door, the Wisconsin Glacier had created the Valparaiso Moraine, a high, crescent-shaped ridge that separates Lake Michigan and the rivers that drain into it from the Mississippi River Valley and its tributaries, such as the Des Plaines and Illinois rivers. Located about a dozen miles west and south of the lake, the moraine averages 15 miles in width and from 100 to 500 feet in height above Lake Michigan. (The eastern rim of the Valparaiso Moraine today is followed by the Tri-State Tollway.) Once the Great Lakes' water level fell to about its present height, the moraine determined the function of the Chicago River as one of the eastward-flowing, watershed outlets into Lake Michigan.

The moraine was the divide that had to be crossed by many generations of Indians and then by the white man when traveling the waterways that united east and west. Present-day Summit was the site of a canoe portage for Indians and French fur traders, and through this point canals were later cut so that Chicago could ship into and out of the Mississippi Valley. Eventually even the Chicago River system would be changed to send its sewage flow westward rather than into Lake Michigan—one of many man-made alterations of the landscape.

The Wisconsin Glacier also put Lake Michigan at Chicago's doorstep. At one point, the lake was little more than a river running through a gently sloping valley, but gradually the glacier dug a deep gorge. As the glacier melted, the

GLACIAL GEOLOGY
OF
CHICAGO
AND VICINITY
BY
J HARLEN BRETZ

SCALE

LEGEND

Beach deposits

Glacial lake bottom

Glacial river bottom

Valley train deposit

Dune sand

Lake Border moraines

Lake Border ground moraines

Tinley moraine

Tinley ground moraine

Valparaiso moraine

Valparaiso ground moraine

Above: The story of a city does not start with its discovery; it begins, rather, with the formation of the land and the appearance of the first forms of life. Chicago's story is no exception. The city's existence and successful development are based on resources that took hundreds of millions of years to accumulate. Painting by Charles R. Knight. Copyright Field Museum of Natural History

Left: Scientific evidence records the presence of glacial ice and water in the Chicago region. The changes to the landscape wrought by glaciation were far greater than all subsequent changes by agents and processes now at work. From Bretz, *Geology of the Chicago Region,* 1939, 1953

Facing page: Ten thousand years ago mastodons and woolly mammoths coexisted with man as evidenced by the fact that the skeletons of these animals have been found with spear wounds. Painting by Charles R. Knight. Copyright Field Museum of Natural History

waters filled and then overflowed the gorge. Lake Michigan was formerly more extensive, covering the area that is now the city. Only a few land formations, such as Blue Island and Stoney Island, were tall enough to project above the lake. Hundreds of years later, however, the lake receded drastically. For a while, it was 50 miles away from the site where Chicago now stands. Later still, heavy rains filled Lake Michigan to its present level.

The first humans probably came to Chicago about 10,000 years ago. Scientific evidence indicates that they hunted mastodons on the skirt of the Wisconsin Glacier. Archaeologists have uncovered signs of 10,000-year-old habitations along the Illinois and Mississippi rivers, at sites now known as Cahokia and Koster, with more recent ones at the Dixon Mounds.

The business of the local Indians was not unlike that of later "civilized" Chicago residents. The tribes were composed of hunters and farmers, traders and builders, fishermen, and transporters. One of Chicago's great industries, meatpacking, which enabled meat to be prepared and shipped to far-flung places, was anticipated by the Indians who long before had learned how to preserve buffalo meat and fowl by drying it and by soaking it in brine. They grew maize, beans, squash, and tobacco. They hunted fish by spearing them through holes cut in the ice during the winter and using nets when the water flowed free. Beneath their wigwams, they kept their earthen larders well-stocked with food gathered and prepared in summer and autumn, so that they largely devoted their winters to ease and keeping warm. Before white men came to the region, the Indians probably lived for the most part in peace. Their culture, passed on from generation to generation, survived a remarkably long time.

The first Indians whom the French missionaries and explorers met in the Chicago area in the late 17th century were the Iliniwek (meaning "men" or "the people"). The French changed the pronunciation of that phonetically spelled name to "Illinois." A hardy people, they were a confederation of various interrelated tribes: the Cahokia, Kaskaskia, Michigamea, Moingwena, Peoria, and Namaroa. The Illinois were allied, especially in language, with the Miami.

These Midwestern Indians were not directly descended from the earlier pre-Columbian Indians inhabiting the area. Their languages had Algonquin roots, indicating a connection with tribes from the Eastern Woodlands in general and the New York region in particular—supporting the theory that many tribes had been driven westward as Europeans began colonizing the East Coast in the early 1600s. Many tribes were thrown into turmoil by the immigration of white settlers, whose determined land seizure was aided by their firearms.

The white invaders, whether French, British, or Dutch, made clever use of the Indians' tribal territorial disputes, ancestral rivalries, and competition over the spoils of the growing fur trade. Unfortunately amongst themselves the

About 500 years ago a Chicago artisan carved this sad face on a marine shell. This emotional portrayal, found on a chest of skeletal remains, was uncovered at the Anker site just south of Chicago. The mask belongs to David Pedric of Dolton, Illinois. Courtesy, Field Museum of Natural History

Facing page, top: Postholes for a house similar to the one portrayed in this diorama entitled "Winter Village of the Indians of the Chicago Region" were found at the Anker archaeological site along the Little Calumet River. Between A.D. 1400 and 1500 the site was the center of a village. Artifacts, including copper items from northern Michigan, face pipes from the East, and trade beads and other objects from throughout the Mississippi Valley demonstrate that the village must have been a trade center. Courtesy, Field Museum of Natural History

Bottom: Starved Rock (pictured here) was the scene of the annihilation of the Illinois Indians by the Miamis and Potawatomis in 1769 in retaliation for the assassination of Pontiac. From Andreas, *History of Chicago*, 1884

Native American groups too often chose to use the warclub rather than the peacepipe when caught up in the Europeans' complex intrigues.

In 1769, just prior to the Revolutionary War, a member of the Illinois tribe assassinated the great Ottawa chief, Pontiac. The Ottawa and their confederates—angered by this and Illinois conspiracies—allied to annihilate the Illinois. They virtually succeeded, creating bloody battlegrounds along the Calumet and Illinois rivers, particularly at Starved Rock. A few Illinois escaped to St. Louis to live as inconspicuously as possible among other tribes.

The tribes that succeeded the Illinois and the Miami (who moved on to the Wabash area in Indiana) in the Chicago environs were the closely knit tribes of the Potawatomi, Chippewa, Ottawa, and Kickapoo. The Potawatomi were known as the "people of the fire," because they welcomed visitors to their communal campfires. They also saw themselves as "the people of the calumet," a religious symbol of peace and alliance.

The French and British had employed Indian allies in their perpetual wars over controlling the fur trading business as well as in their disputes over the national ownership of the North American wilderness. Neither group as yet had designs for residency on the southwest shore of Lake Michigan. But when permanent settlers arrived they needed the land that Indians had occupied for thousands of years.

Most of northern Illinois was once tall-grass prairie, with roots often hundreds of years old. When fires swept across the plains, as they did from time to time, deeply-rooted grasses survived, but the trees and weeds with shorter roots did not. The Indians had deep roots. They survived in the Midwest probably because they had absorbed the long heritage of geological peace in the region and had also husbanded its abundant and beneficent natural resources. The more dominant-appearing urban features that have sprung up from the white civilization displacing the Indian culture have certainly proven less attuned to nature—and may prove less durable.

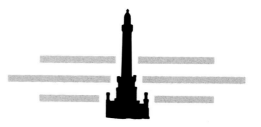

CHAPTER TWO

THE CROSSING PLACE

1763 TO 1829

Often relying on Indians to guide them, French fur traders from Canada would traverse the interior of North America in birch bark canoes using the Great Lakes as their primary transportation system. From Kirkland, *The Story of Chicago,* 1892

Trade begot Chicago. In the beginning, it was the fur trade. The French—who had first discovered the great profits possible in fur trading in North America—sent out teams of explorers primarily to seek new sources for furs. Year by year, they penetrated deeper into the interior of the continent, using the Great Lakes as their primary transportation system from the capital at Montreal. Often Jesuit missionaries accompanied them, to help with the journal keeping, mapping, and report making, while attempting to convert heathen souls to their form of Christianity.

The first European explorers known to have visited the present site of Chicago were Louis Jolliet and Père (Father) Jacques Marquette. In 1673 they traveled southwest from Green Bay through what is now Wisconsin, to the Mississippi River. They were searching for a waterway that supposedly emptied into the Pacific—the mythical "Northwest Passage" route to the Orient's riches. Finally realizing that the great Mississippi which they had discovered rolled ever southward, the explorers—impressed with what they had seen yet disappointed in having failed to achieve their goal—returned to the northeast via the Illinois and Des Plaines rivers, using the Chicago portage to Lake Michigan. In his report to the French governor, Jolliet enthusiastically proposed the possibility of a canal at Chicago to link the lake and the Mississippi Valley.

Father Marquette, excited with the prospect of saving Indian souls, returned to the Illinois River later and spent the winter of 1674-1675 in the Chicago area. The intrepid missionary, famished and ill (he was soon to die), was tended by the first white businessman on record at the site—French fur trader Pierre Moreau, nicknamed Taupine or "The Mole." (Some waggish authors have suggested that because he sold contraband alcohol to the Indians, he might be considered Chicago's first bootlegger.)

In 1682 the ambitious and visionary Rene Robert Cavelier, Sieur de la Salle, passed through this same area to complete Jolliet and Marquette's journey on

Facing page, top: In 1673 Louis Jolliet and Père Jacques Marquette, along with voyageurs, traveled down the Wisconsin and Mississippi rivers and back up the Illinois and Chicago rivers. They were most probably the first non-Indians to visit the site of Chicago. Shown here is a rather romanticized depiction of Jolliet and Marquette being welcomed by the Illinois upon their arrival. It is doubtful that the men traversed the wilderness in clothing such as that in the illustration. From Greely, *Men of Achievement: Explorers and Travellers,* 1894

Bottom left: One year after he first traveled to the Illinois River, Father Marquette sent his Jesuit superior a copy of his journal and a map of the Midwest (a detail of which is redrawn here) showing De la Conception River (the Mississippi) and Lac des Ilinois (Lake Michigan). In his journal Marquette commented on the Mississippi and referred to the Chicago portage: "The river upon which we sailed was wide, deep, and placid for sixty-five leagues, and navigable most all the year round. There is a portage of only half a league into the Lake of the Illinois." From Hurlbut, *Chicago Antiquities,* 1881

Bottom Right: While en route to the mouth of the Mississippi, René Robert Cavelier de La Salle passed through Illinois River country. Claiming the "Father of Waters" for France in 1682, he built a fort on the Illinois River and sent a party of men to establish another fortification at the mouth of the Chicago River. In a report he referred to the portage area near Lake Michigan as "Checagou." From Cirker, *Dictionary of American Portraits,* 1967

the Mississippi, taking it down to the Gulf. He and his lieutenant, Henri de Tonti, saw the area as useful in developing a network of forts in the American heartland that would combine fur trading depots with military outposts, but La Salle's scheme ended with his death in 1687.

La Salle had written a report referring to the portage spot near Lake Michigan as "Checagou," and this name with its variant spellings, eventually to end up as Chicago, often appeared on maps and documents. But the meaning of the word itself has elicited controversy among scholars. Researchers have thoroughly investigated the origin of the name long used for both the river and the region where it enters Lake Michigan. Dominant opinion holds that the word meant "wild onion" or "garlic." Occasionally, "skunk" has been suggested as an alternative. However, Chicagoans with a need for an inspirational definition would prefer "powerful" or "great."

For a few years—1696 to 1700—what had been Father Marquette's temporary parish at the mouth of the Chicago River was occupied by two Jesuit priests. Pierre Pinet and Julian Binnoteau constructed the log-and-bark Mission of the Guardian Angel, but were then ordered to leave the area by the French governor.

Because of fierce rivalries between government-licensed and independent fur traders among the French, as well as ongoing wars among Indian tribes frequently backed by French or British allegiances and weaponry, the area around the southern end of Lake Michigan made dangerous hunting grounds in the 18th century for white fur trappers. The entrepreneurs instead arranged to secure the coveted pelts through Indian trappers and traders.

For almost a century after the closing of the Jesuits' mission the Chicago area saw few white men. The fur activity at regular trading posts began to increase in the late 1770s and early 1780s. This brought to Chicago the man often cited as the city's first settler, Jean Baptiste Point du Sable, who reportedly had a French father and a black mother. A cultivated man, he used his wealth and energy to establish a home on the north side of the Chicago River that seemed more plantation than backwoods outpost.

The Chicago portage was crucial to the Illinois fur trade engaged in by Du Sable. The voyageurs and their flat, wide bateaux—capable of carrying three tons of furs and sometimes used as sledges to be pulled through low water or even mud—used the portage in the fall to move to their winter trapping grounds. They waited until the waters rose in spring to bring their pelts back through it.

Today a sign along Harlem Avenue just north of the Stevenson Expressway commemorates the Chicago portage. The impression is often given that this crossing place was a few miles of dry land between the Des Plaines and Chicago rivers. But historians Robert Knight and Lucius Zeuch maintain that it was entirely navigable for a short time—about 48 days—each year. The Des Plaines river flows southwest to the Illinois river, but at that time in spring it also used a small stream (Portage Creek) to flood eastward toward Lake Michigan, emptying into a five-mile-long body of water unaffectionately but aptly known as Mud Lake, which extended from what is now Harlem to Kedzie Avenue.

Mud Lake had a north-and-south channel, which was more or less navigable for most of the year. (Fur trader Gurdon S. Hubbard said that in his first encounter with it he and his companions spent all day chest-high in mud and bloodsuckers, pushing their canoes through it.) When the water was high, Mud Lake could accommodate a boat drawing 15 inches of water. From the east end of Mud Lake flowed a small creek that was a tributary of the Chicago River. Use of this creek eventually deepened its channel, and it was later regarded as an extension of the South Branch of the Chicago River. Eventually there was a trail alongside Mud Lake for traders' convenience in carrying canoes and supplies. Miserable and limited as it might have been, this Chicago portage served as the "gate" to the West—a gate forced open wider and wider by trade.

The fur trading business in North America was highly organized, carefully administered, and much fought over because of its profits. Although the French had originated it, the English-owned Hudson's Bay Company took control after the French and Indian War gave Great Britain hegemony in the Northeast. For a short period after the Revolutionary War British fur traders ignored the transfer of the land south of Canada to the American nation. Even though the United States officially acquired the Northwest Territory in the Treaty of Paris in 1783, most of its terrain was still possessed by the Indians. Eight years later, General Arthur St. Clair attempted to take control in an ill-fated expedition, when his forces were routed by the Indians and he lost 900 men. In 1794 "Mad" Anthony Wayne led a better-prepared army into battle and defeated the Indian forces at Fallen Timbers, near present-day Toledo. In August 1795 General Wayne and the Indians—who felt abandoned by the British—signed the Treaty of Greenville. Among its terms, the treaty conveyed to the United States "One piece of Land Six Miles square at the Mouth of the Chickago River emptying into the Southwest end of Lake Michigan where a fort formerly stood."

Archaeologists have never found evidence of such a fort, but historians do know that the United States wanted one at that place to establish an American presence in the wilderness, protect the waterway linkage to the West, and be part of a line of defensive fortifications.

By 1800 Jean Baptiste Point du Sable probably had grown weary of the Chicago scenery and felt ready to move on. A bill of sale to his property still exists. For 6,000 livres Jean La Lime of St. Joseph bought the 40-by-22 foot cabin, a horsemill, a pair of millstones, a bakehouse, a large number of tools,

Facing page: In 1779 Chicago consisted of a slow moving river, an Indian encampment, and two traders' cabins. Jean Baptiste Point du Sable (bottom right), who had come to Chicago in the 1770s as a fur trader, is thought to have been the area's first settler. He built a cabin (bottom left) on the north bank of the river. Not depicted in this etching is the cabin of French trader Gaurie, which was located on the North Branch of the river. For years afterward that branch was called the Gaurie River. From Andreas, *History of Chicago,* 1884

Below: One opinion concerning the etymology of the word "Chicago" is that the name means "wild onion" or "garlic." In a 1695 report Antoine de la Mothe Cadillac stated that "Chicagou" meant "river of the wild onions"; Henry R. Schoolcraft wrote that "Chi-Kaug-ong" translated into "wild onion or leek"; and a 1773 Indian treaty referred to "Chicagou" as "Garlick Creek." From Currey, *The Story of Old Fort Dearborn,* 1912

household goods, paintings, furniture, 30 head of cattle, 2 calves, 38 hogs, 2 mules, and 44 hens. Some historians believe that La Lime actually purchased it for trader John Kinzie, who ended up living there.

This area at the mouth of the Chicago River was swampy and needed men to perfect nature's work. But when Jean Baptiste Point du Sable left, money in hand, for a post along the Mississippi River he had already proven Chicago could be a good place for enterprise.

In the early 1800s competition went on between independent fur traders and the U.S. government's "factories" established at settlements and forts to conduct business with the Indians, who exchanged furs and other Indian-produced goods for food supplies, blankets, fabrics, metal pots and tools, and the inevitable trinkets. Factories offered useful goods to the Indians at fair prices and were forbidden to use whiskey as a means of exchange in buying and selling. Their agents or factors were also encouraged to help, however they could, in the "civilizing" or acculturation process with the Indians.

Building began on Fort Dearborn, named after Secretary of War Henry Dearborn, in August 1803 on the south side of the Chicago River, in the area of what is now Michigan Avenue and Wacker Drive. The acquisition of the Louisiana Territory in the same year had made the fort imperative as a visible assertion of American authority in this wilderness. The remoteness of the area itself was demonstrated by the fact that it had taken the new troops 17 days to go from Detroit to Chicago. Work on the fort was plagued by illness ("bilious fevers"), lack of food (especially corn for the oxen), and pilfering by the Indians. The outpost was to function as a military garrison as well as a factory for trading with the Indians. According to most accounts, Fort Dearborn was a boring place to be stationed.

One man who helped to enliven things around the fort was John Kinzie, who functioned as an independent supplier of goods to the soldiers and their families, other settlers, and local Indians. Kinzie had left his trading post on the St. Joseph River at the eastern shore of Lake Michigan to settle with his family in Chicago. In 1804 they moved into du Sable's "mansion." (The site, now called "pioneer court," is at the northeast corner of Michigan Avenue and the river.)

Kinzie, a forceful but enigmatic man, was well-liked by the Indians. With his white companions, however, he could be both manipulative and belligerent, and in a personal feud Kinzie had killed fellow Chicago resident Jean La Lime. (The garrison buried La Lime in Kinzie's front yard, and Kinzie cared for the grave until his own death.)

In early 1812, nine years after it was erected, Fort Dearborn remained little known to the American public. Regarded as part of the Army of the Northwest, in newspapers it was sometimes called Fort Chicago, or else its location was

Facing page, top: Workmen under the direction of Captain John Whistler and engineer Lieutenant James S. Swearingen construct Fort Dearborn—the most isolated fort in the nation in 1803. It was located near the Chicago portage to protect the newly acquired Louisiana Territory. Courtesy, Wilmette Historical Museum

Bottom: Henry Dearborn (left) ordered the establishment of the fort (right). This outpost in the wilderness lasted until 1812. The site is marked in the pavement and sidewalk at the south end of the Michigan Avenue bridge. Dearborn: From Currey, *The Story of Old Fort Dearborn,* 1912; Fort: From Andreas, *History of Chicago,* 1884

given as "Chicago, on the southwest shore of Lake Michigan." In the summer of 1812, however, Great Britain and the United States went to war. And the nation soon thereafter heard much of Chicago and Fort Dearborn.

For years many of the "Old Northwest" Indians kept Britain—still possessor of the land north of the Great Lakes—as an ally, hoping to prevent the invasion of American settlers. British fur traders "poaching" in the area often encouraged disruptive or hostile Indian behavior toward the American residents. Such aggressive tactics included attacks upon isolated settlers, such as the murder in April 1812 of two residents of a farm at Hardscrabble, in the area around the river's South Branch now known as Bridgeport.

The United States, infuriated by British interference with shipping during the Napoleonic War in Europe, declared war against the nation in June of 1812. An attack mounted against Canada failed but roused British Canadians to fight hard. American General William Hull, headquartered at Detroit, considered Fort Dearborn indefensible and ordered its evacuation in August. Days later, he surrendered his own army at Detroit to the British, fearful of what the Indians might do to both soldiers and settlers during or after battle.

Indian fighter William Wells arrived on the 13th of August with a band of friendly Miami Indians to help protect the garrison during its departure, scheduled for the early morning of the 15th. The night before, Kinzie insisted on destroying the fort's liquor and ammunition supplies and forged an order from General Hull to this effect. The fort's commander, Captain Nathan Heald, had hesitated maintaining it was not sound policy to lie to Indians. The supplies were thrown into the river. The destruction of the liquor may have been a precipitating element in the Indians' violent action the next morning.

As the soldiers and settlers began to leave, with the settlers' wagons accompanied by troops and Wells' Miami warriors acting as front and rear guards,

Above: This map depicts Chicago as it was during the year of the massacre. It shows both the original mouth of the Chicago River and the battle site south along the lakefront. At that time the river had many small inlets, including one that helped drain what is now the Loop. From Andreas, *History of Chicago,* 1884

Facing page: On April 6, 1812, four months before the massacre at Fort Dearborn, two farmers were killed and scalped by an angry band of marauding Winnebago Indians at a farmhouse located a few miles from the fort. The house, which belonged to Charles Lee, was known as Lee's Place or Hardscrabble. From Currey, *The Story of Old Fort Dearborn,* 1912

some 600 Indians were lying in ambush at what is now 18th Street. (The shoreline then was a half-mile inland from where it is now.) Most of the Miami fled the grisly scene. According to new research by Allan Eckert in *Gateway to Empire* all 12 of the Chicago-raised militia were killed, as was Wells, 53 of the regulars, six women, two men, and 12 children. The others were taken captive. The fort itself was burned to the ground.

The survivors—some of whom had been rescued by a chief named Black Partridge—were mostly handed over as prisoners and slaves to the various tribes. Captain Heald and Lieutenant Helm and their wives were among the captives and eventually won their freedom. The Kinzies, in their home north of the river, had been protected by Indians friendly to them. They and other whites were taken to Detroit, where for a short time they were prisoners of the British. The only residents remaining in Chicago were Antoine Ouilmette and his Indian wife, who operated a river and portage transportation service for years. (This early settler's name is perpetuated in the suburb of Wilmette.)

The British and American war ended in 1815, but the United States did not rebuild and regarrison Fort Dearborn until July 4, 1816. The government still intended to break the dominance of British traders, who continued using the Chicago portage, and to halt their influence with the Indians, who gathered annually in the vicinity to hunt waterfowl.

The troops arriving at Chicago found ghastly reminders of the massacre. The fort was reconstructed and the government factory for the Indians was reestablished. Early entrepreneur John Kinzie and his family returned to their property and began bringing in supplies and slowly the population increased around the fort and to the north of the river. The new settlement included a trader named Jean Baptiste Beaubien and a few farmers.

The United States, however, had bigger plans for the Chicago area. A canal

to be cut across the portage, which had occurred to Jolliet long before, was first proposed to Congress in 1810. The government now asked Ninian Edwards, territorial governor of Illinois and Indian affairs agent, to acquire the necessary land. In 1816 Edwards helped negotiate the Treaty of St. Louis with the united Potawatomi, Chippewa, and Ottawa tribes. The Indians ceded to the government a 20-mile-wide strip of land stretching 90 miles from Chicago to Ottawa on the Illinois River—eventually the route of the canal.

But Chicago was not the only possible terminus for the desired canal. The Wisconsin portage and the nearby Calumet River were also contenders. Congress finally approved the canal plan itself in 1827 but left the final decision about the exact location to the Illinois legislature.

There had been the predictable inspection tours when federal funding was involved. One of the less enthusiastic observers was geologist William H. Keating, who in 1823 accompanied army surveyor Stephen M. Long on a tour of the entire area. Reporting later on the "Disadvantages of Chicago," a place he considered dismal: " *The land scenery ... consists merely of a plain, in which but few patches of thin and scrubby woods are observed. ... The village presents no cheering prospect as ... it consists of but few huts, inhabited by a miserable race of men, scarcely equal to the Indians from whom they are descended. Their log or barkhouses are low, filthy and disgusting. ... As a place of business, it offers no inducement to the settler; for the whole annual amount of trade on the lake did not exceed the cargo of five or six schooners. ... It is not impossible that at some distant day, when the banks of the Illinois shall have been covered with a dense population, and when the low prairies ... shall have acquired a population proportionate to the produce which they can yield, that Chicago may become one of the points in the direct line of communication between the northern lakes and the Mississippi; but even the intercourse [will] ... be a limited one; the dangers attending the navigation of the lake, and the scarcity of harbours along the shore, must ever prove a serious obstacle to the increase of the commercial importance of Chicago.* "

The unimpressed Keating perhaps failed to meet two young, vigorous, new Chicago residents: future meatpackers Archibald Clybourn and Gurdon S. Hubbard. The latter at this time was still in the employ of the booming American Fur Company; in its business heyday John Jacob Astor of New York had created this first major American monopoly, whose men were instructed to drive all competitors out of local business either by undercutting and underselling them, or else by absorbing them into the company itself.

Astor had been successful in persuading Congress to pass a law in 1816 that forbade all foreigners from engaging in the fur trading business. In 1822 a second law, lobbied by his boodlepaying minions, effectively killed the government factory system—thereby destroying a good part of Fort Dearborn's raison d'être.

Facing page, top left: During the summer of 1820 Lewis Cass, governor of Michigan Territory, came to Fort Dearborn to inspect the area that was one of the possible termini for a canal that would link East and West. Cass declared himself a proponent of the proposed canal. Courtesy, National Portrait Gallery, Smithsonian Institution, Washington, D.C.

Middle: Ninian Wirt Edwards was instrumental in negotiating the Treaty of St. Louis in which the Potawatomi, Chippewa, and Ottawa Indians relinquished a 20-mile-wide piece of land stretching from Chicago to Ottawa on the Illinois River. Eventually this became the route of the Illinois and Michigan Canal. Courtesy, Illinois State Historical Society. From Cirker, *Dictionary of American Portraits,* 1967

Right: The Potawatomi Metea was a great orator among his people and spoke strongly against ceding any of Northern Illinois to the whites. In his journals Major Stephen H. Long described Metea: ''His features are strongly marked, and expressive of a haughty and tyrannical disposition ... . We behold in him all the characteristics of the Indian warrior to perfection.'' This painting, though unsigned, may be the work of Samuel Seymour, an artist who accompanied the Long expedition. From McKenney and Hall, *The Indian Tribes of North America,* 1933

Bottom: This drawing depicts Chicago in 1820, the year Lewis Cass and young geographer/ethnologist Henry R. Schoolcraft visited Fort Dearborn. At the time Schoolcraft saw the Chicago area as a potential ''great thoroughfare for strangers, merchants, and travellers.'' From Hurlbut, *Chicago Antiquities,* 1881

Eventually, by dint of hard work and a good reputation, Hubbard became so successful that in 1828 he actually bought out Astor's interest in the Chicago area. He himself was strongly ''sold'' on the place, in spite of an unkempt or dull appearance it might have to strangers. He was determined to turn the small settlement into a thriving town.

Chicago's major disadvantages were all too obvious even to its few residents. Located virtually in swampland because of a low-lying site and poor drainage, its streets were little better than mudholes in the spring. During much of the year it was cut off from other places by lack of decent roads. The Great Lakes water system was frozen for at least several months of the year, and in any case voyages could be hazardous. The Chicago River ended in a sandbar that prevented developing the much needed harbor on a lake with notoriously inhospitable shores. And Chicago was still threatened by the possibility of Indian attack, having to call hastily gathered militia to race up fron Danville in 1827.

Illinois, which became a state in 1818, was being settled from the south northward as immigrants came via the Ohio River. The National Road was being built into the center of Illinois, and maps from the era depicted northeastern Illinois mainly as marsh. The Chicago area, according to the original terms of the Northwest Ordinance, should rightly have belonged to Wisconsin Territory. But the Illinois citizenry to the south had insisted on having a piece of land that gave them access to Lake Michigan upon 63 miles of shoreline and thence to the important waterways beyond it, for already the Erie Canal was being dug. Not that Chicago, with its crude, sandbar-blocked port, had any ostensible virtues then ... but it might someday to the young state.

Chicago in the 1820s did not seem to possess much value as real estate. The talk of any canal building apparently had stalled in the Illinois legislature. But Gurdon S. Hubbard had driven a herd of several hundred pigs into the dusty streets of Chicago in the late 1820s—having purchased them from farmers in the hinterland—and then sold their meat, at a good profit. He saw great new possibilities in commerce connected now with farm products, not furs. Getting himself elected to the state assembly, he determined to lay siege to the Illinois capital and obtain a canal for Chicago that would link East and West.

CHAPTER THREE

CHICAGO SPECULATES ON ITS FUTURE

THE 1830s

Chicago sent its first shipment of wheat to the East in 1838 aboard the steamer *Great Western*. One year later the city's second wheat shipment was made on the brig *Osceola* (pictured here). Courtesy, Chicago Historical Society

In the 1830s Chicago tried to cash in on its future and in the effort it became a city. The long debate over the canal site finally ended in the Illinois legislature in 1829, when Gurdon Saltonstall Hubbard, who had gone there to represent Chicago, argued that choosing the Calumet Lake and River route would create a major city at the site that would benefit Indiana more than Illinois. Obtaining the money to finance this major construction work would be another problem.

Although estimates of Chicago's population in 1830 range widely the best guess is 40 to 50. Three of Chicago's buildings at that time were taverns: Elijah Wentworth's, Samuel Miller's, and Mark Beaubien's. These inns, which housed travelers and newcomers, were at best rudimentary. One of Wentworth's problems on Wolf Point was literally keeping the wolves away from his door. Mark Beaubien was probably a better fiddler and populator of Chicago (he had 24 children by two wives) than innkeeper. But his Sauganash Hotel, located centrally, kept expanding the number of its guests and provisions. There people usually slept in shifts in dirty beds, several at a time, and the menu was execrable, with diners all grabbing from a common plate.

To encourage both trade and settlement, the ferry service across the river at Wolf Point was free for all Cook County residents in 1831. Some choice lots adjoining the canal-to-be were sold in order to pay for Thompson's survey and other expenses. Bidders were mainly local people. The highest payment for any lot was $138, and the average lot sold for about $50. Large tracts elsewhere sold for prices as low as $1.25 an acre.

The story of Chicago in the 1830s is often told in terms of the spiraling prices of these lots. An 1835 newspaper account reported that one lot had "increased 100% everyday" in the five years between 1830 and 1835. The reporter obviously meant it had increased by an average of its original $50 every day over those years, since it was "worth" $85,000 in 1835.

The factors behind these dramatic increases reveal the changes in Chicago.

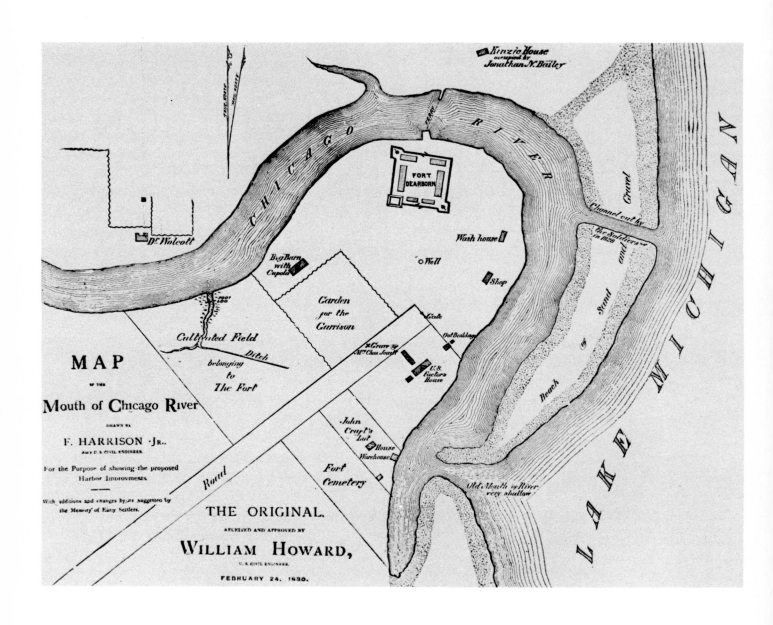

MAP

of the

Mouth of Chicago River

DRAWN BY

F. HARRISON Jr.,

ASST U. S. CIVIL ENGINEER.

For the Purpose of showing the proposed Harbor Improvements

With additions and changes by me suggested by the Memory of Early Settlers.

THE ORIGINAL.

RECEIVED AND APPROVED BY

WILLIAM HOWARD,

U. S. CIVIL ENGINEER.

FEBRUARY 24, 1830.

Kenzie House occupied by Jonathan N. Bailey

CHICAGO RIVER

FORT DEARBORN

Dr. Wolcott

Big Barn with Cupola

FOOT LOG

Cultivated Field

Garden for the Garrison

Ditch belonging to The Fort

Wash house

Well

Shop

Gate

Out Buildings

Grave of Mrs Chas Jouett

U. S. Factory House

John Crafts Lot

House

Warehouse

Fort Cemetery

Road

Channel cut by the Soldiers in 1829

Gravel

Beach of Sand

Old Mouth of River very shallow

LAKE MICHIGAN

This 1830 map of the mouth of the Chicago River demonstrates not only the dramatic geographical changes that took place, but also the difficulties that existed. Though the small creeks and sandbar were gone and the river was straightened, an adequate channel still needed to be dug. Legal questions as to who owned the land under the fort, however, continued for decades. From Andreas, *History of Chicago,* 1884

The land speculators sensed Chicago's future and responded to it. However, major difficulties would have to be overcome before Chicago properties were actually worth the prices asked and received for them by the mid-1830s. The value of the canal lots, which rose the most spectacularly from 1830 on, did not rise immediately nor steadily. At first other signs of growth were more dramatic. Chicago acquired its own post office in 1831 and that year became the county seat for Cook County.

Then there was a war to be reckoned with. It is ironic that throughout its history, except for the War of 1812, Chicago has benefited financially from wars. The economic breakthrough for Chicago came from the Black Hawk War in 1832. Some members of the Sauk and Fox tribes had signed a treaty giving up their lands in northern Illinois and agreeing to settle west of the Mississippi River. Black Hawk, a Sauk leader, argued against the validity of such treaties between the Indians and the white settlers. With a band numbering almost 1,000, including tribe elders, women, and children, he recrossed the Mississippi in April to plant corn and to hunt. When Governor John Reynolds of Illinois called out the militia, Black Hawk inflicted a stinging defeat. Northern Illinois settlers and pioneers feared that if other tribes joined this rebellious group, Fort Dearborn-style massacres would ensue. Indian support for Black Hawk's cause did not materialize, but United States troops did. Black Hawk was hunted down and most of his band slaughtered in a battle in August at the Bad Axe River in Wisconsin. Although he escaped, he was recaptured and humiliated.

Additional U.S. troops from the East sent to fight in the Black Hawk War, were transported by schooners across the Great Lakes and disembarked at Chicago. While on ship, they suffered an epidemic of Asiatic cholera in which 58 men died. The survivors ultimately headed west to find the war, but it was over by the time they got there. Although these troops could not brag about a military victory over the Indians, they did return to the East praising the rich black soil in Illinois, which compared favorably to the rocky, infertile land farmers were trying to till in New England. Meanwhile, almost the entire central third of Illinois had been turned into a military tract to be given to veterans of the War of 1812. And speculators in Illinois lands were promoting a land boom.

The last major barrier for widespread white settlement in Illinois fell as a result of the Black Hawk War. The Potawatomi, Ottawa, and Chippewa, all of whom had refused to join Black Hawk in his rebellion, were called to a great council in Chicago. The purpose of the meeting was to make a treaty whereby the Indians would cede to the United States all their remaining land east of the Mississippi River and would "be removed" to lands west of it.

In September 1833 some 5,000 Indians gathered in and around Chicago. Governor George Porter of the Michigan Territory opened the council by stating that "As their great father in Washington had heard that they wished to sell their land, he had sent commissioners to treat with them."

The Indians did not think they were hearing correctly. They politely responded that the "great father in Washington must have seen a bad bird which told him a lie, for that far from wishing to sell their land, they wished to keep it." Nevertheless, the commissioner urged the Indians to consider the matter. After using delaying tactics, the Indians at last succumbed to a combination of blandishments, whiskey, and military threat. They signed (mainly with "X's") the Treaty of Chicago, which bought their lands for about two cents an acre. Two years hence they were to be uprooted and moved to Iowa—from which they would be removed westward again by yet another treaty when that land too was recognized as desirable.

In August of 1835 Chicago would see the last of its Indians as some 800 representatives of different tribes gathered there to collect their annuity payments in the form of 50 cent pieces and goods. Too many exchanged their money or blankets for drams of whiskey. Intoxicated and divested of their tribal lands (some even of their clothing), the outcasts finally moved through the town's streets, dancing wildly and gesturing menacingly at householders who watched the motley parade from their windows, behind locked doors. Billy Caldwell, though invited to remain among his white friends, chose to accompany his own people in their pitiful passage. He was after all, Chief Sauganash. The local Indians' culture was best remembered by John H. Kinzie, son of the former Indian trader, who sometimes fascinated visitors by performing ritualistic aboriginal dances.

Meanwhile, entrepreneurs, lawyers, speculators, wide-eyed dreamers, ambitious black freedmen, and all manner of folk packed their bags to go to Chicago—or to pass through it. They traveled by ship, and stage, or Conestoga wagon. Many simply walked, and among them was young "Long" John Wentworth, who came in barefooted, carrying his shoes.

Financier Charles Butler of New York, intrigued by the reports coming from the war veterans, visited Illinois in 1833 to look it over. He arrived in Chicago. Fascinated with Chicago's potential, Butler asked his young brother-in-law, William B. Ogden, to go there and handle real estate and railroad-building business for him. Ogden, at first unimpressed with the crudely built place containing several hundred permanent residents and many more in transit, decided to stay on when a portion of a lot he considered valueless earned enough to pay for the whole property.

The United States government, wanting a safe harbor along the southwest shore of treacherous Lake Michigan, also became more interested in Chicago. In 1832 it built a lighthouse there and in 1833 it appropriated $25,000 to construct a harbor at Chicago. Interestingly, one of Chicago's promoters was Jefferson Davis, then a young army engineer, who argued against placing the harbor

Facing page, top: When this log cabin at South Water Street (Wacker Drive) and the Forks (Lake Street) began serving unincorporated Chicago as a post office in 1832, postage was 25 cents a letter. Postmaster Jonathan Bailey lived in the Kinzie House and first distributed mail from there. Courtesy, Chicago Historical Society

Bottom: Mark Beaubien (left), one of Chicago's first innkeepers, owned the Sauganash Hotel (right), which was located on the east side of the river just south of the fork. Beaubien had 24 children from two marriages. Beaubien: From Andreas, *History of Chicago*, 1884; Hotel: From Kirkland, *The Story of Chicago*, 1892

at the mouth of the Calumet River.

On August 5, 1833, an important meeting was held in Chicago to decide whether or not to incorporate as a town. The vote—at a time when the population was more than 300—was a mere 12 to 1 for the proposal. The lone opposition vote came from Russel E. Heacock, who owned a business in Chicago but lived beyond the borders of the proposed town.

The boundaries of the new town were set at Jackson Street on the south, Jefferson and Cook streets on the west, Ohio Street on the north, and State Street on the east. Within two years, Chicago would add Wabash and Michigan avenues to the east and extend north to North Avenue, west to Wood Street, and south to 22nd Street.

In the mid-1830s Chicago was still a scrappy town with a small population. The tallest landmark was Fort Dearborn's 50-foot flagpole. Most homes and stores were located along a three-block stretch south of the river, between Fort Dearborn and the river's South Branch. The first public building was a pen for stray animals. In 1834 a drawbridge was constructed to link the main settlement with the North Side residents occupying the old Du Sable and Kinzie domains. The South Siders, however, grew obstreperous about this convenient bridge, believing that it interfered with their commercial well-being by conferring new advantages to the people across the river. (In 1839 the city council finally ordered the bridge pulled down, partly to please the South Side constituents, who arose at dawn to hack down the bridge with axes. Actually, the early Dearborn Street bridge had insufficient horizontal draw and impeded ship traffic in the river.)

On November 26, 1833, John Calhoun printed the city's first newspaper, the *Chicago Democrat*. Its mailing list included the Librarian at Fort Dearborn; "Doct. Maxwell" (later the city physician, after whom Maxwell Street is named); meatpacker Archibald Clybourn; many men who would become famous Chicago businessmen, such as John S. Wright, P.F.W. Peck, Walter L. Newberry, George W. Dole, John Gage, and Peter Cohen; lawyers (later judges) Walter Kimball and John Dean Caton. Not listed among these early subscribers however, are the names of prominent men who were newcomers then to the town or would shortly arrive thereafter: William B. Ogden, Stephen A. Douglas, Jonathan Young Scammon, and John Wentworth.

Editorially the paper proclaimed, "The rapidly increasing importance of Chicago, in a commercial point of view, calls aloud for the speedy commencement and completion of the long contemplated canal or Rail-Road [at that time the word meant a waterway], which is to connect the waters of Lake Michigan with those of the Illinois River."

The building of the canal had been discussed for years. Financing for construction was finally obtained in 1834 by a legislative enactment that authorized

Chief Black Hawk led a band of 400 Sauk warriors and about 1,000 women and children across the Mississippi in 1832 to lands that other members of his tribe had sold to the Americans. When a messenger sent to negotiate was killed by whites, Black Hawk routed the poorly disciplined militia and struck deep fear into the early settlers who had begun to trickle into Northern Illinois. He was defeated, however, and his people were slaughtered near Bad Axe, Wisconsin. "These lands are now yours," he said, "keep them as we did." Courtesy, National Portrait Gallery, Smithsonian Institution, Washington, D.C.

Former Indian agent John. H. Kinzie, son of John Kinzie, was nine years old when his family escaped from the massacre at Fort Dearborn. In 1834 he and his wife Juliette returned to Chicago. There Kinzie served as village board president. Three years later he lost to William B. Ogden in Chicago's first mayoral election. During the Civil War, President Lincoln appointed him paymaster. From Gilbert and Bryson, *Chicago and Its Makers*, 1929

a loan to be floated in the East. Eastern investors' interest in Chicago became clear when Gurdon Hubbard, visiting among them, managed to sell for $80,000 Chicago property he had bought for $5,000.

The fast upward spiral in property values had begun. It gained momentum in 1835 and peaked in 1836. In a speech given a few years later, Joseph Balestier gave a ringside remembrance of the wild speculation: *Visions of the glorious future filled the imaginations of the multitude ... The mechanic laid aside his tools and resolved to grow rich without labor. The lawyer sold his books and invested the proceeds in lands. The physician "threw physic to the dogs" and wrote promissory notes instead of prescriptions. Even the day-laborer became learned in the mysteries of quit-claim and warranty, and calculated his fortunes in the thousands. Quickly built shanties in Chicago too had maps of such future cities and suburbs plastered on their walls and local "experts" willing to extol the virtues of their town, while offering a piece of land at a special, once-in-a-lifetime price ...*

At this very time the sharply observant English traveler, Harriet Martineau, happened upon the town and afterwards described it in *A Retrospect of Western Travel:* *Chicago looks raw and bare, standing on the high prairie above the lake-shore. The houses ... run up in various directions, without any principal at all.*

I never saw a busier place than Chicago. ... The streets were crowded with land speculators. A negro, dressed up in scarlet, bearing a scarlet flag, and riding a white horse with housings of scarlet, announced the times of sale. At every street corner where he stopped, the crowd flocked round him; and it seemed as if some prevalent mania infected the whole people. The rage of speculation might fairly be so regarded. As the gentlemen of our party walked the streets, storekeepers hailed them from their doors, with offers of farms, ... advising them to speculate before the price of land rose higher. A young lawyer, of my acquaintance there, had realized five hundred dollars per day the five preceding days, by merely making out titles to land. Another friend had realized in two years, ten times as much money as he had before fixed upon as a competence for life. ... A bursting of the bubble must come soon. The absurdity of the speculation is so striking, that the wonder is that the fever should have attained such a height as I witnessed.

Later, John Wentworth analyzed this first Chicago land boom and bust and put the situation in the proper national perspective in the Jacksonian era with its encouragement of emigration to the West. There government-owned lands had been bought up for $1.25 per acre by speculators, who then sold and mortgaged them at much higher prices to the eager, but cash-poor new settlers. Banks and speculators kept exchanging notes of credit and debenture based on increasingly inflated prices. There were few real assets involved except the land itself. The government itself was the fundamental creditor since it had sold the land precipitating this buying and selling spree. As the debt-free government actually accrued profits, Jackson promised new federal money to be spent in worthy

public projects in the states—which simply precipitated more speculative activity based on paper. As Wentworth saw it— *" Money was taken from every branch of business to invest in these western speculations. The President of the United States had no power to stop the sales of lands or to limit bank discounts. He saw the immediate necessity of arresting this condition of things, and he had no other way to do it than to issue an order that nothing but gold and silver should be received for the public lands. "*

The Panic of 1837 which started in May was like a collapsing house of cards. It swept westward from faltering, then failing, Eastern banks and businesses affected by the demand for hard money. In Chicago property values based on financing that used other inflated property as collateral totally crumbled.

But before the frantic land speculation bubble burst, Chicago had become a city. On March 4, 1837, a city charter was conferred by the Illinois legislature. William B. Ogden was elected the first mayor (a one-year term) by a two-to-one margin over John H. Kinzie. The first census, taken on July 1, 1837, says much about the robust city of some 4,000 souls. It listed 1,800 adult males, 845 adult females, 831 children, 104 "sailors belonging to vessels here," and 77 "persons of color."

During the financial crisis of the times, Mayor Ogden determinedly held Chicago's head above water. "Above all, do not tarnish the honor of our infant city!" he asserted when others proposed a moratorium on the city's growing—and staggering—debt. The city began to do what merchants and other government bodies were doing: it issued $5,000 in paper money in one-, two-, three-dollar demoninations in July of 1837. This scrip actually proved better than virtually declaring bankruptcy.

Above left: The city's first drawbridge was built across the river at Dearborn Street in 1834, but the residents and merchants on the South Side were angered by the commercial success the bridge brought to North Siders. Five years after its construction, the bridge was torn down when the city council deemed it a danger to river navigation. From Andreas, *History of Chicago,* 1884

Above: Philo Carpenter arrived in Chicago in 1832 and opened the city's first drugstore in a 16-foot by 20-foot log building on Lake Street near the river. After merchant George W. Dole vacated his larger building, Carpenter moved into it. Then, in the summer of 1833, the druggist erected a store on South Water Street between LaSalle and Wells and added general merchandise and hardware to his stock of drugs. From Andreas, *History of Chicago,* 1884

Apart from all the hoopla of speculation, Chicago was taking strides important for its future. The town got into manufacturing in this decade. The first commercial shop was begun by Mathias Mason in the fall of 1833, with Clement Stose and Lemuel Brown establishing themselves in the trade at about the same time. The city's clay had proven excellent for making bricks, and in the spring of 1833 Tyler Blodgett opened a brickyard on the North Side. In early 1834 John T. Temple started manufacturing the "Bull" plow, with a wooden mould-board, the first farm implement known to be manufactured commercially in Chicago. David McGee, who had been the government blacksmith at Fort Dearborn, set up his own shop after the fort closed down in 1836. Charles Morgan in 1837 initiated a furniture-building plant.

Other commercial and manufacturing industries that commenced in Chicago during the 1830s included: sash and door factories (Ira Miltmore was first in 1837); flour (Lyman and Gage had a mill on the South Branch at Canal Street); brewers and distillers (William Haas had his business where the Water Tower now is); foundry (work was begun in 1834 on the "Chicago Furnace" at Polk Street, on the west bank of the Chicago River); candle and soap makers (the biggest was Charles Cleaver's on The Point, between the North Branch and the main river).

During the 1830s an architectural innovation originating in Chicago helped the town grow into a city with hundreds of buildings, impermanent and flimsy though many were. This was the "balloon frame" building, the first of which was St. Mary's Catholic Church, erected in 1833 by a nameless carpenter who devised a fast new way of putting up houses, offices, and public structures. Other examples of this easy and sensible construction technique literally popped up all over town, and the idea spread elsewhere.

In 1835 too Chicago got its first courthouse, as well as town offices. The one-story brick building was put up at the northeast corner of Randolph and Clark streets. Behind it was the log-house jail, in operation since 1832.

But most importantly, work had finally begun on the canal. The state had pledged payments of principal and interest on the loans from Eastern investors. The monthly influx of $75,000 would help Chicago get through its worst financial times.

On July 4, 1836, an impressive civic ceremony was attended by many townspeople going upriver by boats with food for a huge picnic. They met at the site where the great ditch was about to be dug to join the Chicago, flowing eastward to Lake Michigan, with the Illinois River and thence to the Mississippi. Locks would be used to permit boats to adjust to the differing water levels. A canal commissioner lifted the first shovelful of earth, and as resounding speeches were given—one, appropriately, by Gurdon Hubbard—in the distance the crew of Irish immigrants impatiently waited to begin the real work. Cutting

Juliette Kinzie's 1856 novel *Wau-Bun* is a forceful and moving account of the Fort Dearborn Massacre, though its lack of historical accuracy has obscured the actual history of the event. From Andreas, *History of Chicago,* 1884

Facing page, top: The Wolf tavern (left), Samuel Miller's house (right), and the Reverend Jesse Walker's cabin (in the distance) are depicted in this view of Wolf Point as it appeared in 1835. Drawing by W.E.S. Trowbridge, 1902. From Gale, *Reminiscences of Early Chicago*, 1902

Bottom left: When printer John Calhoun traveled to Chicago in 1833, his ship floundered in Lake Erie. Fortunately, he had shipped his press on a different boat. With the safe arrival of both printer and press, Calhoun began issuing the city's first newspaper—the *Chicago Democrat*. Three years later ill health forced him to sell out. From Kirkland, *The Story of Chicago*, 1892

Bottom right: Jonathan Young Scammon exemplified the early successful and civic-minded Chicagoan. A lawyer, he was deeply involved with the city's courts, banks, railroads, and newspapers. Having arrived in Chicago in 1835, Scammon soon began advocating common schools and caused a free school clause to be inserted in the city charter in 1837. From Andreas, *History of Chicago*, 1884

through the limestone subsoil, however, would prove harder, more time-consuming, and therefore more costly than anticipated.

Transportation also carried Chicago through both its dizzy and depressed times. In 1834, 11 steamboats served Chicago in Great Lakes water traffic. The next year the number increased to 18. The canal would not be completed until 1848, but its route was being followed by pack horses. St. Louis merchants banded together to ship goods from the East via Chicago—by wagon to the Illinois River, and from there by flatboat.

The alarming fact, however, was that there was no balance of trade. The farmlands of Illinois were not as yet creating a surplus, and what little food they did produce could be used by Chicago. The goods were still all going westward, often paid for with title to land or indebtedness on it. In the 1830s Chicago bought 30 times as much as it sold. The balance of trade for northern Illinois was not much better.

This economic imbalance could only be corrected when the main item of trade was not land but farm commodities and their by-products, with Chicago becoming a far more facile conduit for them. And a favorable turn in this direction was foreshadowed in the fact of 1838, when Newberry and Dole sent out the first shipment of Midwestern wheat to go by boat from Chicago on a steamer, the *Great Western*. Next year the same freighting firm sent out a second batch on the *Osceola*.

For all the criticism that can be made of the wild real estate speculation in the Chicago of the 1830s, it was symptomatic of the nation's reckless, rocketing times, rather than a peculiar sign of local irresponsibility. And it did help to create a city out of a backwater town.

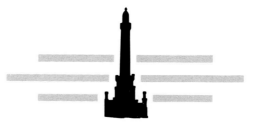

CHAPTER FOUR

GOING PLACES AT LAST

THE 1840s

From the cupola of the Galena and Chicago Union Railroad station, railroad company president William B. Ogden would watch trains traverse the prairies. The "Pioneer" was the first train to use the station, which was built in 1848 at Kinzie and Canal streets. From the author's collection

Chicago started the 1840s without money—good money, that is. Michigan's "shinplasters," increasingly worthless scrip, continued to flood the Chicago area, especially hurting the farmers. Illinois was bankrupted in 1841 by costly public works projects of which the politically-minded, Illinois legislator Abraham Lincoln was a major supporter.

Lincoln at this time led the "Long Nine" group in Springfield, members of the Whig party averaging over six feet tall and 200 pounds in weight. Their vision for the state matched their size. They pushed for internal improvements that included a railroad from Galena to the Ohio River, as well as railways crisscrossing the state—in all, 1,350 miles of track. They also allotted $4 million for finishing the Illinois and Michigan Canal, plotted other canals, and set in motion plans to improve the Rock River as well as the Western Mail Route. Their schemes, to be financed by state bonds, were to cost $12 million. What they mainly accomplished, in addition to some financing of the Illinois and Michigan Canal, was the construction of a small railroad line in the center of the state that eventually failed.

Work on the canal system using the old Chicago portage route was often interrupted when funds ran out. The Irish canalers often had to fall back on the dole in Chicago. Reflecting on Chicago in 1841, 35 years later, Joseph N. Balestier wrote: *At that day, all that remained to support life in Chicago was hope. The poverty of the place was visible and unfeigned. The more land a man had, the worse off he apparently was. Money and the people had long been strangers. But there were few who despaired, for the Genius of the place forbade. To the dullest eye it was evident that a great destiny awaited our muddy little town, squatted upon the low banks of its sluggish bayou.*

Balestier's family, however, could not survive on such hope and he was among those "who left the city for his ancient home." But others stuck it out, like John Wentworth, who much later sounded nostalgic when recalling

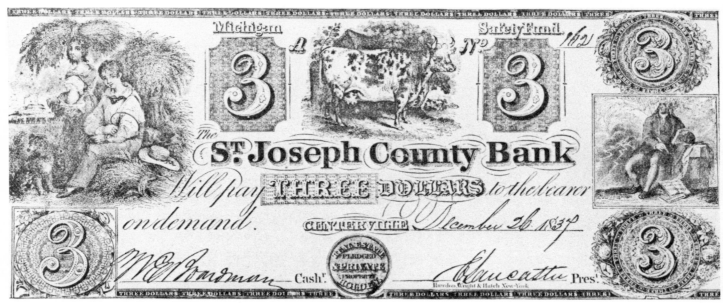

Chicago's early years and the natural democracy and internationalism of its populace: *Here in Chicago, in early times, we had not any one prevailing class or interest; nor was there any sufficient number of people from any particular locality to exercise a controlling influence in molding public sentiment. We had people of almost every opinion. We had Jews and Christians, Protestants, there were Calvinists and Armenians. Nearly every language was represented here. ... We had every variety of people, and out of these we had to construct what is called society. The winters were long; no railroads, no telegraphs, no canal, and all we had to rely upon for news were our weekly newspapers. We had no libraries, no lectures, no theatres or other places of amusement ... and the gentlemen outnumbered the ladies by about four or five to one. You ask what society lived upon in those days? I answer, upon faith. ... Our faith consisted principally in the future of Chicago.*

Yet the pivot on which Chicago balanced was beginning to turn. Perhaps, had it not been so headstrong in its rollicking ride toward early good fortune, Chicago would have recognized the signs of the upswing sooner.

By the fall of 1839 farmers close to Chicago found themselves with surpluses of pork and wheat, which they turned over to Chicago merchants to ship to the East. Shortly thereafter produce commission dealers came on the scene, eager to purchase grain and meat for New York and Canada markets. From then on, the commerce grew with Chicago at its center. Certainly the most vital element in Chicago's selection in the early 1840s as the shipping point for the Illinois and Mississippi river valleys, which were already building up a surplus of wheat, was the nature of grain itself. Since it was relatively imperishable, with a concentrated bulk, it could be transported over rough roads for long distances.

For more than a decade, grown, harvested, and then hauled and stored, wheat dominated the agriculture of the opening prairie lands. It was the only crop that could repay the costs of harvesting and transporting to Chicago from farmlands in the interior. Often it served as the farmers' own medium of exchange. Merchants in towns on the Illinois River did not have the same storage and transportation facilities as Chicago. When shipping to the East through the Mississippi River and thence up the Ohio, they charged higher prices than those available in Chicago. In such towns the farmer also received lower prices for the wheat itself, the difference ranging from $.37 to $.66 per bushel.

During the 1830s Chicagoans had seemed too busy with the future to be overly concerned with the discomforts and inconveniences of everyday life, but in the economic mire of the early 1840s Chicago began to recognize more fully its physical morass. The city was built virtually on swampland. The water table was just below the ground. In the spring the streets became mud traps in which carriages and teams of horses got stuck.

"The first year or two we were here there was not a cellar in Chicago," re-

Facing page, top: In 1845 Chicago showed few indications of becoming the great commercial success as we know it today. This pastoral view contains elements that make the mid-19th-century city appear more developed than it was at the time. It is doubtful that on any one day in 1845 one would see many ships' masts in Chicago's inadequate port. Also, in their 19th-century city views artists frequently included chimneys bellowing smoke to symbolize prosperity. From Andreas, *History of Chicago,* 1884

Bottom: Beginning in the late 1830s and continuing into the 1840s Michigan banks began flooding Chicago and the rest of the Midwest with poorly secured and depreciated currency. The slang word "shinplasters" was often the nicest used for these bills frequently forced on laborers for their work and farmers for their crops. From Andreas, *History of Chicago,* 1884

ported Charles Cleaver when reminiscing about Chicago in the 1840s and '50s. He described an attempt to dig out Lake Street to a depth of three feet and to lay down heavy planks or timber. It was, he said, a good street until heavy teams going over it worked the timbers into the mud—"and it was consequently squash, squash, until at last, in wet weather, the mud would splash up into the horses' faces, and the plan was condemned as a failure."

Cleaver's business was meatpacking, which Archibald Clybourn had begun in Chicago in the late 1820s. By 1833 Clybourn had a small log slaughterhouse on the east side of the river's North Branch. In the 1830s Clybourn mixed land speculation with his business as did most entrepreneurs. He continued in the steadier of the two ventures in the 1840s, so that by the winter of 1842-1843, he slaughtered and packed 2,000 to 3,000 head of cattle to ship to New York through the Erie Canal.

The largest meatpacker in 1844, according to the Norris Directory for that year, was former fur trader Gurdon Hubbard. He packed 300 to 400 hogs a day that season. Some packers were located on the North Branch and others along the lakeshore. Some eventually opened slaughterhouses in Bridgeport and along the South Branch. (Not until 1865 were the city's scattered stockyards sensibly unified, when the Union Stock Yards opened on the South Branch.)

During shipping season Clybourn and the other Chicago meatpackers shipped cattle. In the days before refrigeration and technologically scientific meatpacking, Cleaver reports, "Packing was quite an experiment and few were willing to risk their money in it, as they had to carry everything packed till spring and then ship east by vessel."

Packing operations generally began in autumn with beef and continued until the end of navigation, when packers turned their attention to pork, which they could barrel in brine. Actually, though, in the 1830s Hubbard conducted a notable experiment in fresh-frozen meatpacking when he brought 400 pigs to market too late to be transported across the iced-in Lake Michigan. He butchered them and stored their carcasses in a snowbank, retrieving them in the spring thaw to find them quite palatable.

The thriving stockyards did not bode well, however, either for the quality of the city's air or of its drinking water. Wastes from the livestock and meatpacking activities got into the water supply. Chicago attempted to filter water from wells or lakeside through hollow logs to help keep it pure, but disease and poor taste would long be a problem because of water pollution.

In the early and mid-1840s Chicago was unable to start resolving most of its dilemmas. There were simply too many and the resources were stretched too thin. Nonetheless, the undercurrent of the city's success was growing stronger. The introduction in 1843 of a new kind of steamship propelled by the Ericsson screw instead of a sidewheel meant far more fuel-efficient vessels. By 1844

Facing page, top: Rotten Row was a dilapidated block on the north side of Lake Street west of Clark in 1843. Though the streets were muddy and the grass grew two feet tall, the area drew high rent for years because of its location. From Gale, *Reminiscences of Early Chicago,* 1902

Bottom Left: Archibald Clybourn started the meatpacking industry in Chicago in the late 1820s. Successful in this venture, during the 1842-1843 winter Clybourn slaughtered and packed close to 3,000 head of cattle for shipment through the Erie Canal to the East. From Kirkland, *The Story of Chicago,* 1892

Bottom right: Former fur trader Gurdon Hubbard contributed to the city in a multitude of ways and became one of its leading industrialists, meatpackers, and ship owners. If there had been a "Chicagoan of the Century" award in the 1800s, Hubbard would have received it. From Andreas, *History of Chicago,* 1884

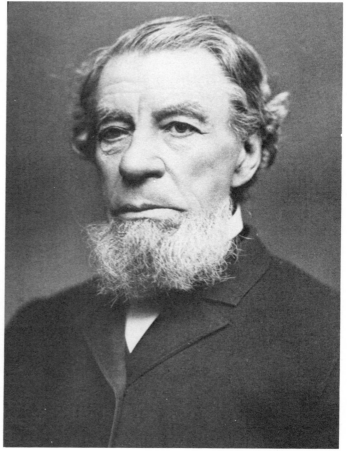

AMERICAN TEMPERANCE HOUSE,

By C. W. COOK,

Corner of Lake and Wabash streets, near the Steamboat
Landing,

CHICAGO, ILL.

N.B.—Passengers and Baggage carried to and from the
Steamboats free of charge.

there were 10 such vessels engaged in the Chicago trade.

Historian Andreas' list of Chicago imports and exports for the early to mid-1840s shows that it was becoming a major trade center, especially when one considers its relatively small population.

IMPORTS	EXPORTS
1842 . . . . $ 800,427.24	1842 . . . . $ 659,302.20
1843 . . . . 1,135,886.70	1843 . . . . 1,008,207.94
1844 . . . . 1,686,416.00	1844 . . . . 785,504.23
1845 . . . . 2,043,445.73	1845 . . . . 1,543,519.85
1846 . . . . 2,027,150.00	1846 . . . . 1,813,468.00
1847 . . . . 2,641,852.52	1847 . . . . 2,296,299.00

The leading articles of export were:

	WHEAT, bu.	FLOUR, bbls.	BEEF, PORK, lbs.	WOOL, lbs.
1842	587,207	2,920	16,209	1,500
1843	628,966	10,876	21,795	22,952
1844	891,894	6,320	14,938	96,635
1845	956,860	13,752	13,268	216,616
1846 . . .	1,459,594	28,045	31,224	281,222
1847 . . .	1,974,304	32,538	48,920	411,488

More than ever the city needed a decent harbor. A sandbar persisted in reforming at the mouth of the river, so that the city resurrected a dredging scow scuttled by the federal government. In 1846 Congress appropriated $80,000 to improve the harbor again, along with some others on Lake Michigan. When President Polk vetoed the bill, Chicagoans were furious. As a result their representative in Congress, ''Long John'' Wentworth, requested that a national meeting be held in his city to debate the important issue of federal aid to improve rivers and harbors. Representatives from various sections of the country took up the call, and July 5, 1847, was set as the date for a ''River and Harbor Convention.''

The convention itself actually did little immediate good for Chicago's harbor. Congress's next appropriation was not made until 1852, and then it was only $20,000 to improve the inner harbor. But the River and Harbor Convention had some lasting effects on Chicago itself for it attracted a large number of outsiders to the city. Among them was the Whig Congressman Abraham Lincoln, who addressed the convention. The visitors beheld a city on the verge of gaining impressive commercial momentum. They also noted that Chicago could successfully handle a large convocation. (Lincoln would remember this 13 years later when he was in line to be nominated for President at the Republican party's national convention held in Chicago.)

The *New York Tribune's* Horace Greeley also attended the River and Harbor Convention, and would henceforth advise, "Go West, young man. ..." There too was Albany's influential journalist-politician, Thurlow Weed. Riding a few miles outside the city to see the prairies, Weed "found the road all the way occupied with an almost unbroken line of wagons, drawn generally by two yokes of oxen, bringing wheat to the City." He had seen the famed "prairie schooners" of the West.

The first stirrings of new physical growth were also felt in 1847. Chicago acquired its first permanent stage, the Rice Theater, founded by John B. Rice— who some 20 years later would be elected mayor. The city added another newspaper to its many journals when 400 copies of the *Chicago Tribune* were issued on June 10, 1847. Unfortunately, none of these first-day copies has survived.

Chicago's trade picture had broadened by 1847, as shown by Andreas who provided a table showing the general kinds of goods and merchandise and their values when received in Chicago in 1847 to be sold there.

SALEABLE GOODS AND MERCHANDISE, 1847

Dry goods	$837,451.22	Liquors	$86,334.67
Groceries	506,027.56	Tobacco and cigars	3,716.00
Hardware	148,811.50	Ship chandlery	23,000.00
Iron and nails	88,275.00	Tools and hardware	15,000.00
Stoves and hol'ware	68,612.00	Furniture trimming	5,564.07
Crockery	30,505.00	Glass	8,949.24
Boots and shoes	94,275.00	Scales	4,044.55
Hats, caps and furs	68,200.00	Coaches, etc	1,500.00
Jewelry, etc	51,000.00	Looking glasses, etc	2,500.00
Books and station'y	43,580.00	Marble	800.00
Printing paper	7,284.11	Oysters	2,500.00
Presses, type, and		Sportsmen's articles	2,000.00
printing materials	7,432.50	Musical instruments	6,426.00
Drugs & medicines	92,081.41	Machinery, etc	30,000.00
Paints and oils	25,460.00		

Total value of imports of merchandise $2,259,309.83

The dry goods figure indicates how strong Chicago had already become in that trade. The sales of retail dry goods—encompassing textiles, clothing, and "notions"—dated back to the 1830s. The wholesale trade in dry goods was

Facing page, top left: When Thurlow Weed of Albany came to Chicago in 1847 he noted the many wheat-carrying prairie schooners just outside the city. These ox or mule-drawn large wooden wagons with their white canvas covers received their name because when seen from a distance they resembled ships with billowing sails. Courtesy, Chicago Board of Trade

Bottom left: John Blake Rice, an actor, founded the first permanent theater in Chicago—the Rice Theater—in 1847. Once, when a fire reportedly broke out in it, the audience panicked. "Do you think I would let my theater catch on fire?" Rice demanded. It did. The patrons, who escaped, balked when Rice tried to get donations from them to replace the building. From Gilbert and Bryson, *Chicago and Its Makers,* 1929

Right: After attending the River and Harbor Convention in Chicago, the *New York Tribune's* Horace Greeley advised "Go West, young man and grow up with the country." Watercolor by Thomas Nast. Courtesy, National Portrait Gallery, Smithsonian Institution, Washington, D.C.

started in 1845 by Hamilton and Day with Cooley, Wadsworth and Company wholesaling on a large scale two years later. Chicago increasingly began handling a variety of goods for outlying areas, involving the ordering, receiving, storing, shipping out, and billing of products received from eastern manufacturers. Eventually, of course, this healthy traffic encouraged Chicago business interests to commence their own manufacturing ventures rather than rely on firms far away—thus multiplying the possibility for profits as well as contributing to greater employment.

The population of Chicago in 1848 was 20,023, which represented only 1/150th of the population it would attain in its next 50 years. Yet several phenomenal events happened in 1848 in the little city mired in the mud and smelling of its stockyards.

The Illinois and Michigan Canal was completed at last. The canal had been proposed in Congress in 1810, had been started 26 years after that, and was finally finished with the help of European loans. On April 10, 1848, the *General Fry* sailed into the Chicago River from Lockport to the cheering of crowds. Later, starting on April 19, the *General Thornton* made the entire canal trip, from LaSalle to Chicago, arriving on April 23.

Although traffic through the canal nearly stagnated for the first few months because of an insufficient supply of both water and canal boats (only 16 were in use), traffic became heavy by the end of the summer. St. Louis was the first major city to experience an adverse impact from this new route to the East, thus beginning the perennial rivalry with Chicago that sometimes grew intensely acrimonious. In 1848, St. Louis shipped 316,625 fewer bushels of corn and 237,588 less of wheat than the year before, and again in 1849 it suffered a decrease in shipping volume.

As a result of the burgeoning wheat crops from the hinterland, Chicago's grain storage elevators began to spring up along the river. These enormous buildings—which stand out in old etchings of Chicago—were for generations a primary key to Chicago's prosperity.

The Illinois and Michigan Canal gave the farmers in areas close to the new waterway the opportunity to ship their produce by barges to Chicago, rather than using the dusty roads that, after rainfall, became muddy and tended to trap their heavily-laden wagons. From Chicago, across Lakes Michigan, Huron, and Erie, schooners filled with the grain harvest of the Midwest would enter the Erie Canal, bound for New York City—or points along the way, from Buffalo through to Mohawk Valley and on to the Hudson River and Albany. Some also headed for Canadian ports.

The possibility of profit making attracted the middlemen—merchants and traders—to Chicago near the time when the crops were ready to arrive, in order to speculate on the grain market. Already some of them tried to "corner the

Facing page, top: Midwestern farmers brought their grain to Chicago before it was shipped to the East. Because traders and middlemen-merchants would gather in the city to speculate on the grain market, Chicago businessmen decided to establish the Board of Trade where buyers and sellers could meet and engage in an open auction to set prices for current and future grain crops. Courtesy, Chicago Board of Trade

Bottom left: McCormick's reaper revolutionized 19th-century farming. With this incredible machine a farmer could reap a thousand acres as easily as he could a 10-acre patch by hand. Pictured here is McCormick's first reaper, designed in 1831. Sixteen years later, McCormick moved to Chicago and began manufacturing an improved reaper under the firm name of McCormick and Gray. From Andreas, *History of Chicago,* 1884

Bottom right: Cyrus McCormick, unlike most prominent 19th-century Chicago residents, was a Southerner (from Virginia) rather than a Yankee (from the Northeast). His McCormick Reaper Works, despite heavy competition, became the leading manufacturer and distributor of reaping machines in the world. From Andreas, *History of Chicago,* 1884

market'' in grain, or else engaged in unsavory and unethical ''bucket shop'' tactics to cheat other would-be profiteers. Thus the resident Chicago businessmen wisely created a Board of Trade to provide a single, convenient place for all buyers and vendors to meet together and engage in an open auction that set prices for current or future grain crops. This facility set definite rules for behavior that endure to this day. The Board's administrators, anxious to retain a good name in their city's primary form of commerce, tried to supervise all trading activities relative to grain and to make sure that the funds involved in the transactions—increasingly considerable—were solid. Thus a close connection was established between the Board of Trade (and other commodity exchanges to come) and the growing number of banking firms.

Wheat and corn were far from being the only commodities shipped on the canal, which of course offered two-way traffic. The other main ones—sugar, merchandise, and lumber—interestingly enough, proved much more stable, both for Chicago's economy and for the operation of the canal. This was partly because merchandise and lumber traveled westward, to the plains and its small towns and farms. The following table, offered by Putnam in *The Illinois and Michigan Canal,* shows the volume of trade in the six years following the opening of Chicago's canal.

YEAR	WHEAT, bu.	CORN, bu.	SUGAR, lbs.	MDSE., lbs.	LUMBER, ft.
1848	454,111	516,230	3,219,122	4,948,000	15,425,357
1849	579,598	754,288	4,218,298	9,176,943	26,882,000
1850	417,036	317,674	5,680,324	10,372,623	38,687,528
1851	78,062	2,878,550	4,591,471	14,175,928	56,845,027
1852	117,441	1,810,880	4,822,297	15,390,346	52,510,051
1853	340,277	2,490,675	7,332,032	10,687,598	58,500,438

In Chicago, with the canal's opening, the word ''commerce'' began to take on increased meaning. The little city, its harbor filled with multimasted schooners, was still principally involved in shipping raw goods, and volume was increasing geometrically. Even if businessmen found themselves with four or five competitors, all of them might prosper. The competition usually was not for more business but rather for the labor to build more facilities such as grain elevators and boat slips. Fortunately the ships that came from the East to pick up grain, corn, and sugar also began to carry the workmen to build the city. Steamboats on Lake Michigan brought the necessary lumber from areas such as Green Bay, Wisconsin, although they never seemed to bring enough of it, since wood was also sent out on canal boats to the almost treeless prairie settlements.

Another industry that eventually would help increase Chicago's commerce and overall prosperity arrived in 1847 when Cyrus Hall McCormick and Charles M. Gray, a local manufacturer of cradles and scythes, began construction of a "large establishment" along the North Bank of the Chicago River. They intended to construct 500 mechanized reapers in the 1848 season. Eventually McCormick bought out his partners, Gray and William B. Ogden. The McCormick harvester—at first pulled by horses, mules, or oxen, then engine-driven—would soon begin to revolutionize the agricultural activity of the Midwest. Farming machinery would mechanize procedures from plowing and planting through reaping, binding, and threshing.

The city that had waited 12 years for its canal to be finished also saw its first railroad, the Galena and Chicago Union Railroad, another transportation innovation proposed in 1836, completed in 1848. In the 1830s, Galena, Illinois, was a flourishing city on the Fever River, navigable a few miles upriver from the Mississippi. A center for lead mining, it begged to be bonded with Chicago. A company with plans to connect the two towns by rail was chartered by the state of Illinois on January 16, 1836. Because Galena's future looked brighter, its name came first in the railroad's title. The incorporators of the railroad were granted three years to begin work and were given the option of using animal or steam power. The capital stock was placed at $100,000, but could be increased to one million dollars.

The year 1836 had been an ambitious one for railroad dreams in the state. The Illinois Central was incorporated two days after the Galena and Chicago Union. The state legislature drew plans and granted charters for more railroads and canals to form a network in Illinois as part of the Internal Improvement Act of February 27, 1837. Only one rail system was completed at the time: a six-mile stretch of track from the Mississippi River to East St. Louis. Another one, The Northern Cross between Springfield and Meredosia on the Illinois River, was eventually finished, but it proved so unsuccessful that its steam engine was replaced by mules.

In 1837 a route for the Galena and Chicago Union was surveyed from North Dearborn Street west to the Des Plaines River. In 1838 laborers began driving piles along Madison Street for the track bed. But the economic depression ended the venture almost at once.

Four years later the idea of the Galena and Chicago Union was revived with a rally in Rockford, the halfway point between Galena and Chicago. Three men created new impetus for the infant railway: William B. Ogden, Chicago's first mayor; lawyer Jonathan Young Scammon of Chicago; and Thomas Drummond, then of Galena and later of Chicago. They arranged to purchase the charter from those who had started the road, for $20,000 "in full paid stock"—half payable upon organization of the board of directors, and the other half upon the railroad's reaching the Rock River.

In September 1843, at the instigation of John S. Wright and his *Prairie Farmer,* Chicago sponsored a cattle show and fair. Because times were hard, Wright encouraged farmers to bring cheap cotton tents and their own provisions. The show and fair signified the beginning of Chicago's future in the convention business, cattle trade, and farm implement manufacturing industry. From the author's collection

PRAIRIE FARMER.

DEVOTED TO WESTERN AGRICULTURE, MECHANICS AND EDUCATION.

Vol. III.   CHICAGO, SEPTEMBER, 1843.   No. 9.

EDITED BY
JOHN S. WRIGHT AND J. AMBROSE WIGHT.
OFFICE, 112 LAKE STREET, CHICAGO, ILLINOIS.

ADVERTISEMENTS inserted on the following terms: for one square or under, first insertion, one dollar fifty cents; second, one dollar; subsequent ones, seventy five cents. More than one square will be counted as two; more than two, as three, and so on.

Yearly advertisers charged eight dollars for one square, and four dollars for each additional square. A square contains twelve lines.

Cards of six lines or less inserted for four dollars for the year.

Communications upon patent implements and machines, accompanied with cash, inserted for $3 for one column or less; $2 for each additional column or part of a column.

☞ Payments for advertisements to be always in advance.

For terms of the Prairie Farmer, see last page.

THE CATTLE SHOW AND FAIR.

POSSIBLY you will not see another No. of the Prairie Farmer till it will be too late to urge your attendance at the exhibition of the Union Agricultural Society, and we embrace the present opportunity to say one word about it.

That this exhibition is to be most creditable to the great West—that the attendance is to be fully equal to what the most sanguine have anticipated—there is no reason to doubt. We have travelled pretty extensively in the district of the Society and the adjoining counties, and the farmers appear to be making calculations to attend. It is indeed to be the Farmer's Holiday, for all northern Illinois, and those who take no part in it will most certainly regret their negligence. The expense will be almost the only hindrance, and the only one which ought to operate with farmers, and if they will adopt the plan recommended by the Society, to unite in companies, taking along a cheap tent made of cotton cloth, with their own provisions, &c., the expense will be almost nothing in money. It will be really a beautiful sight to see several hundred tents spread on such an occasion, and it is to be hoped that all who can add to the sight, will do so.

It has been impossible to make arrangements definitely, so that we can state what they are to be; but addresses are expected from several individuals from abroad, who have been written to, besides some of our own members.

The trial of plows alone will excite interest sufficient to insure a very large attendance, and the number of competitors will probably be larger than at the last exhibition. This part of the arrangements is justly considered to be of primary importance. Farmers are desirous of knowing where the best plow is to be obtained, and every manufacturer is anxious to convince the public that his pattern is exactly the thing. Both are wide awake to avail themselves of this grand opportunity for each to gain his object.

The show of stock will be large; and in Stark and Knox counties we were informed several farmers were going from that region expressly to purchase at the Fair. If those who have more than they need understand their true interests, they will be sure to show them at this time. They will probably be able to dispose of their surplus at fair prices.

In exhibitions of mechanical skill, we can only say, the interest of mechanics will prompt them to do all they can. Another more favorable opportunity to introduce specimens of their handiwork to the notice of their best customers, they need not expect soon to have, and wisdom will therefore dictate to them to improve the present. Will they not do it?

In butter and cheese, and articles of domestic manufacture, dependence is placed chiefly upon the ladies to see the exhibition made creditable, and we have too much gallantry to doubt them, even if we had not a tithe of the evidence already in our possession, that they will nobly sustain their part. May the rest of the exhibition be as well supported as this!

To the inhabitants of this district—to every farmer—yes, to every citizen, would we make a special appeal in behalf of this exhibition. Our reputation is at stake, for whether deserved or not, this Society is looked to as an example; and shall we not all take that interest in it that will cause the necessary exertions and sacrifices to be made, by which our reputation will not only be saved but increased? From all the surrounding counties there will be a large attendance; and having passed through Bureau, Stark, Knox, and Warren, we know there will be quite a number from those counties. We have heard also of companies that were coming from Henry, Mercer, Hancock, Peoria, Fulton, Adams, Tazewell, Sangamon, and Morgan; and from other of the central counties there will probably be individuals present, and from all the northern counties there will be more or less in attendance. And now shall there not be an exhibition of stock, implements, &c., that will correctly indicate the zeal in agricultural improvement in this part of the State? We doubt not there will be. If we cannot show as large herds of blooded stock, we can exhibit individual animals from which will spring herds as fine as any others in the West. Let not an animal or implement be left at home that is worth showing. †

THE PLOWING MATCH.—Let it not be forgotten that the premium for the best specimen of prairie plowing is the PREMIUM PLOW. Who, of the many young men that will be in attendance, would not like to obtain it? Try then and see if *you* cannot win the prize. †

ERRATUM.—On page 198, 2d column, 7th line from top, instead of "unworked," read, unwashed.

With financing the primary problem, Drummond attempted to sell stock to Galena citizens, while Scammon went to residents of Chicago, and Ogden traveled on horseback to farmers living in between. Ogden proved the most successful of the three because he could appeal to the farmers' own best interests. One tavern keeper in Marengo, however—possibly because he was allied with other transportation forms—showed the kind of opposition the three men faced. He denounced railroads as "undemocratic, aristocratic institutions that would ride rough-shod over the people and grind them to powder." He declared that "the only roads the people want are good common or plank roads upon which everybody can travel."

Eastern railroad financiers too were equally skeptical of Ogden and his approach to financing the railroad, but certainly left the door open to some future advantage to them. "Railroad King" William F. Weld of Boston told Odgen, "You must go home, raise what money you can, expend it upon your road, and when it breaks down as it surely will, come and give it to us and we will take hold of it and complete it."

Ogden and his associates were selling stock to farmer-investors for as little as $2.50 each, although payment was often deferred until harvest. Odgen oversaw the railroad's successful scrimping. Property owners were granted six cents each for the right-of-way. The tracks were laid with used strap rail, which the eastern railroads had begun to replace with T rail. Finally, the railroad decided to purchase a secondhand engine, with payment to be made in stock. It seemed an impossible assignment at a time when engines were at a premium, but one was fortuitously found in New Buffalo, Michigan. Actually third hand, it had already put in 11 grueling years of service, the last stint in building the just-completed Michigan Central Railroad.

The little engine was shipped across the lake by boat. Its name changed from "The Alert" to "The Pioneer," it chugged out of Chicago for a 10-mile trip to Oak Ridge (now Oak Park) on the afternoon of October 25, 1848. A farmer had been induced with the promise of a free ride to allow his wheat to be shipped on the train for the return trip.

Chicago and northern Illinois had launched themselves into the new railroading era. The Galena and Chicago Union Railroad was a small operation with a big debt, but the future would pay for it. The total earnings of the railroad in 1849 were $23,763, but they rose to $104,359 the next year. By January 1850 the line had been extended to Elgin, 40 miles west of Chicago.

Dissension on the board of directors caused Ogden to quit in disgust. In the mid-1850s he acquired and consolidated what became the prosperous Chicago and North Western Railroad that serviced northern Illinois and Wisconsin. It, in turn, fittingly merged on June 2, 1864, with the Galena and Chicago Union Railroad, so that Ogden was once more the boss of Chicago's pioneer railway—

Facing page, left: William B. Ogden, who made a fortune in Chicago land, served as the city's first mayor in 1837. After establishing the area's first railroad in 1848, during the following decade he started the Chicago and North Western Railway and extended it through Wisconsin. President of the Union Pacific Railroad in the 1860s, Ogden helped to drive the golden spike (at Ogden Flats, Utah) that united East and West by rail. His two towns, Chicago and Peshtigo, Wisconsin, burned on the same day in 1871. From Andreas, *History of Chicago,* 1884

Right: By 1839 Frink, Walker and Company operated a stage service three times a week to the booming lead mining town of Galena. Each trip took 24 hours. By the late 1840s the firm controlled 2,000 to 3,000 miles of stage line and mail routes throughout the Midwest. Courtesy, Chicago Historical Society

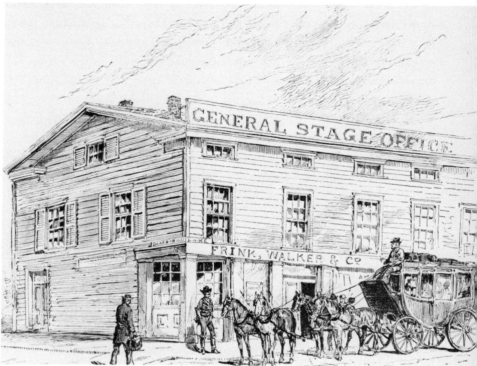

which never did get to Galena anyway.

Historically, 1848 was Chicago's pivotal year. Two other major events besides the canal and railroad had immediate impact on the city. One was the opening of a telegraph line to Milwaukee, followed later in the year by an eastward line. And the end of that year the *Chicago Tribune* announced it was subscribing to O'Reilly's telegraph line, which was actually a combination of telegraph and stage-coach lines connecting it to the East. Chicago's shell of isolation was broken. News of congressional and federal legislation no longer arrived weeks after the actual event.

The fourth event making that year memorable was the building of a plank road to the southwest into prime farming country. In September the road was opened to the Des Plaines River. It was eight feet wide and consisted of planks three inches thick. A toll road, it earned $1,500 in its first month of operation. A route that had been pure mud in wet weather was now passable all year round. This was the first of many such roads leading to and from the farmlands south and west of Chicago.

If Chicago felt that at last it was conquering its environment's limitations, it had become too self-confident. The year 1849 would teach the city two severe lessons. On March 12, 1849, Chicago suffered a freak calamity sent by Mother Nature. A major flood made local residents wonder about the future of Chicago and its river. A contemporary newspaper, the *Chicago Daily Journal* described how at 10 o'clock an ice mass on the South Branch broke loose and moved downriver, crushing every bridge and many wharves on the Chicago River. Almost all boats in port—four steamers, six propeller crafts, 24 brigs, 27 canal boats, and two sloops—were damaged or destroyed. Most of the vessels and pieces of bridges and wharves were swept out into Lake Michigan as a huge collection of debris. But there was also the human toll. A boy was crushed to death at the Randolph Street bridge, a little girl was killed by the falling of a topmast, and a number of men were reported lost upon canal boats which had been sunk, and upon the ice and bridges as the jam broke up. One poor fellow on a canal boat waves his handkerchief as a signal of distress, about ten miles out, during the afternoon; but there was no boat which could be sent to his assistance.

As if this had not been enough, cholera broke out. From July 15 to August 28 an epidemic raged; 1,000 persons were victims of the disease, and 314 of them died. Cholera would reappear periodically to scourge Chicago until the start of the new century, when Chicago at last found a clever way to handle its wastes.

As the 1840s ended, Chicagoans could look back on a dramatic period. The city had suffered an almost decade-long depression along with an epidemic and flood. By 1848, however, Chicago's destiny was swinging toward untold progress and prosperity. Some of the lessons learned as a result of tragedy and hard times helped Chicago face its future, which would include more bubbles burst, a divisive war, and some terrible fires. Still, the strongest belief to come out of the 1840s was that Chicago would be an American hub city—the center of Midwestern commerce and, ultimately, of the the whole continent.

A few men, such as William B. Ogden, John S. Wright, John Wentworth, and Wiliam "Deacon" Bross already believed that the future of American business rightly belonged to Chicago—and went around the country saying so. For others, the new prosperity seemed more accidental than purposeful. They had gambled on the city just by settling there. Whatever their abilities to predict Chicago's future, all of them put their money down on the city—and the spinning wheel of fortune often came up with Chicago's lucky number.

The Chicago River demonstrated a violent nature only once in history— March 12, 1849. The bridges were knocked out and for the next few months it cost one cent to cross the river by schooner. This etching made from a daguerreotype of the flood's aftermath represents the first "news" photo in the city's history. From Andreas, *History of Chicago,* 1884

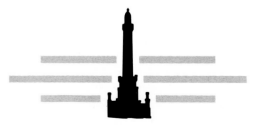

CHAPTER FIVE

THE OPEN GATE
TO THE WEST
THE 1850s

By 1857 Chicago had become both a residential and commercial city. The North Side at this time was highly residential and the swing bridges over the river were kept busy if one is to believe the number and size of ships shown. The disproportionately large structure at bottom left is the Illinois Central terminus. Lithograph by C. Inger from a drawing by James Palmatary. From the author's collection

During the decade from 1850 to 1860, Chicago evolved from a minor city of small industries and modest commerce into a major trade and manufacturing center. As the whole Midwest began exploding economically, Chicago was its nucleus.

Suddenly, it seemed, the wood-burning "iron horses" came chugging into Chicago from every direction. They brought rapid, extensive development and a cornucopia of wealth to the city. They exchanged loads with lake steamboats and schooners, long lines of canal barges, and team-pulled wagons, overloaded with Midwestern produce that was coming in on the new plank roads.

Zestful and youthful, Chicago gained national fame for its astoundingly successful commercialism. People everywhere wanted its formula. Reporters analyzed the city with statistics and anecdotes. Since many such tabulations and accounts still exist, the dramatic growth of Chicago in the 1850s can be examined in retrospect.

The decade started well when Chicago rated a favorable mention in Daniel S. Curtiss' *Western Portraiture and Emigrant's Guide,* which set down notable features that might well attract any vigorous and enterprising fellow eager to move to a place of strong economic action. " " *The leading articles of export from this city are wheat, flour, pork, beef, horses, wool, cattle, lard, etc., eastward by steamboat and sail vessels; lumber, merchandise, ironwood, wood and iron machinery, farming utensils, etc., southward by canal, and westward by railroad. ... In a single year the value of exports from that place has been between two and three millions of dollars; besides its vast lumber trade, of nearly two hundred million feet, distributed in all directions, to supply the wants of a vast country, so rapidly being settled and ornamented with fine buildings, fences, etc. " "*

Meanwhile, Chicago's extensive railroad system was being born. In 1851 the Galena and Chicago Union, *Hunts' Merchants Magazine* reported, was completed to the distance of "almost 80 miles." The Rock Island line stretched six miles from Chicago, at which point it was intersected by the Michigan Southern Road. "It is expected," the article continued, "that the road will be completed to Joliet by the month of July, 1852, and that Rock Island will be reached in two to three years." The Chicago branch of the Central Railroad had "recently disposed of four millions of its bonds, and will commence the construction of this branch immediately." Subsequently known as the Illinois Central, the railroad received this comment: "Of all the railroads connected with Chicago, we anticipate the largest benefit from this one."

Like the great Chicago and North Western Railroad with its humble yet dramatic start in the Galena and Chicago Union through Ogden's persuasive powers with farmer investors, another key Chicago railroad can boast of a romantic inception. John S. Wright, ever the Chicago booster, drafted petition after petition to congress to help initiate the Illinois Central. He asked that railroad companies be granted lots along its right-of-way which could then be sold to finance building costs. It was a revolutionary idea because the country had been building railroads for over 20 years without such subsidies. Chicago's Stephen A. Douglas was working in Congress as hard as Wright to get the land grants. They succeeded. The plan later allowed the railroads to expand westward and to capitalize the construction of the transcontinental Union Pacific and Central Pacific railroads.

Chicago's geographical isolation from the East was ending. It took at least 20 days for passengers and mail to arrive from New York City through the waterways, through the Erie Canal and on Great Lakes steamers, or about eight days by train and then boat or stagecoach. In 1853 the New York Central Railroad made a connection with the Michigan Southern so that traveling time was further reduced. By 1870 it would be possible to travel from New York to Chicago without changing trains.

Through the eyes and financial reporting of "Deacon" William Bross, we can view Chicago's economic progress in the 1850s. Bross was editor and publisher of *The Daily Democratic Press,* a paper later merged with *The Tribune.* In 1854 he published a booklet called "The Railroads, History and Commerce of Chicago" which reported the following railroads leading into Chicago completed and in operation:

CHICAGO'S RAILROADS, 1854

ILLINOIS & WISCONSIN to Deer Grove	32 miles
GALENA & CHICAGO UNION to Freeport	121 miles
Beloit Branch of the Galena	20 miles
GALENA AIR LINE, to Lane, Ogle Co.	75 miles
CHICAGO, ST. CHARLES & MISSISSIPPI	10 miles
CHICAGO & AURORA	89 miles

After many hours of hard work, John S. Wright and Stephen A. Douglas were able to get Congress to approve land grants to railroad companies. This land would then be sold to finance railroad construction. By about 1860 the Illinois Central was selling its land for "$7 to $12 and upward per acre." Courtesy, Illinois Central Gulf Railroad

ILLINOIS CENTRAL RAILROAD COMPANY

OFFER FOR SALE

ONE MILLION ACRES OF SUPERIOR FARMING LANDS,

IN FARMS OF

40, 80 & 160 acres and upwards at from $8 to $12 per acre.

THESE LANDS ARE

NOT SURPASSED BY ANY IN THE WORLD.

THEY LIE ALONG

THE WHOLE LINE OF THE CENTRAL ILLINOIS RAILROAD,

For Sale on LONG CREDIT, SHORT CREDIT and for CASH, they are situated near TOWNS, VILLAGES, SCHOOLS and CHURCHES.

For all Purposes of Agriculture.

The lands offered for sale by the Illinois Central Railroad Company are equal to any in the world. A healthy climate, a rich soil, and railroads to convey to market the fullness of the earth—all combine to place in the hands of the enterprising workingman the means of independence.

Illinois.

Extending 380 miles from North to South, has all the diversity of climate to be found between Massachusetts and Virginia, and varieties of soil adapted to the products of New England and those of the Middle States. The black soil in the central portions of the State is the richest known, and produces the finest corn, wheat, sorghum and hay, which latter crop, during the past year, has been highly remunerative. The seeding of these prairie lands to tame grasses, for pasture, offers to farmers with capital the most profitable results. The smaller prairies, interspersed with timber, in the more southern portion of the State, produce the best of winter wheat, tobacco, flax, hemp and fruit. The lands still further South are heavily timbered, and here the raising of fruit, tobacco, cotton and the manufacture of lumber yield large returns. The health of Illinois is hardly surpassed by any State in the Union.

Grain and Stock Raising.

In the list of corn and wheat producing States, Illinois stands pre-eminently first. Its advantages for raising cattle and hogs are too well known to require comment here. For sheep raising, the lands in every part of the State are well adapted, and Illinois can now boast of many of the largest flocks in the country. No branch in industry offers greater inducements for investment.

Hemp, Flax and Tobacco.

Hemp and flax can be produced of as good quality as any grown in Europe. Tobacco of the finest quality is raised upon lands purchased of this Company, and it promises to be one of the most important crops of the State. Cotton, too, is raised, to a considerable extent, in the southern portion. The making of sugar from the beet is receiving considerable attention, and experiments upon a large scale have been made during the past season. The cultivation of sorghum is rapidly increasing, and there are numerous indications that ere many years Illinois will produce a large surplus of sugar and molasses for exportation.

Fruit.

The central and southern parts of the State are peculiarly adapted to fruit raising ; and peaches, pears and strawberries, together with early vegetables, are sent to Chicago, St. Louis and Cincinnati, as well as other markets, and always command a ready sale.

Coal and Minerals.

The immense coal deposits of Illinois are worked at different points near the Railroad, and the great resources of the State in iron, lead, zinc, limestone, potters' clay, &c., &c., as yet barely touched, will eventually be the source of great wealth.

To Actual Settlers

the inducements offered are so great that the Company has already sold 1,500,000 acres, and the sales during the past year have been to a larger number of purchasers than ever before. The advantages to a man of small means, settling in Illinois, where his children may grow up with all the benefits of education and the best of public schools, can hardly be over-estimated. No State in the Union is increasing more rapidly in population, which has trebled in ten years along the line of this Railroad.

PRICES AND TERMS OF PAYMENT.

The price of land varies from $7 to $12 and upward per acre, and they are sold on long credit, on short credit, or for cash. A deduction of *ten per cent.* from the long credit price is made to those who make a payment of one-fourth of the principal down, and the balance in one, two, and three years. A deduction of **twenty per cent.** is made to those who purchase for cash. Never before have greater inducements been offered to cash purchasers.

EXAMPLE.

Forty acres at $10 per acre on long credit, interest at six per cent., payable annually in advance ; the principal in four, five, six, and seven years.

	INTEREST.	PRINCIPAL.
Cash payment,	$24.00	
Payment in one year,	24.00	
" two years,	24.00	
" three "	24.00	
" four "	18.00	$100.00
" five "	12.00	100.00
" six "	6.00	100.00
" seven "		100.00

Or the same farm, on short credit :

	INTEREST.	PRINCIPAL.
Cash payment,	$16.20	$90.00
Payment in one year,	10.80	90.00
" two years,	5.00	90.00
" three		90.00

The same farm may be purchased for $320 in cash.

CHICAGO & ROCK ISLAND to Geneseo	158 miles
CHICAGO & MISSISSIPPI, Alton to Bloomington	132 miles
Great Western, Naples to Springfield	65 miles
ILLINOIS CENTRAL	245 miles
MICHIGAN SOUTH & NORTH, Indiana to Toledo	242 miles
MICHIGAN CENTRAL, New Albany & Salem	155 miles
Total	1,626 miles

Of all the Chicago railroads, the Illinois Central would have the greatest physical impact. The Illinois Central wanted, and got, a 300-foot-wide swath of submerged land along the lakeshore, in spite of early city ordinances that forbad commercial use of the waterfront. At first the railway was built across trestles above the water. The company, however, had agreed to create a breakwater that would protect the shoreline from the pounding of waves. Through the years boulders and miscellaneous landfill (notably rubble from the Great Fire of 1871) created a sea wall, then many acres of dry land. As if to announce its importance, the new railroad built the nation's largest and grandest depot. Ridiculed at first as cavernously large, within a dozen years it would be too small for its needs.

Hunt's Merchants Magazine had showered abundant enthusiasm on the city's new and projected plank roads. In 1851 the bushels of corn that came by plank road doubled the number arriving by railroad. Most of this corn was a product of the fertile Illinois River Valley. Downriver from the valley was St. Louis. Upriver and through the canal was Chicago. In the competition for handling the corn, Chicago was outdoing St. Louis almost two to one because of "superior facilities for receiving and forwarding grain, the less expense of storage, reshipment and commissions."

Another potentially important advance in transportation took place in 1855, when the canal and locks were completed at Sault Ste. Marie at the entrance to Lake Superior. By passing the rapids that had thwarted commercial traffic, the Soo Canal would permit the shipping of the northern region's abundant timber. Later its iron ore came to Chicago's port, once the fabulously rich iron mines were opened and special scows were devised for the heavy freight.

Mid-19th century visitors to Chicago were inclined to reveal its attributes and deficiencies. Rapid growth created a number of municipal problems for the new city. One of the latter often mentioned in the late 1840s was its lack of gaslight. Writing of his memories of Chicago in the 1830s, E.O. Gale had said:

" " *Added to the discomforts enumerated. We must not lose sight of the gloom that evening shadows cast, when no cheerful light could be obtained and families were doomed to sit in almost absolute darkness. A whale oil lamp was but little better than the tallow candle or the saucer of grease in which floated in an ignited rag. Kerosene,*

Facing page, top: Seth Paine, who intermingled wit, sarcasm, Christianity, and banking, also issued his own newspaper—the *Christian Banker*—and his own money (shown here). Eventually all Paine's Bank of Chicago notes had to be turned in. From Andreas, *History of Chicago*, 1884

Bottom left: Robert Schuyler became the Illinois Central's first president in March of 1851. He served in this position until July of 1853. Courtesy, Illinois Central Gulf Railroad

Bottom right: Chicago booster William "Deacon" Bross edited and published *The Daily Democratic Press*, a newspaper through which he disseminated information about the city's economy. Courtesy, Chicago Historical Society

though first used to a limited extent in 1826, was not burned in this part of the country for many years later. 　　Finally, on September 4, 1850, the city of Chicago was lighted with gas for the first time. At two in the afternoon, the city's gas pipes were filled and the humming sound at the top of lampposts indicated that the streets would be lighted that night. The firm responsible for this wonder was the Chicago Gas Light and Coke Company, chartered in perpetuity by the state legislature on February 12, 1849. A decade later, when the 10-year exclusive charter had run its course, a competitor entered the arena: the People's Gas Light and Coke Company. High rates and charges of monopoly were among the reasons for chartering this new firm. Between 1862 and 1864, the companies split up the city. Subsequently, the Chicago city council regulated prices. For decades, charges would be made that rate setting and franchise extending were done principally by bribery payments to the aldermen—a situation repeated later in the traction companies' connection with municipal corruption.

The public street transportation issue was relatively simple in the early 1850s. In 1850, intracity transit was initiated with an omnibus line that ran from the business district to what is now Lincoln Park. At first simply a stagecoach, the omnibus was eventually elongated to serve more passengers.

The condition of Chicago's undrained streets, however, wreaked continuous havoc with schedules, profits, and people's patience. As early as 1854 the city council passed an enabling ordinance for a street railway and requiring that only horse power be used; the fare would be five cents for a mile or less and 10 cents over a mile. The Panic of 1857 stifled the venture, but it was renewed in the following year when the city council granted a charter to Henry Fuller, Frank Parmalee, and Liberty Bigelow, giving them the right to construct and operate a street railway in the South and West Divisions for 25 years. Then the press and many members of the public objected that the charter did not limit prices nor did it state when the city could buy it back. This remained a crucial issue for years to come.

Chicago's bridges, essential in a city that stretched across three waterways—the outlet of the Chicago River and its North and South Branches—created their own problems for travelers needing to pass over when boats with masts demanded passage. A *Putnam's Monthly Magazine's* reporter drolly described the complications in the 1850s—some of which endure to this day.

　　The level of the streets is not more than three or four feet above the level of the river; the river being navigable, of course all bridges must be draw-bridges. Police-men are stationed on either side, to prevent persons from driving, jumping, or being pushed into the water, and the motive power (two men with a cross-bar, standing in the middle of the bridge) keeps up ... a perpetual "grind." People jump on and jump off as long as the policemen will let them. ... A bridge, however, cannot be turned in a minute (I think it usually takes about two), and, while the process is going on, a row

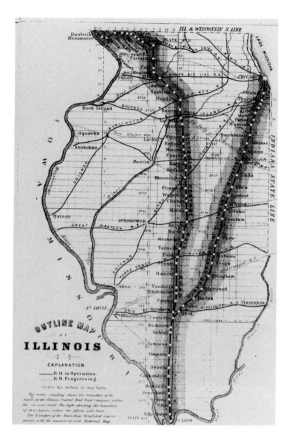

In the 1850s the destiny of the Midwest was signed, sealed, and delivered as the region became girded with railroads. Cities sprang up where railroads met waterways or other railroads. Most railroads headed toward Lake Michigan and Chicago. This single fact, more than any other, accounted for the phenomenal growth immediately ahead for the city. From *The Illinois Central Rail-Road Company,* 1856

of vehicles and impatience frequently accumulates that is quite terrific. There is a great deal of scolding on such occasions, and alas for human nature—sometimes, I fear, a slight degree of profanity. 99

People who lived in the North Side and worked in the main part of town across the river, or those who had appointments involving a river crossing, sometimes took as long as an hour to reach their destinations. Partial relief of the vehicular congestion would be obtained, in 1869 and 1871, when tunnels were burrowed beneath the river bed at Washington and LaSalle streets.

Another municipal problem difficult to ignore was the water supply, surely an essential element in any city's growth, maintenance, and its residents' health. William Bross, in spite of his reputation as one of Chicago's best boosters, was not reluctant later to describe how it was in the 1840s.

66 *At first, water was pumped in from the lakeshore, to be stored in a cistern and then piped through hollow logs. In rough weather the water would be muddy. Neighborhood wells were often contaminated. Many houses purchased their potable water by bucket or barrel from water-carts. In 1854 a large new water works was built, but that too pumped in water from the shoreline and presented unsavory problems.*

In the spring and early summer it was impossible to keep the young fish out of the reservoir, and it was no uncommon thing to find the unwelcome fry sporting in one's washbowl, or dead and stuck in the faucets. And besides they would find their way into the hot-water reservoir, where they would get stewed up into a very nauseous fish chowder. 99

The strong growth of Chicago attracted people from all parts of the country and the world. Such, certainly, was the observation of Isabella Lucy Bishop, an author who had to lodge in a fleabag hotel—which sounds suspiciously like the Sauganash—because the better establishments were filled to capacity. She later reported in *The Englishwoman in America* (1856) how she had sat down for dinner in a room that had a long table with plates—none too clean—laid out for 100 people. Four "brigand-looking waiters with prodigious beards and moustachios" proceeded to set down the common meal, partly consisting of greasy mutton legs and "antiquated fowls" which guests pulled apart with their hands or hacked at with drawn bowie-knives. After satisfying her own immediate hunger, the visitor looked at her fellow diners: 66 *There were Scots, for Scots are always to be found where there is any hope of honest gain—there were Irish emigrants, speaking with a rich brogue—French traders from St. Louis—Mexicans from Santa Fe—Californians fitting out, and Californians coming home with fortunes made—keen-eyed speculators from New England—packmen from Canada— "Prairie-men," trappers, hunters, and adventurers of all descriptions.* 99

Rubbing elbows with colorful characters was one thing; allowing them to become voters or to occupy jobs with any authority was quite another. Jacksonian democracy had already put the common man, the workingman, into the

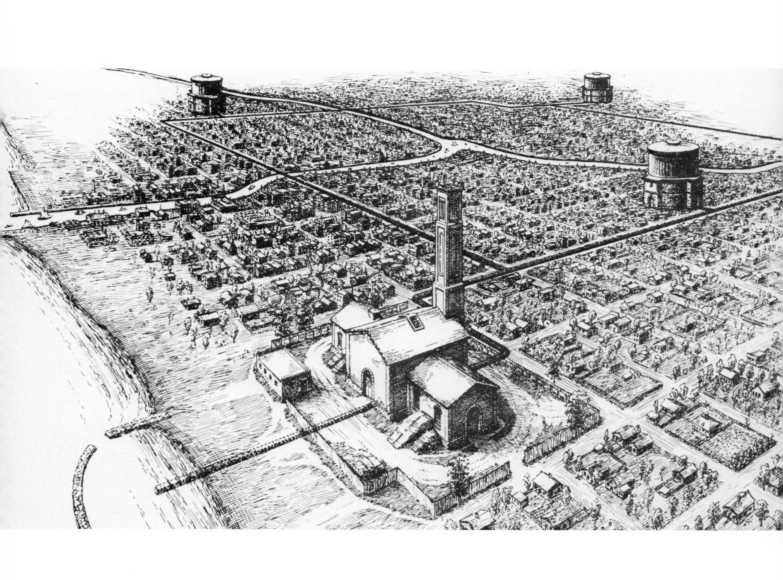

Chicago's municipal waterworks, built in 1854, served the city's 35,000 residents. Its pumps operated just nine hours a day and not at all on Sundays, except in case of fire. Of the cylindrical reservoirs in the background, *Ballou's Pictorial* said: "The style of the building affords a pleasant contrast to the massive square structures usually erected for that purpose." From the author's collection

polls of America. Now that the country was becoming increasingly a haven for the indigent and the politically restless, the entire issue of suffrage and office-holding qualifications was being reexamined.

Individuals wanted the republic to be a meritocracy, if not a plutocracy. Such prejudices led native-born citizens to organize the "Know-Nothing" or Native American political party, which for a time concealed even its name and always hid its purpose (basically anti-immigration and anti-Catholicism) in the cloak of ritualistic secrecy. According to the Know-Nothings, only native-born Americans and those Protestants who had been naturalized should vote. "Put none but Americans on guard," was their slogan.

The majority of Chicago's voters chose a Know-Nothing candidate, Levi D. Boone, as mayor in 1854. He started off his administration by making native birth a requisite for serving on the police force, thereby infuriating the Irish already employed as policemen. Then, in 1855, he decided to put the German population equally on the defensive by upping the saloon license fee from $50 to a prohibitive $300. He also decreed a Sunday closure of the beer parlors, where the Germans and Scandinavians on the North Side drank, ate, met, and argued politics. Boone apparently thought he was satisfying not just his Know-Nothing constituents, but also the growing number of temperance advocates.

Boone's actions proved fatal to several citizens and eventually to himself, politically. Enforcing the new rules, his magistrates arrested a handful of German saloon keepers, and on the day of their trial a gigantic mob of Germans began marching on the courthouse to demonstrate their wrath.

Bearing bricks, clubs, knives, and guns, several hundred of these civilian warriors approached the river. The first group got across before Mayor Boone ordered the drawbridge swung, thereby stranding the rioters until the policemen could be lined up along Clark Street, ready to receive them as they crossed over. As the furious Germans shouted orders to "Shoot the police!" and "Pick out the stars!" one blasted his shotgun and tore off a policeman's arm, only to be killed in the next instant by another officer. Wild warfare ensued as the men were prevented from advancing southward, and the melee ended at last with a retreat by the Germans, carrying their wounded with them. Mayor Boone had poised cannon around the city hall to ward off new attacks, but none came. Instead, the local citizenry began to express disapproval of both the Know-Nothings and Prohibition and soon voted in a liberal new administration.

A succeeding mayor attempted other reforms. In 1857 "Long John" Wentworth, after some years as a congressman, was elected mayor and took his new role seriously. He aimed at the reform of various forms of vice—prostitution, gambling, and other shady activities—that offered alluring opportunities for profit to some and entertainment to others.

Many of Mayor Wentworth's associates and their wives had expected, by

Above: Senator Stephen A. Douglas, founder of the original University of Chicago, was the man around whom swirled the slavery question. When the Civil War began, he rallied his fellow Democrats to the Union cause in support of Abraham Lincoln who had defeated him for the Presidency. The "Little Giant" is buried near his home at 35th Street just west of the Illinois Central Railroad. Courtesy, National Portrait Gallery, Smithsonian Institution, Washington, D.C.

Facing page: In the late 1850s Mayor John Wentworth practiced a highly personalized form of rule in Chicago. He once fired the entire police force, raided the redlight district known as The Sands, and introduced the Prince of Wales "to the boys." Also, as this illustration indicates, he ordered that all nonconforming street signs in Chicago be torn down. From Andreas, *History of Chicago*, 1884

electing him, to get something done once and for all about "The Sands," the notorious shanty town on the North Side inhabited by many in the city's underworld population. Wentworth chose to attack the settlement at a time when most of its residents were away, attending a rowdy dog fight which may actually have been arranged by the mayor. Wentworth, accompanied by 30 policemen, raided the settlement. They destroyed it by sledgehammer and fire—ousting its vice vendors. Unfortunately, they settled elsewhere in the city.

Meanwhile, Chicago's popular and eloquent senator, Stephen A. Douglas, had decided in 1854 that the city needed a good university and therefore offered 10 acres south of 31st Street to the Baptists, who began gathering funds for a building program. Because of a series of financial problems the project did not take off for several years.

Concurrently, Douglas had been beset by serious political problems. He had courageously combatted the Know-Nothing party, which not only gained him the loyalty of immigrant voters, the Irish in particular, but also vilification from various native-born citizens. Baffling and infuriating to the liberal-minded population was his promoting of the Kansas-Nebraska Act in Congress, which left the slavery issue up to the settlers. Douglas' motivation was his customary espousal of states' rights and his view that this measure would secure conditions for getting a northern transcontinental railroad—one of his big dreams—started in Nebraska Territory.

Chicago became a divided camp of "pro-Nebraskans" and "anti-Nebraskans." The bill's passage in 1854 reversed the Missouri Compromise of 1820, which prohibited the extension of slavery in the Louisiana Territory north of 36°30′.

Antislavery and abolitionist voters, on the increase in northern Illinois, were furious with Douglas. The senator wryly admitted that on the train ride back from Washington, D.C., he could have read a newspaper by the light of all the effigies of him being burned along the route. In his home city on a Saturday night, a heckling crowd of 10,000 would not permit him to deliver a speech. At last, at midnight, after waiting cooly for hours, he told them: "It is now Sunday. I am going to church, and you can go to Hell."

Chicago had not heard the last about the problem of slavery. In 1858 the Tremont House balcony would be the scene of the initial speeches of the crucial, much publicized debates between Stephen A. Douglas—the "Little Giant"—and Springfield's gangling ex-congressman, lawyer Abraham Lincoln. Douglas, Chicago's champion politician, had done much in the nation's capital to promote the city's commercial welfare. But he was increasingly encountering opposition to his tendency to occupy a compromising or accommodating position regarding slavery. Like Daniel Webster before him, Douglas found many of his own loyal followers now deserting him, to join new political alliances like the Republican party.

Chicago, with its many entering and exiting railways also had a hardworking "underground railroad," providing terminals for escaped slaves coming from the mid-south and Missouri. "Operators" put their black passengers on ships heading for Canada and freedom. Among the best-known local abolitionists were "Deacon" William Bross, private detective Allan Pinkerton, and Leo Eastman. Chicagoans never permitted the return of a single slave to the South, defying the Fugitive Slave Law.

Feminism, another social reform movement of the decade that had been initially started by abolitionists, indirectly affected Chicago. In the early 1850s Bloomerism—the wearing of pantaloons beneath a skirt—had outraged or amused Chicagoans as a passing fad of female defiance. But Woman's Rights advocates, like Lucy Stone, Anna Dickinson, and Wendell Phillips were finding a hearty response among Midwestern women, who played crucial roles in the "civilizing" of frontier society.

The 1850s saw the blooming of culture in many forms in Chicago. Once the first millions were made in speculating, meatpacking, and railroad deals, it was time for the men to settle down, get wives, dress fashionably, and build mansions to impress others. Especially as they began having children, the once single-minded entrepreneurs began to concern themselves with schools, health-care facilities, and municipal issues such as fire protection and the quality of the drinking water. To enhance the life with "culture" seemed a good idea, and a busy businessman was usually glad to let his wife pursue the work of bringing culture to Chicago, using his name with a "Mrs." attached, which naturally meant using his money and influence too.

And culture did come to Chicago. Architect John M. Van Osdel commenced a long tenure of designing Chicago's most elegant homes and business premises. Portraitist George P.A. Healy came to stay. Sculptor Leonard W. Volk returned to make busts of the illustrious. Alexander Hesler photographed the city's faces and places. When John B. Rice's Theater burnt in 1850, a new and better one was built. There were also McVicker's Theater, the Tremont Music Hall, and the Metropolitan Hall for dramas, concerts, and operas. The Mechanics' Institute offered lectures. Traveling theatrical and music companies and noted speakers all visited Chicago. And there were activities such as charity balls, and literary-club meetings. Rush Medical College, the Baptists' new University of Chicago, and Northwestern University (with the affiliated Female Institution) in Evanston were offering courses in higher learning to the citizens.

Women probably deserve the credit for encouraging the start of a commercial enterprise closely linked to Chicago's business success—that of retail merchandising. Traditionally, they were responsible for feeding and clothing their families and furnishing their homes. As ready-made relatively inexpensive

Above: Allan Pinkerton, who arrived in the Chicago area in the 1840s, started his own detective agency the following decade. He specialized in railway theft cases. Once, he helped thwart an assassination attempt on Abraham Lincoln. Pinkerton was among Chicago's best known abolitionists. From Cirker, *Dictionary of American Portraits,* 1967

Facing page: "Long" John Wentworth was many things to Chicago: editor of its first newspaper (after John Calhoun); congressman (in the days of Webster, Clay, and Lincoln); mayor for two terms; farmer and landowner on the city's Southwest side; and lecturer in Chicago's early days. From Andreas, *History of Chicago,* 1884

Facing page, top: McVicker's Theatre provided entertainment for Chicago residents in the second half of the 19th century. Lithograph by Jevne and Almini. Courtesy, Chicago Historical Society (ICHi-06872)

Bottom left: Portrait painter George P.A. Healy, shown in this self-portrait, became Chicago's first professional artist when he arrived in the city in 1855. Prominent personalities who sat for him included the U.S. Presidents from John Quincy Adams to Ulysses S. Grant, Daniel Webster, and Henry Wadsworth Longfellow. The prolific painter died in Chicago in 1894. Courtesy, National Portrait Gallery, Smithsonian Institution, Washington, D.C.

Bottom right: An 1857 credit report on dry goods merchant Potter Palmer reads: "Making money, economical, business not too much extended, attends closely to business, does not pay large interest, good moral character, credits prudently, not sued, pays promptly. Credit good. Capital $25,000." A decade later Potter sold out to Marshall Field and Levi Z. Leiter. He subsequently became the city's most famous hotel owner (the Palmer House) and real-estate developer (32 buildings). Photo by Charles D. Mosher

products became available, women relied less on their own or others' handiwork.

Among Chicago merchants who astutely appealed to the lucrative women's trade, the leader in the 1850s was clearly Potter Palmer. He arrived from Oneida County, New York in 1852 and established P. Palmer and Company on Lake Street, the city's main but muddy business thoroughfare. Palmer treated his customers, whether wealthy or working people, with courtesy. He offered to exchange goods if the customer was not satisfied, a revolutionary gesture at the time. And he bought the best and most stylish goods, imported directly from Europe when this became easier through shipping from Liverpool via the St. Lawrence canal. (The ships could take back Midwestern grain.)

In the spring of 1856 another fledgling merchant came to Chicago from the East. Marshall Field, 21 years old, went to work for Cooley, Farwell and Company, Palmer's competitor on Lake Street. Field, who emulated Palmer's deferential respect for customers, would take over Palmer's business in partnership with Levi Z. Leiter in the 1860s.

The 1850s saw not only a proliferation but a sophistication in the building, expansion, or remodeling of the city's hotels. One of the best examples was the Briggs House built at Randolph and Wells in 1854 by William Briggs. Other hotels of the period were the Sherman House, the Lake View House, and the Planter's House. But the most famous hostelry of the era was the Tremont House built in 1850.

Englishman Anthony Trollope, coming later in the decade, provided an entertaining appraisal of the hotel—and the spirit of the city and citizenry around it. *At Chicago the hotel was bigger than other hotels, and grander. There were pipes without end for cold water which ran hot, and for hot water which would not run at all. The post-office also was grander and bigger than other post-offices—though the postmaster confessed to me that the delivery of letters was one which could not be compassed ... It was being done as a private speculation; but it did not pay, and would be discontinued. The theatre too was large, handsome, and convenient; but on the night of my attendance it seemed to lack an audience.*

The hotel trade would be the bedrock on which Chicago would build, eventually becoming the "convention capital" of the United States. They would also serve business people, cattle barons, cowboys, and new residents. They would be filled when, in 1859, some 70,000 people visited Chicago to attend a week-long agricultural fair. The climax, however, would be achieved in 1860, when every room was used for delegates to a convention that would change Chicago and national history.

In the 1850s the city still had an unkempt appearance, particularly to a critical eye—like that possessed by Swedish author Frederika Bremer, who visited in the early 1850s and wrote about Chicago in *The Homes of the New World:*

       Chicago is one of the most miserable and ugly cities which I have yet seen in America, and is very little deserving of its name, "Queen of the Lake," for she resembles rather a huckstress than a queen. Certainly, the city seems for the most part to consist of shops. And it seems as if, on all hands, people came here merely to trade, to make money, and not to live.

The Swedish visitor's acerbic comments were affirmed a few years later when a Rhode Island-based botanist named Edward L. Peckham came through Chicago: *Chicago, the world renowned Chicago, is as mean a spot as I ever was in, yet. The streets are laid out in squares and are in miserable condition of soft clay mud, which in many places, shakes and trembles as it is passed over. The side walks are very uneven, up hill and down, the buildings put up before the streets were graded and filled in, being the lowest from 3 to 8 feet below the foundation of houses raised upon the new grade, the ascent and descent being made by very steep steps to save room.*

The city's first approach to the drainage problem had been to remove soil from the streets, but this made them even muddier because of run-off from the sides where buildings stood. Shopkeepers, particularly those along the much-frequented Lake Street, would put up sidewalks outside their premises. The different periods in which contiguous buildings had been erected determined how they sat in relation to the street. As planks and dirt were periodically added to regrade the streets traveled by thousands of wagons, and other wheeled and

The Sherman House (above) and Tremont House (facing page) were two of Chicago's hotels in the 1850s. By the mid-19th century many of the city's hotels were built, expanded, or remodeled. Courtesy, Chicago Historical Society (ICHi-06875, ICHi-06891)

four-footed traffic, the older structures appeared to have settled into the dust or mire. Meatpacker Charles Cleaver delighted in reminiscing about the Tremont House's, situation. Built to the grade of earlier time, as the street in front of it got added to, it found itself about four feet below the surface. Steps and a wooden walkway were constructed so that people could walk around it.

In 1854 an especially severe cholera epidemic necessitated the elimination of the board walkways beneath which standing water and refuse collected and putrified. The dangerous sidewalks, which provided hideouts for rats, also offered ready fuel for the fires that periodically wracked sections of the city. A decision was made to raise the streets and, where necessary, the existing buildings to a higher and uniform level. A young contractor from New York state named George M. Pullman volunteered to try using screwjacks located at crucial points in a foundation's structure. With the Tremont House selected as the candidate, Pullman assembled more than a thousand workers to turn the jacks in unison. Such was the confidence, apparently, in the outcome of this maneuver that some hotel guests remained inside—dining and wining without experiencing a tremor. Charles Cleaver recalled later that: *The building was afterward raised eight feet, bringing it up to the grade, and making cellars and basements underneath. It was the first brick building ever raised in Chicago, and the raising was done at a cost to the proprietors, Ira and James Couch, of some $45,000 ... Many were the prophecies that the building would fall down during the process; but*

Facing page: Built on a swamp, Chicago faced insurmountable drainage problems. In the mid-1850s City Engineer Ellis Sylvester Chesbrough boldly proposed that the grade of streets and buildings be raised 12 to 16 feet so that sewers could be built that would drain into the lake and river by gravity. This 1857 view of Clark Street shows some sidewalks raised to the new levels and others not. This practice continued throughout the city until the 1890s. The old grade can be seen in the sunken front lawns found in Chicago's old neighborhoods. From Andreas, *History of Chicago,* 1884

Below: The city's courthouse, viewed here in 1858 from the northwest was an imposing three-story structure complete with a basement and columned tower. When President Lincoln's body was brought to Chicago en route to Springfield for burial, it lay in state in this courthouse while 130,000 citizens filed in to pay their respects. From Kirkland, *The Story of Chicago,* 1894

it was raised without the breaking of a pane of glass, although it was 160 by 180 feet. After the success attending the raising of the Tremont many others were raised to grade.

By 1857 Chicago was clearly America's "boom town," boasting over 3,000 miles of railroad track. While its population was still behind those of Cincinnati and St. Louis, the Illinois city was outdistancing both in the rate of growth and the increase in trade. Around 90,000 residents lived there, but Chicagoans gladly claimed it was well over 100,000.

The East still regarded Chicago as "the West," as did the city itself. A group of Chicagoans belonging to the liberal and literate Mechanics' Institute rallied around printer Zeb Eastman to publish a promising monthly, *Chicago Magazine: The West as It Is Illustrated.* The monthly—a forum for local history, illustrations, poetry, and "western literature"—lasted for five issues and 460 interesting pages. Its view of Chicago, in the ads, illustrations, and text, lushly portrayed the best that the exhilarating young city and surrounding area had to offer. Crisp writing, inviting advertising, and perceptive editorials were characteristic.

The magazine quoted the *Chicago Daily Journal* on the much-feared recession the county was facing. Many attributed the economic downturn to a comet that "was dallying about our outer sphere, and drawing off the vital currents, so that grass wouldn't grow, and water would hardly run downhill ..." The doomsayers predicted that Chicago would be hurt the most by the recession, as it had been 20 years before. However, the Journal said: *Grave predictions are made of a general crash in Chicago. But those who are acquainted with the business of Chicago smile at such predictions. In the published records of failures, no city of its size has presented so small a list. Indeed the failures have been so insignificant, that the first knowledge of them has been through the New York papers. The business of Chicago cannot keep pace with the demand. ... Hence a general crash is impossible.*

The Panic of 1857 did hit Chicago hard as another business recession, but its duration was short. The more stable companies weathered the storm handily, while new and overextended firms did not survive. Unfortunately, on the list of those that failed was *Chicago Magazine: The West as It Is Illustrated.*

However, the printing and publishing business that had been thoroughly launched in the 1850s continued. It introduced new and faster presses, capitalized on an expanding Chicago and Midwest population—among which many were avid readers—and used an ever-extending network of railroads to send out a variety of publications. By the mid-1850s Chicago had 30 newspapers; by 1860, about 30 literary journals, with children's magazines and other specialized publications on the increase.

In the last year of this important decade, a single event brought in the

FROM AN AMBROTYPE

Livestock dealers exhibited their prime beef cattle in a "Fat Cattle Fair" held in Chicago in 1856. That same year saw the opening of John B. Sherman's cattle yards north of 31st Street along the Illinois Central line. The location was well suited to the needs of the livestock traffic. Note the photographer in the foreground. From Andreas, *History of Chicago,* 1884

greatest number yet of Chicago visitors: the Seventh Annual United States Fair and Agriculture Exhibition, sponsored by the U. S. Agriculture Society. Chicagoans had been anxious to host it. South of town and next to Lake Michigan, just where the new horsecar railroad would have its terminus, 45 acres were readied for Chicago's first great exposition. It would feature the latest in agricultural machinery demonstrations, the best in livestock shows, a race track, horticultural wonders, and new domestic appliances.

On September 13, 1859, this wonderland opened for one week only. A parade opened it with traveling bands, wagons converted into "floats" celebrating Chicago's primary assets, and even prize livestock herded along by their proud owners. Some 60,000 people attended the first day. On the third day, a much publicized contest took place between two gigantic steam-driven plows, each about 16 yards long, and specially imported for this important trial from Detroit and Lancaster, Pennsylvania. Spectators by the thousands gathered to watch the proceedings—some laying bets on the winner. The Detroit model created by James Waters had the first turn. Snorting black fumes, the creature began digging into the ground. After two minutes, though, it came to a halt, stunned by a mechanical failure. Then Joseph W. Fawkes' contraption took to the field. Within 17 minutes it had turned an acre of prairie soil and earned a gold medal and $3,000.

But the ultimate winners were the people and firms who had homesteaded or invested in the Great Plains for they now had the promise of a device that could break the tough sod far faster than a pair of oxen or draft horses pulling a small plow. And Chicago, manufacturing center for agricultural machinery, and poised to work with iron and steel, would try now to perfect, produce, and ship out its own mechanized plows.

But this new marvel of agricultural technology engendered by the Industrial Revolution would have to take a back seat in the first half of the next decade to a very different kind of competition—war. And in some ways Chicago was where the war began.

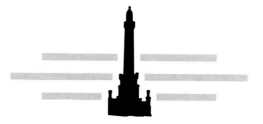

CHAPTER SIX

THE BOOM OF WAR

THE 1860s

Soon after war broke out with the attack on Fort Sumter on April 12, 1861, about 3,500 Chicago men volunteered for military service. One was Colonel Elmer E. Ellsworth, formerly of the United States Zouave Cadets, once the Chicago-based National Guard Cadets. According to Frank Leslie, these men were known for their "striking and gay uniforms; their flowing red pants; their jaunty crimson caps; their peculiar drab gaiters and leggings, and the loose blue jackets, with rows of small, sparkling buttons, and the light-blue shirt beneath. In all their evolutions the Zouaves displayed great precision." From *Frank Leslie's Illustrated History of the Civil War*, 1895

The decade in Chicago began with a crucial event. The future convention capital had secured the first of many national political conventions to come. Chicago had invited the four-year-old Republican party to bring in delegates from the 33 states to debate their presidential nominee choices. Once the offer was accepted, the derelict Sauganash Hotel on Lake Street was torn down and hundreds of carpenters were engaged to erect the largest convention hall yet built. It was dubbed the "Great Wigwam," as befitted this crucial political "powwow." Just before May 16, 1860, Chicago became so full of people that hotel space proved inadequate. Private homes opened their doors, and even saloons' billiard tables served as beds. Since the town celebrated the event with boisterous enthusiasm, some of the staid and temperate citizens took boats out on the lake to hold more subdued gatherings.

But the convention issues were serious. The Democrats were already split. When they first met in Charleston, S.C., they failed to nominate a candidate. When they had gathered again in Baltimore and selected Illinois' own Senator Stephen A. Douglas, a Southern splinter group withdrew to nominate John C. Breckinridge. Still another candidate, John Bell, decided to run on a Constitutionalist-Union ticket.

Enemies called the Republican gathering in Chicago "a sectional convention," although there were representatives from some Southern states. Nonetheless, the feud within the Democratic party's ranks offered the Republicans a good chance, especially with a distinguished candidate like William H. Seward of New York. The selection of Seward looked certain when Chicago's Mayor John Wentworth declared for him.

But a solid "dark horse" candidate was being touted vociferously and skillfully by other local Republicans. He was the man from Springfield whom the incumbent Douglas had defeated (because the choice was made in the Illinois legislature) in the Senate race of 1858—Abraham Lincoln. The loudest editorial voice calling for him was the *Chicago Tribune*. Its editors—Charles H. Ray, John L. Scripps, and Joseph Medill—knew Lincoln personally and well. They had helped him, for example, by working late into the night editing his Cooper Union speech. But he cast aside all the editing in giving the talk. This was the time when Lincoln virtually showed the nation his mettle in the concluding words: "Let us have faith that right makes might, and in that faith let us to the end dare to do our duty as we understand it."

If the *Tribune's* editors couldn't make Lincoln over, at least they might make him President. And they did—commencing with the help of a few hundred delegates and a shrewdly orchestrated claque in the Wigwam balcony. Medill and Norman Judd, in charge of seating the delegates, isolated Seward's New York delegation. Taking advantage of a Seward-boosting parade on the streets, they packed the convention hall with Lincolnites. When the proceedings began, pro-Lincoln ripples were pushed into a tide. Thus on May 18, 1860, Lincoln was nominated as the presidential candidate on the Republican ticket. Backroom politicians had helped wheel-and-deal him into the position by promising cabinet positions without his knowledge. They now wired him in Springfield: "WE DID IT GLORY TO GOD."

And so two Illinois politicians became the major contenders for the presidency. Chicago's Stephen A. Douglas campaigned vigorously. He believed he could avoid a rupture in the Union by allowing the South to retain its stubbornly held institution of slavery without interference in their own territories. Scarcely a proslavery advocate, Douglas—basically a sensible businessman—figured that in time Southerners would realize that not only was black bondage unethical but it was also a poor business practice.

Most white workingmen of the North simply did not welcome the economic competition from slave labor, whether or not they believed slavery itself to be immoral. Thus there had been a difference between the crusading abolitionists and the "free-soilers" who wanted the territory they lived in, whether city or farmland, to be free of slaves. Both groups, however, combined in the antislavery movement reaching its crescendo in the Republican party platform of 1860. An exception among the working class was the Irish population. They did not want slavery to end in the South because they feared that the freedmen would come North to hinder their own chances for jobs and also deflate wages that were already low.

The bellicose South would have none of Douglas. In the North he did better but not well enough, with the Democratic vote split in three ways nationwide as the Republicans picked off many of his former admirers. Southern Illinois liked him, but Chicago and the northern part of the state did not. When the votes were counted in Cook County, there were 9,846 for Douglas and 14,589 for Lincoln, who also carried the state in the electoral college. In spite of receiving

Facing page, top: During the 1860 Presidential campaign, John C. Breckinridge (left) was nominated by Southern Democrats who were opposed to the nomination of Stephen A. Douglas. John Bell (middle), who was also nominated at the time, ran for the hastily organized Constitutional Union party. Courtesy, National Portrait Gallery, Smithsonian Institution, Washington, D.C.

Top right: Chicago's first city clerk, Isaac Newton Arnold, was an early and staunch supporter of Abraham Lincoln for President. He later wrote a biography of Lincoln, served in Congress from 1860-1864, and helped found the Chicago Historical Society. From Andreas, *History of Chicago,* 1884

Bottom: Chicago businessmen underwrote the cost of the Wigwam building to house the Republican National Convention in 1860. Having been built in only five weeks, the structure reminded people of a wigwam—a flimsy, fir bough hut used for temporary housing by the Great Lakes Indians. The building was located on Lake Street and what is now Wacker Drive. From Andreas, *History of Chicago,* 1884

only a third of the collective vote, Lincoln was elected the next American President.

After the election the Southern states, led by South Carolina, began seceding, to form the Confederate States of America; Douglas did his utmost to convince the wavering ones at the border to remain in the Union with Lincoln at its helm. As Lincoln assumed office on March 4, 1861, he made it clear that he was unwilling to let the South shatter the once-united states. He refused to give up federal forts in the South, which resulted in the attack on Fort Sumter on April 12, 1861. The belligerent move made war unavoidable.

In the first three weeks of the war, some 3,500 Chicago men volunteered for 90-day military service in regiments being outfitted by different local groups. Many of them were already prepared for militant marching, having drilled for months as fervid Republican "Wide-Awakes." Best known were the Zouaves trained by Elmer Ellsworth.

A long article that appeared in the *Chicago Tribune* on April 23, 1861, telling of the war excitement, was itself meant to excite others to volunteer:

“ *Yesterday was but a continuation of the military bustle and preparation of several days preceeding. The streets were alive all day with the movement of volunteers. Everything gives way to the war and to its demands. Workmen from their shops, printers from their cases, lawyers from their offices, are busily drilling, and the enlistments are marvelously rapid.* ”

Just as Stephen Douglas had dedicated his past efforts to preventing war at all cost, he now rushed to help his former opponent, Lincoln. Douglas stumped to gain popular support for the war, especially in the southern part of Illinois, where many people favored the South. He also worked on the large Irish population in Chicago who had always supported him loyally because of his stand against the Know-Nothings. Overtaxing himself, Douglas developed typhoid fever and then pneumonia, and died in the Tremont House on June 3. Some 50,000 mourners escorted his remains to a resting place on his property on the South side of Chicago, where a memorial would eventually be erected. Ironically, the greatest laments came from the "Little Giant's" past political foes, whose pro-Union cause he had been wholeheartedly advocating. And the South, whom he had vainly wooed for years, expressed a grim satisfaction over his demise.

The breakdown of relations with the South caused financial panic in the city, since banks and businesses had considerable funds tied up with Southern investments now virtually valueless. And as before in troubled times, paper currency, credit slips, and bonds issued by an assortment of banking houses proliferated. Few held up in the rush for hard cash. In the year following November 1860, some 6,000 Chicago business firms failed. Lincoln's new Secretary of the Treasury, Salmon P. Chase, established a national bank system

Facing page: Colonel Elmer Ellsworth, who was shot by a civilian while attempting to haul down a rebel flag, was the first officer killed in the Civil War. To commemorate this well loved organizer of Chicago's Zouave Cadets, two of the city's music publishers—Root and Cady and A. Judson Higgins—published "Col. Ellsworth Requiem March" by A.J. Vaas and "Sadly the Bells Toll the Death of the Hero" by A.B. Tobey. Courtesy, Chicago Historical Society (ICHi-16765)

Below: During the Civil War Chicago composer, music publisher, and music educator George Frederick Root wrote songs to which soldiers could march: "Tramp, tramp, tramp, the boys are marching .../Bearing the colors as they come;/Tramp, tramp, tramp, the boys are marching/'Til victory is won." From Cirker, *Dictionary of American Portraits*, 1967

TO THE MEMORY OF
COL. E. E. ELLSWORTH.
WHO FELL AT ALEXANDRIA. VA. MAY 24TH 1861.

"I am perfectly content to accept whatever my fortune may be, confident that He who noteth even the fall of a sparrow, will have some purpose even in the fate of one like me.

Ed. Mendel. Lith. Chicago.

COL. ELLSWORTH REQUIEM MARCH.
BY A. J. VAAS.
PUBLISHIED BY ROOT & CADY. CHICAGO.

"SADLY THE BELLS TOLL THE DEATH OF THE HERO."
PUBLISHED BY A. JUDSON HIGGINS. CHICAGO.   "SONG" BY A. B. TOBEY.

Facing page, top: Chicago's population had grown from about 100 in 1831 to over 100,000 in 1861. This contemporary cartoon, which appeared in *The Illustrated Chicago News* in 1868, demonstrates the effects of the tremendous population growth on city life. From the author's collection

Bottom left: The Chamber of Commerce Building (right) was located at the southeast corner of LaSalle and Washington streets. The Board of Trade used a two-story trading room within the building. During the Great Fire in 1871, the building burned to the ground. From the author's collection

Bottom right: J.M. Loomis represented the leading fashions in hats in Chicago in the early 1860s. He had established his business in the city in 1851. From Guyer, *History of Chicago: Its Commercial and Manufacturing Interests and Industry,* 1862

to issue "greenbacks" and counter the insecure, uncontrolled banks run by states, communities, and private companies. But the measure came too late to halt the financial ruin of many enterprises and investors.

But if the economic scene at first was troubled, it soon became clear that this War Between the States might well benefit firms that had survived the crash. It also would launch new enterprises. Chicago, chosen as a primary quartermaster depot for the nation, was an excellent central source for the Union Army's food provisions, weaponry, leather goods, clothing, and other supplies. Chicago also had an unexcelled transportation network, with both railroad and waterway link-ups with the Mississippi and the Atlantic.

This view of Chicago's real and potential might was quickly discerned by a British journalist, William Howard Russell, while traveling on assignment for the *London Times:*   *In warlike operations ... Chicago, with its communication open to the sea, its access to the head waters of the Mississippi, its intercourse with the marts of commerce and of manufacture, may be considered to possess greater belligerent power and strength than the great city of New Orleans; and there is much greater probability of Chicago sending its contingent to attack the Crescent City than there is of the latter being able to dispatch a soldier within five hundred miles of its streets.*

If the word for Chicago in the 1850s was "hundreds," often used in exaggeration, then in the 1860s the word became "thousands" even without boasting: thousands of buildings built, books and periodicals published, fortunes made, miles of railroads laid, businesses begun, barrels of flour and bushels of wheat and corn shipped daily, cattle and hogs slaughtered, and McCormick reapers produced. And thousands of gamblers and con men and prostitutes too, as the city's reputation for wickedness grew along with its commercial prowess.

A large portion of the booming business and population came because of the Civil War. During its four years the number of Chicagoans expanded from 109,000 to 178,000, so that it overtook Cincinnati and now was approaching St. Louis in population.

Isaac D. Guyer's book, *History of Chicago: Its Commercial and Manufacturing Interests and Industry,* chronicles what Chicagoans in its publication year of 1862 were telling the world: *The commerce of the West (meaning what is now the Midwest) is fast becoming the controlling power of the nation. As the geographical and the commercial center of the Mississippi Valley ... within the past ten years this city has taken her rank as the greatest primary grain mart ... not only in the United States, but in the world; and during the present year, 1862, in her exports and trade in Lumber and Pork she has outstripped every other city on the face of the globe.*

People wanted news, and they got more of it and faster. Battles were often reported within hours, with casualty lists soon after. Old people learned to read in order to follow the course of the war and to learn, often sadly, of the fates of friends and relatives.

And the *Tribune* was ready to bring news to them. In 1861 it had installed a Hoe steam-powered four-cylinder press. By the end of the war, the paper had replaced it with an eight-cylinder press, for its daily circulation had jumped from 20,000 to 40,000. By 1864 its payroll rose to 265, of whom 18 were editors and reporters. The *Tribune* also had 29 correspondents in Washington and various state capitals, and with the armies in the field. The *Tribune,* under Joseph Medill's editorship, took its role seriously. Telegraph costs for the paper jumped from $1,200 to $12,000 a year during the Civil War. The *Tribune* was never at a loss for strong editorial words; for the most part it loyally supported Lincoln. And it early championed Ulysses S. Grant.

Meanwhile the *Chicago Times* berated Lincoln. In spite of the ardent patriotism of many Chicagoans, the city harbored a large population of antiwar as well as pro-South dissidents. The fractious Democrats demanding a cessation of the war were called "Copperheads." They were regarded by others as a nest of vipers engaged in sabotage, propaganda, and even treason. The man considered the most pernicious Copperhead of them all was newspaperman Wilbur F. Storey, who had moved to Chicago in 1861. Acquiring the *Chicago Times* in June, he intemperately assailed Lincoln as a "mean, wily, illiterate, brutal, unprincipled, and utterly vulgar creature."

Storey was scarcely the only prominent voice in opposition to Lincoln's war policies. Many people who backed the war maintained that it was not being conducted properly. The Radical Republicans demanded immediate emancipation of the slaves. They had been infuriated when their presidential candidate of 1856, General John C. Fremont, was reprimanded and removed from command by Lincoln for freeing all slaves who came into Union camps under his jurisdiction. During the build-up to the Republican national convention in 1864, the party was split between the pro-Lincoln contingent and the Radicals or "black" Republicans who hoped to run Fremont again. Before unity was achieved for the good of the country, some Chicagoans turned against Illinois' "native son" occupying the White House.

The prowar newspapers assigned themselves the task of keeping up public enthusiasm for the ongoing combat with the Confederacy. Illinois had exceeded the enlistment quotas set by the government, so through most of the war there was no need for a draft. Chicago was spared the ugly 1863 draft riots which erupted in other large cities, where vicious attacks were made on black residents blamed personally for having brought on the war.

Chicago would later boast of and build memorials to its involvement in the Civil War, claiming it had proportionately sent more "sons" to the front than any other city. Although the figures were there to prove it, they were deceptive.

Facing page, top left: General John C. Fremont had been removed from command by Abraham Lincoln because of serious ineptitude. He also proclaimed all slaves in Missouri free. Engraving by John C. Buttre. From Cirker, *Dictionary of American Portraits,* 1967

Top middle: Joseph Medill, who helped purchase the *Chicago Tribune* in April 1855, used the paper to promote the Republican Party and to help elect their subscriber, Abraham Lincoln of Springfield, to the U.S. Presidency. Medill also campaigned to get the vote for soldiers in the Civil War. He was elected mayor in 1871 immediately after the Great Fire. From Cirker, *Dictionary of American Portraits,* 1967

Top right: During the Civil War Ambrose Everett Burnside, who had at one time worked for the Illinois Central Railroad, was military commander of the district that included Northern Illinois. Courtesy, National Portrait Gallery, Smithsonian Institution, Washington, D.C.

Bottom: The number of men from Illinois who volunteered for military service exceeded the government's enlistment quotas. Pictured here is the company mess tent of the 13th Illinois Volunteers in their camp at Corinth, Massachusetts. From *Frank Leslie's Illustrated History of the Civil War,* 1895

Chicago was so prosperous both in its own right and as a result of the war trade that many Chicago men could afford to pay handsome bounties to out-of-towners to fight in their places. Once the first rush to enlist had taken place in the early weeks of the war, ardent patriotism was subdued among the well-to-do and their sons.

The county offered a $300 bounty for enlisting in Chicago, so immigrants and farmers flocked to the city to help it meet all enlistment quotas. A special business started up, in fact, in Chicago with "bounty brokers" who for a percentage would find the best deal for a prospective enlistee. Unscrupulous men might join up with one regiment and soon afterward disappear, and using an assumed name enlist somewhere else to gain another bounty, then go AWOL again.

On the home front, a variety of new industries started up while a number of well-entrenched ones prospered in aiding the war effort. Chicago supplied beef, pork, and grain. It made boots, canvas, tents, and blue uniforms.

Heavy industry manufacturing arrived in Chicago when southern Illinois' coal deposits were joined with the iron ore starting to be shipped from the Lake Superior region. Conveniently nearby were limestone deposits used in the conversion of iron to the firmer, more durable steel. Chicago acquired more foundries and rolling mills to produce railroad tracks and rolling stock, artillery, field ambulances and other large metal machinery and pieces needed in conducting the war.

Chicago also manufactured the reapers that freed the farmers in the North to fight in the war—an irony when one considers that harvester king Cyrus McCormick hailed from Virginia and sympathized with the South. McCormick's reapers proved so successful that Lincoln's Secretary of War Edwin Stanton would say, "Without McCormick's invention, I feel the North could not win."

The war that Northerners thought would be over in a few months dragged on. War can sometimes be highly profitable, and in the Civil War Chicago received what some urban rivals considered far more than its fair share of lucrative government contracts. Chicago merchants, industrialists, and speculators were widely accused of unscrupulous profiteering. Removed geographically from the war fronts, the city suffered no physical damage. Although wages went up, scarcities in lodging, food, and merchandise pushed prices up too, and the erratic valuation of paper currency caused both insecurity and inflation.

Since Chicago attracted outsiders to work in the war effort, its population swelled. Among the influx was a host of undesirables. Some men appeared in Chicago who had escaped service in the Confederate Army by going to the North, but were decidedly proslavery in their attitudes. Combining with the Copperheads elements in Chicago, they made their views known, and few

Facing page, top: In 1863, under the leadership of Mary Livermore and Jane Hoge, Chicago held a "Sanitary Fair" to raise funds to help the Sanitary Commission. This commission was formed during the Civil War to assist sick and wounded soldiers and their families. President Lincoln offered a copy of the Emancipation Proclamation to be auctioned off. The event more than tripled its goal of raising $25,000. The *Voice of the Fair* was initiated by Andrew Shuman to develop interest in a subsequent Northwestern Sanitary Fair. From the author's collection

Bottom: Because Chicago was located far from the war fronts, it was physically untouched during the Civil War. This 1864 view of the city looking from the foot of Madison and Michigan depicts pleasure boaters and strollers seemingly oblivious to the cruel war going on in other parts of their country. Courtesy, Illinois Central Gulf Railroad

VOICE OF THE FAIR.

PUBLISHED UNDER THE AUSPICES OF THE } NORTHWESTERN SANITARY FAIR.

"The world will little note, nor long remember, what we say here, but it can never forget what our brave men did here."
[President Lincoln's Address, dedicating the Soldiers' Cemetery, at Gettysburg.]

{ SINGLE COPIES TEN CENTS. { ADVERTISEMENTS $1.25 PER SQUARE.

VOLUME I. NUMBER 9.]

CHICAGO, SATURDAY, JUNE 3, 1865.

{ ROUNDS & JAMES, Printers, No. 46 State Street.

THE WORLD HARVEST.

They are sowing their seed in the daylight fair,
They are sowing their seed in the noonday's glare,
They are sowing their seed in the soft twilight,
They are sowing their seed in the solemn night,
What shall the harvest be!

They are sowing the seed of pleasant thought,
In the spring's green light they have blithely wrought,
They have brought their fancies from wood and dell,
Where the mosses creep and the flower-buds swell,
Rare shall the harvest be.

They are sowing their seed of word and deed,
Which the cold know not nor the careless heed,
Of the gentle word and kindly deed,
That have blessed the heart in its sorest need,
Sweet will the harvest be.

And some are sowing the seed of pain,
Of late remorse and madden'd brain;
And the stars shall fall and the sun shall wane,
Ere they root the seeds from the soil again,
Dark will the harvest be.

And some are standing with idle hand,
Yet they scatter seed on their native land;
And some are sowing the seed of care,
Which their soil hath borne and still must bear,
Sad will the harvest be.

They are sowing their seed of noble deed,
With a sleepless watch and earnest heed,
With a careless hand o'er the earth they sow,
And the fields are whitening where'er they go,
Rich will the harvest be.

Sown in the darkness, or sown in light,
Sown in weakness, or sown in might,
Sown in meekness, or sown in wrath,
In the broad workfield, or the shadowy path,
Sure will the harvest be.

MORE ANECDOTES OF MR. LINCOLN.

HIS STORY-TELLING PROPENSITIES—REMINISCENSES.

The artist Carpenter contributes to last week's *Independent* another interesting chapter of reminiscenses of Mr. Lincoln. He says:

In my former communication the incidents related were mostly of a tender, pathetic character. With the multitude of cases convicted of military offences and crimes, together with those constantly appealing for relief or redress from hardships imposed by the war, of course, scenes like those described, were of frequent occurrence. I desire,

"Why yes," he replied, manifesting some surprise, "but has it leaked out? I was in hopes nothing would be said about it, lest some oversensitive people should imagine there was a degree of levity in the intercourse between us." He then went on to relate the circumstances which called it out. "You see," said he, "we had reached and were discussing the slavery question. Mr. Stephens said, substantially, that the slaves, always accustomed to an overseer and to work upon compulsion, suddenly freed, as they would be if the South should consent to peace on the basis of the emancipation proclamation, would precipitate not only themselves but the entire Southern society into irremediable ruin. No work would be done, nothing would be cultivated, and blacks and whites would starve."

"Said the President," I waited for Seward to answer that argument, but as he was silent, I at length said: Mr. Stephens, *you* ought to know a great deal better about this matter than *I*, for you have always lived under the slave system. I can only say in reply to your statement of the case, that it reminds me of a man out in Illinois by the name of Case, who undertook a very few years ago, to raise a very large herd of hogs. It was a great trouble to *feed* them, and how to get around this was a puzzle to him. At length he hit on the plan of planting an immense field of potatoes, and, when they had sufficiently grown, he turned the whole herd into the field and let them have full swing, thus saving not only the labor of feeding the hogs, but also that of digging the potatoes! Charmed with his sagacity, he stood one day leaning against the fence counting his hogs, when a neighbor came along. 'Well, well,' said he, 'Mr. Case, this is all very fine. Your hogs are doing very well just now, but you know out here in Illinois the frost comes early, and the ground freezes for a foot deep. Then what are you going to do?' This was a view of the matter Mr. Case had not taken into account. Butchering time for hogs was way on in December or January. He scratched his head and at length stammered, 'Well, it may come pretty hard on their *snouts*, but I don't see but that it will be 'root hog or die.'" He did not tell me that either of the "Commissioners" made any reply to this way of "putting the thing." It is very evident that there was little more argument necessary on one side of

ABOUT AUTHORS AND BOOKS.

Old periodicals are dying and new ones are being born in England and elsewhere. It is understood that the *Fine Arts Quarterly Review* will not be issued any more. As a commercial speculation it has not proved fortunate, and as a venture it has been pronounced a failure, even by persons interested in its success. Mr. G. H. Lewes, the biographer of Goethe, is to edit the new *Fortnightly Review*, a magazine which has, for London, the merit of an original idea. All the article are to be signed by their writers, and every writer is to be left free to express his opinions in his own way, regardless of editorial or other consistency. Mr. Samuel Lucas, author of "Secularia," is marshalling a host of writers for his experiment in the periodical way, under the good title of the *Shilling Magazine*. Mr. Lucas' troop is very strong in travelers.

——English light literature has suffered quite a loss in the decease of Mrs. Theodosia Trolope, at Florence. Though this lady be only known by scattered contributions to the periodicals, mostly signed by her initials—many of them graceful pictures of life and character, full of original observation—she will be remembered and missed for her bright and pictorial record of Italian events as they passed during these late days of awakening. Besides this, Mrs. Trollope had poetical powers of no common order, as was shown in her translation of Nicolini's "Arnaldo da Brescia," and fugitive verse which it might be well to collect; further, descended from a musical ancestry, her accomplishments in that art were such as to place her high among amateurs. Such a woman has died too soon.

——The London *Pall Mall Gazette*, smarting under the inhospitable treatment it has recently received at the hands of the French censorship, having seen its editions sent to France several times confiscated by the authorities—addresses the Emperor Napoleon as "Imperial Seizer."

——"Is the following statement by a popular lecturer a joke?" asks a correspondent in the English *Notes and Queries*, "or has it any true historic foundation?" The statement referred to is this: "A curious example of *Nolo Episcopari* was offered by the Rev. Dr. John Bull, Canon of Christ-church, who refused the See of Oxford for the reason that he would not give up the venerable signature of

A LESSON FOR THE ROMANTIC.

ADVERTISING FOR A WIFE, AND WHAT CAME OF IT.

The Toronto *Leader* gives the particulars of a matrimonial romance, in which a Vermont clergyman was the main character, the denouement of which was, however, anything but romantic to him. It seems that a farmer in McHenry county, Illinois, named W——, had advertised in a Chicago paper for a wife, which was replied to by a dashing young law student of Toronto, ripe for fun, under the name of Helen Christopher. A warm correspondence ensued, imitating the hand and style of a lady anxious to make a good match, and describing herself as an orphan of respectable family connections, and of means, residing in Toronto. The correspondence was finally broken off by W——'s neglect in paying his postage, which in Canada amounts to something, and he married some one in his own neighborhood. But the sequel contains the pith of the story. W——'s father, a minister in Vermont, and a widower, by some means got hold of "Helen's" letters to his son, and, being struck with her style, wrote to her with a view of marrying her himself. He told her that:

"I am a minister of the gospel, am unmarried, buried a nice little wife years ago, and have no children to tax the attention of a companion. My family is provided for and off my hands. I think sometimes of discontinuing preaching, and of retiring to private life. My age people judge to be thirty-five, though I am older. I am above the middle size of men, though not large; have perfect health, and a fair position in society. My complexion is dark, with dark eyes and hair—hair not tinged with gray in the least. What makes my complexion still darker, I wear full beard and moustache."

And queried:

"May I ask my little girl (if I may be allowed to call her so), if you are a Christian? If you can sing and play on the melodeon? If you have good health? What is your complexion?"

Helen promptly replied, and an animated correspondence ensued, resulting in the Rev. inviting himself to visit Toronto to obtain an interview with his fair correspondent. This was rather more than "Helen" desired, and thinking it imprudent to bring the old man on a fool's errand, some 600 miles from his "local" habitation, sent him a note over another name, pretending to have accident-

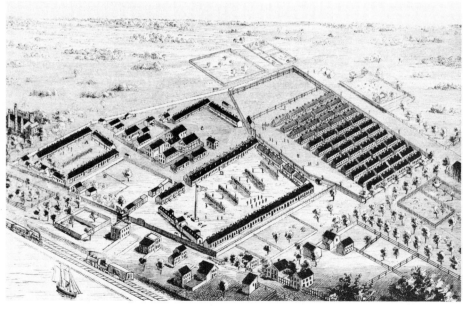

attempts were made to crack down on free speech, however treasonable it sounded. After the war, many of these underworld denizens remained in Chicago, devising schemes to pry money loose from the unwary and gullible.

The Copperheads of Chicago attempted to dictate the platform and candidate selection in the Democratic party's national convention to be held in Chicago in late August of 1864. William Bross recalled the event later, as a Union loyalist who could never forgive the Copperheads' stance in the Civil War years.

The "man for the hour," according to Bross, was Camp Douglas' commander, General Benjamin J. Sweet. But parts were also played by detective Allan Pinkerton and William Bross himself. They learned that the city contained 10,000 caches of arms, and perhaps as many rebels to use them, if the Copperheads could not prevail—first in their desire to capture the Democratic convention, and second in controlling the election itself. General Sweet, when informed, at once stationed detectives in all parts of the city, increased the guards at the prison camp and alerted the militia to possible civil disorder. Democratic politicians from the East were determined to run the show themselves and not permit Chicago street people to select the candidate. Their choice was General George B. McClellan.

Just before the election, General Sweet and his many assistants, both military and civilian, arrested at least 150 of the rebel and purported plotters. News of this action was telegraphed to incoming insurgents, halting them in their tracks. So ended a strange and desperate plot to stuff the ballot box while laying waste to the North's pre-eminent supply depot.

That bitter, fratricidal war, however, was drawing to a close in the winter of 1864-1865 as Sherman marched across the South toward the sea and Grant and other generals struck at vital places. When surrender came at Appomattox on April 12, four years to the day after the shelling of Fort Sumter, Chicagoans like other Northerners rejoiced.

But before the future could be contemplated, shocking news arrived by telegraph on April 16. The night before, President Lincoln had been assassinated. Crosby's elegant new Opera House cancelled its gala opening that evening, and the city went into mourning. The grief now poured out for the slain President, and people warmly expressed an admiration few had shown during his tenure in office. The deep sorrow was also cumulative and collective. It was for all lives lost in an irrepressible conflict that neither side had wanted yet somehow could not avoid.

The murder of the President by a pro-Confederacy plotter indicated that the reconstruction of the Union would not be readily accomplished. Few people in the North now felt conciliatory. The Radical Republicans capitalized on this infuriated mood that now demanded vengeance.

It was proposed to Mary Todd Lincoln that after her husband's body had lain

Facing page, top: At the beginning of May in 1865 the train bearing President Lincoln's body arrived in Chicago. Here it pauses on the Illinois Central trestle. Courtesy, Illinois Central Gulf Railroad

Bottom left: The locomotive "John B. Turner" was constructed in the shops of the Chicago and North Western Railway. It was in service from 1867 until 1898. During the 1860s the locomotive carried through the wilds of Wisconsin the picture of John B. Turner—a member of the C&NW railroad board of directors and former president of the Galena and Chicago Union before it consolidated with the Chicago and North Western. From White, *Early American Locomotives*, 1972

Bottom right: Crosby's Opera House on Washington Boulevard had a seating capacity of 2,500. Considered the finest theater west of the Alleghenies, the building also contained a restaurant, art gallery, and shops. From the author's collection

in state at various cities on the train route back to Springfield for burial, she should join him in Chicago for the last leg of the long journey. The distraught woman first balked at the suggestion. But then George Pullman of Chicago offered the use of several of his luxurious new parlor cars. When she accepted, Pullman hurriedly arranged for necessary changes in trestles and other features along the line in order to accommodate the wider, heavier cars he was designing for manufacture. By accepting the Chicago entrepreneur's generous offer, Lincoln's widow gave Pullman Palace Car Company priceless publicity. In 1867 the corporation was launched with Andrew Carnegie as a partner.

Chicago had grown into the lumber capital of the continent with huge yards next to the miles of wharves in the lumber district or the South Branch. Timber coming mainly from northern Wisconsin and Michigan by water was used not only in Chicago's own buildings but also in the construction needs of prairie settlers. By 1867 the annual sale of all wood totaled almost 1.5 billion feet, and lumber yards numbered well over 100. Shingles too became readily available. In the 1860s some of the lumber companies began creating pre-cut and packaged-up houses—early "pre-fabs"—for shipping to wood and carpenter-scarce regions.

Lumber had also assisted in the construction of the tall grain elevators along lakeside and river banks, which gave Chicago one of its characteristic skyline features. By 1870, the largest of these gigantic monoliths was the Sturges and Buckingham elevator located in the Illinois Central Railroad yard, just at the edge of Lake Michigan, which could store almost 3 million bushels. "The elevator swallows the grain like a hungry dog devouring a mouthful of meat, and is ready for more before any is ready for him," one spectator commented after watching it in operation.

The city's largest business during the Civil War had been meatpacking. Much of the corn grown went to hogs—"condensed and reduced in bulk by feeding it into an animal form, more portable," as one observer concluded. "The hog eats the corn, and Europe eats the hog. Corn thus becomes incarnate; for what is a hog but fifteen or twenty bushels of corn on four legs?" It was said that if all the hogs slaughtered in Chicago in 1863 had been lined up one after the other, the line would have reached New York. Fully a third of all the meat processed in the West during the 1860s came from Chicago.

In 1864 Chicago had 68 meatpacking firms located in various sections of the city. Since cattle, sheep, and swine had to be herded through city streets to take them to the slaughterhouse, no location close to the yards or meatpacking establishments was considered desirable as a residence. In 1864 the Pork Packers Association asked for better facilities, and the consensus wanted to unify the scattered stockyards and meatpacking plants for efficiency purposes. On Christmas Day, 1865, the Union Stock Yard and Transit Company of

Chicago was officially opened for business.

By 1868 the Union Stock Yards was well established, and in that year was described by a guidebook: ❝ *Out on the prairie, four miles south of the city ... may be seen the famous Yards. Two million dollars have been expended there in the construction of a cattle-market. The company owning it has nearly a square mile of land, 355 acres of which are enclosed with cattle pens—150 of these acres being floored with plank. There is at the present time penroom for 25,000 cattle, 80,000 hogs, and 25,000 sheep, the sheep and hogs being provided with sheds. ... One hundred tons of hay are frequently used in the yards in one day. If these yards were in any of the Eastern States, the sale of the manure would be an important part of the business; but the fertile prairie not needing anything of the kind, they are glad to sell it at ten cents a wagon-load, which is less than the cost of shovelling it up.* ❞

This consolidation of the stockyards facilitated further growth in Chicago's meatpacking industry. In 1869 a refrigerated carload of dressed beef reached New England in good condition, a harbinger of advances to be made to revolutionize the business in the next decade.

In the late 1860s retail Chicago also thrived, particularly in the Potter Palmer style. In 1865 Palmer offered Marshall Field and Levi Z. Leiter "very handsome terms" to take over his highly successful Lake Street dry goods store. Chicagoans thought the wealthy young bachelor was retiring early from "mercantile pursuits" in which he had already earned a fortune by speculating in cotton. He wasn't. After a brief vacation he returned to Chicago to invest over $2 million in real estate through purchasing and developing the unsightly State Street. He was determined to have it replace Lake Street as the fashionable place for Chicago women to shop and for businessmen to gather at fine hotels— one to be called the Palmer House. He widened the street and laid down the newly tried Nicholson pavement, consisting of tar-dipped wooden blocks set like bricks, then covered with pitch and gravel.

In October 1868 Field, Leiter and Company enthusiastically opened their dry goods "palace" in a marble-columned, six-story emporium Palmer had built for them at State and Washington streets, paying a rental fee of $1,000 per week. They followed Palmer's policy of taking back any goods "if not entirely approved" and "at our expense." This contrasted with the company's competitor and Field's ex-employer, John V. Farwell, whose receipts read, "Positively no goods will be taken back unless damaged when delivered." Another competitor new on the scene was Carson, Pirie and Company, which opened as a retail dry goods store in 1867 and followed the same pattern as Field's.

Brightly lit, the Field, Leiter and Company emporium was the nation's first real "department store" offering a wide variety of goods. By 1868 the company was bringing in more than $10 million and was third in sales, after two New York City retailers. Field, Leiter and Company and its competition also sent

Facing page, top left: Though Levi Z. Leiter is usually remembered as Marshall Field's onetime partner, he was a brilliant businessman who helped the firm stay solvent during the late 1860s. Courtesy, Chicago Historical Society. From Cirker, *Dictionary of American Portraits,* 1967

Bottom left: Following in the footsteps of Potter Palmer, who believed in respect for his customers, Marshall Field offered his shoppers plainly displayed prices, extended credit, and the return of merchandise "if not entirely approved" and "at our expense." Field was the first merchant to install a restaurant in a department store. His investments included real estate, traction, banking, steel, and silver mines. At the time of his death in 1906, Field's estate totaled $130 million. From Cirker, *Dictionary of American Portraits,* 1967

Right: In 1868 Chicago imported 25 million bushels of corn and 13 million bushels of wheat, received 315,000 head of cattle of which it packed 35,000, and contained enough pens in the stockyards to accomodate 80,000 hogs. This drawing appeared in the October 31, 1868, issue of *Harper's Weekly.* From the author's collection

CHICAGO, ILLINOIS—CORN EXCHANGE AND GRAIN MARKET.

CHICAGO, ILLINOIS—THE CATTLE MARKET.

"drummers" out on trains to sell to small stores along the lines, making wholesaling a major adjunct to their business.

Chicago's hotel trade continued to prosper, with the new Palmer House designed by popular architect John Van Osdel as a main attraction. The $200,000 structure finished in 1870, had eight stories and 225 rooms, and the hotel owner had spent $100,000 in furnishings.

In 1863 the city's turbulent banking history had been given some solidity by the organization of a bank having a national charter permitted under new

federal laws devised by Secretary of the Treasury Salmon P. Chase. Called the First National Bank of Chicago, with capital totaling $690,000, its first building was at the corner of Lake and Clark Streets.

Prior to the Civil War, Chicago's banking and mercantile transactions were basically those of a small city. The systems and the institutions existed, but they had small volume and growth. Banks in Chicago could not finance an important railroad, a major hotel, or the serious expansion of a manufacturer. The aggregate commercial transactions of the city in 1860 did not exceed $100 million. The largest mercantile house reported only $600,000 in sales that year. By 1868 the volume of business had quadrupled and 78 houses reported sales in excess of $1 million.

By March 3, 1865, the number of banks and volume of business had grown to the extent that seven men met in the Sherman House to set up the Chicago Clearing House Association. A week later, under the leadership of Lyman Gage and J. Young Scammon, the group sponsored a broader meeting at which 16 banks (10 national, 3 state and 3 private institutions) were represented. Ultimately, 19 banks were charter members. Only one of them, First National, still exists today.

Many of the city's banks focused at first on serving the business interests of a specific group. As the city grew, yet others met the needs of neighborhoods or nationality groups; banks merged or moved, often losing their initial identity. But even those that failed helped Chicago pay for its past and finance its future.

The Radical Republicans feuded with President Andrew Johnson over Reconstruction of the defeated yet scarcely repentant South. Chicago went on

This page: P. Palmer and Company issued this 25-cent scrip from the dry goods and carpet store on Lake Street in the early 1860s. In 1865 Palmer took on partners Marshall Field and Levi Z. Leiter. Two years later Palmer left the partnership to pursue other interests. Courtesy, Chicago Historical Society (ICHi-16670)

Facing page, left: The eight-story, 225-room Palmer House was built in 1869-1870 by Potter Palmer at the northwest corner of State and Quincy streets. The hotel's first proprietor was W.F.P. Meserve. During the fire of 1871, the $200,000 structure was destroyed. From Andreas, *History of Chicago*, 1885

Top right: While working as a traveling salesman for John V. Farwell and Company's wholesale dry goods store, Marshall Field probably distributed advertising cards such as this to customers and prospective customers. Field was later a clerk, the general manager, and in 1862 he became a partner. Three years later he left the company to establish his own store with Potter Palmer and former Farwell partner Levi Z. Leiter. From the Windsor Archives

Bottom right: Before starting his own business John V. Farwell had advanced from clerk to partner in Wadsworth and Phelps, the leading dry goods store in Chicago in the 1860s. He is best remembered for his philanthropy, especially through an organization he helped to bring to Chicago in the 1850s—the YMCA. From Gilbert and Bryson, *Chicago and Its Makers,* 1929

A. M. COMPTON, } Salesmen.
J. S. MILES,

making and distributing goods as well as money. But unemployment became severe, particularly since Chicago had gained so many more residents during the war years.

The industries that had prospered in wartime now attempted to convert over to peacetime production. The great impetus given to the making of heavy machinery continued as Chicago rose closer to Pittsburgh as an iron- and steel-making center. The Pullman Palace Car Company and the McCormick plant produced new equipment. The garment industry now produced ready-made clothing with help from the mechanical sewing machines, opening up a new trade for women workers, especially immigrants.

In the 1860s the shoe industry had achieved a million-dollar volume by using the readily available leather, as did saddle, harness, and furniture makers. Boiled and purified fat was processed in huge vats into soap, tallow, and lard. Dozens of other Chicago businesses developed by using the stockyards' by-products. And the war's technologies were converted wherever possible into making useful peacetime goods.

The city's commercial and financial growth was also paralleled by an unsavory growth of corruption. The city council fell under the sway of a payoff system run by several "rings" or alliances of graft-accepting aldermen. Chicago's underworld in the 1860s took possession of such streets as Randolph and Fifth (later renamed Wells Street because of its reputation for vice). Parts of these streets became known as "Hairtrigger Block" and "Gamblers Alley." In 1868 railroad engineer Rosell B. Mason, on the People's party ticket, was elected mayor on a reform platform, but he—like mayors before and after him—often found the city's criminals hard to dislodge, and frequently their rackets were protected by more "respectable" citizens.

On the other hand, Chicago was also developing a reputation for culture which brought noted performers to the city's theaters and music halls. Its resident German population was particularly attentive to developing an appreciation for music.

The cultural heart of the city was Crosby's Opera House. Its builder, Uranus H. Crosby, in a highly questionable scheme to pay off the construction costs of $600,000, had conducted a lottery offering the building itself as the first prize. A nebulous out-of-town winner quickly sold the structure back to its original owner for $200,000. When suspicion of collusion was inevitably aroused, Crosby turned the building over to his brother and skipped town. In spite of the scandal, the Opera House continued as an admirable theatrical and concert hall and assembly place. In 1868 the Republicans' national convention met in the auditorium. And there in 1869 Chicago welcomed a first visit by Theodore Thomas, a German-born conductor who in years to come would give the city a

Facing page, top: This 1866 Jevne and Almini view of Randolph Street features Colonel Joseph H. Wood's museum. Here visitors could gawk at unconventional exhibits usually reserved for circus sideshows such as the "largest woman in the world, weighing near 900." Courtesy, Chicago Historical Society (ICHi-00952)

Bottom left: As soon as the First National Bank of Chicago was authorized to begin business, Edmund Aiken was elected to the board of directors. Shortly thereafter he was chosen the first president of the new corporation. From Morris, *The History of the First National Bank of Chicago,* 1902

Bottom right: This building located at the southwest corner of LaSalle and Lake streets housed the first offices of the First National Bank of Chicago. The bank soon outgrew these quarters, however, and moved to its own building at Lake and Clark. From Morris, *The History of the First National Bank of Chicago,* 1902

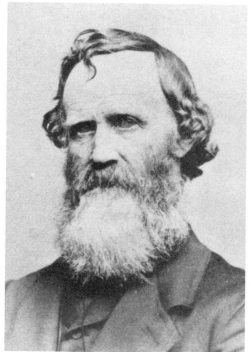

regular diet of musical splendors.

In the mid-1860s Chicago's best water supply came from its artesian wells. The first, at the corner of Chicago and Western avenues, dated back to 1863. According to a handbook published in the 1860s, it was drilled "during the oil fever, for the purpose of boring for oil, under the inspiration of a spiritual medium." By 1869 two wells at the site were supplying an estimated 1.25 million gallons per day. Two more artesian wells in the stockyards were supplying more than a half-million gallons of water per day.

Unlike the inshore lake water the artesian wells offered no "dead fish, newts, and every species of watery animalculae known to the books." They fell far short, however, of meeting the city's needs. A vast project began in 1864 under the direction of city engineer Ellis S. Chesbrough. A tunnel was constructed under the lake to a point two miles from the shore and 60 feet deep, where the water would be pure, and an engine capable of pumping 18 million gallons of water per day was purchased. The plan seemed utter folly to some; to others, a "bore." On March 25, 1867, the water began to flow through nine-foot-wide pipes from the crib out in the lake. Chesbrough's visionary plan worked.

The standpipe for this system that pumped pure water into the city was encased in the "castellated Gothic" tower on North Michigan Avenue, designed by architect W.W. Boyington, that still stands as the city's monument to this busy decade and to a dramatic event that came soon afterward.

Less monumental in scope was the invitation issued in 1869 to noted city landscape designer Frederick Law Olmsted to come and devise a public park and boulevard system for Chicago. He did so, allowing for accessibility to the entire population both through omnibus routes and railroad lines. Lincoln, Humboldt, Central, Douglas, and South parks all date back to Olmsted's planning.

In retrospect the 1860s, apart from the Civil War activities, might be viewed as "pre-fire Chicago"—an Atlantis to be swallowed in the raging sea of the Great Fire of 1871. Scholars and collectors are still discovering books and relics of the era thought to be lost. Many pictures of Chicago in the 1860s exist in photographs and in the form of etchings such as the often reproduced Jevne and Almini prints, 52 of which were published in 1866 and 1867. The scenes include 13 of harbor and lake views, and the rest depict the main streets and buildings of the city. All portray a grand and glorious Chicago, perhaps an unrealistic portrayal. Citizens complained that trees would never grow around City Hall, yet they are in full foliage in these views. In them the treacherous ruts in Chicago streets don't exist nor do the hastily erected shanties that would help fuel the Great Chicago Fire.

By the end of the decade of the 1860s, Chicago was well on the way to becoming *the* commercial center of the North American continent. Still writing

Above: The Washington Street tunnel project, conceived in 1864, had met many delays and construction difficulties such as the high water content of the clay through which it was dug. Finally, on January 1, 1869, the mayor, city council, and other local dignitaries paraded through the completed tunnel. It eventually served as a streetcar tunnel and, although blocked off, still exists. From Andreas, *History of Chicago*, 1884

Facing page: In 1868 the Grand Army of the Republic held their reunion in Chicago at Crosby's Opera House. Pictured here is Lieutenant General William T. Sherman delivering a welcoming address. From Cook, *Bygone Days in Chicago*, 1910

John S. Wright, who had donated funds to build Chicago's first school building in 1835, later became one of the city's biggest boosters. In 1870 he published *Chicago: Past, Present, Future* for the Board of Trade. Painting by Susan Hely Saint John. Courtesy, Chicago Historical Society

and lecturing then was the perennial prophet-booster John S. Wright. He was thrilled with the 1869 achievement, at long last, of the transcontinental railroad that linked the East Coast with the Far West and gave Chicago a handy hook-up with new commerce. (The trip to San Francisco took 106 hours.) In 1870, for the Chicago Board of Trade, he published a book chockfull of statistics, attacks upon other cities and praise for his own—*Chicago: Past, Present, Future*. Wright had first aimed for the ministry but then realized that his best bet was for business proselytizing. As usual, he laced his text with quotations from the Bible. Among those prominent on the title page itself was this passage from the Gospel of Matthew: " " *Ye are the light of the world. A CITY THAT IS SET ON A HILL CANNOT BE HID. Neither do men light a candle and put it under a bushel, but on a candlestick, and it giveth light unto all that are in the house. Let your light so shine before men, that they may see your good works, and glorify your Father which is in heaven.* " "

Fate would soon exchange this "light" for a broken lantern in a cow's stall. And the light and heat of the flame that engulfed much of Chicago's good works, along with some of its bad, would awe the rest of the world—and possibly heaven too, Chicagoans seemed to think.

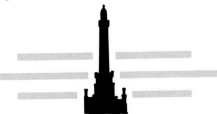

Above: This 1856 panoramic view of Chicago depicts both the residential and commercial sections of the burgeoning city. On the South Side, next to the largest ship in the river, are the final vestiges of Fort Dearborn. Just west of them is the harbor light. Note that little of the North Side was developed by this time. Drawn by G.J. Robertson. Engraved by W. Wellstood. Courtesy, Library of Congress

Right: The Galena and Chicago Dixon Air Line published this broadside in 1856. It shows the railroad's routes through Iowa, northern Illinois, southern Wisconsin, and southeastern Minnesota. As railroads fingered their way throughout the Midwest, they made sure to alert the public to all their destinations. Courtesy, Chicago Historical Society

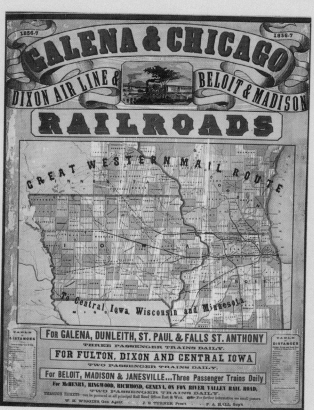

This page: By 1869 the Chicago and North Western Railway provided transcontinental service and billed itself as ''the only line by which berths can be secured in Pullman's Palace Cars from Chicago to Promontory.'' Courtesy, Chicago Historical Society

Facing page, top: In 1866 Chicago was a bustling town whose energy was captured in the etchings published by Jevne and Almini. As indicated by this illustration of city hall and the corner of Randolph and LaSalle streets, the artists took a little liberty. They cleaned up the streets and flushed out the perennially pathetic foliage that attempted to grow in the city square. Courtesy, Chicago Historical Society

Bottom: The wooden-truss Rush Street Bridge depicted in this Charles Kremer painting was built in 1864 after the original bridge collapsed under the weight of a drove of cattle a year earlier. The painting is from an 1869 stereoscopic view by noted Chicago photographer J. Carbutt. Courtesy, Chicago Historical Society

CHAPTER SEVEN

FIRE AND RESURRECTION
THE 1870s

As the city burned around them, men, women, and children surged across the Randolph Street Bridge to safety. It is estimated that 300 lives were lost and 17,450 buildings were burned, most of them on the North Side. Out of this tragic event, however, Chicagoans rebuilt their city, making it an architectural showplace and a commercial success. Lithograph by Currier and Ives. Courtesy, The New-York Historical Society

By the 1870s an overconfident Chicago was beginning to realize something. The city's phenomenal growth and economic success couldn't simply push obstacles and problems aside. And Chicago's very expansion was creating more of them all the time.

Even with the new waterworks bringing in fresh lake water, a sufficient water supply remained questionable at best. The relationship between politics and vice tightened. Space limitations and outdated buildings downtown started to strangle the city's commerce. And public transportation too often got crowded and snarled as people went to and from work.

The presence of many thousands of slaughter-bound animals, as well as their leavings, created highly unpleasant odors which wafted through the town. The stockyards dumped their waste into filth-fermenting Bubbly Creek which flowed into the Chicago River and then into the lake, threatening even the water-intake site two miles out. In July 1871 the city attempted to correct its water pollution problems. It dug the river and canal channels deeper and installed new large pumps at Bridgeport to reverse the flow of the river, sending some of Chicago's sewage toward the Illinois River. The technique only partially worked in the sluggish waterway.

The southward expansion of the downtown area in the late 1860s had lessened the cramped quarters of the burgeoning commercial center of Chicago, but the alleviation period was brief. The difference can be seen in the rise of land costs as supply diminished. The site of the Palmer House had sold for $1.50 per square foot in the mid-1860s. A year later, a new site for the First National Bank close by, at Washington and State streets, went for $25 per square foot.

Fire alone cleared space quickly. In October 1857 a major fire had destroyed a large part of Lake and South Water streets and took 21 lives. Another major fire in 1859 had destroyed a half-million dollars' worth of property. There were two more in 1866. The first conflagration sizable enough to be called a "Great Chicago Fire" leveled a block of Wells Street in 1868 and caused $3 million in damage. Records show Chicago had an average of two fires a day during 1871, more than New York City, which was much older than Chicago and had three times its population.

In *Tale of Chicago* Edgar Lee Masters vividly depicted the city's 59,500 buildings in the autumn of 1871—a city of "Sham magnificence" awaiting an auto-da-fé in a fiery inquisition that would sorely test its faith in its destiny:

66 *Although the city presented a splendid appearance, it was flimsily built, because it had gone up in haste. Walls of the thinness of one brick were sent up a hundred feet into the air, and in the high winds, cornices insecurely fastened, rattled down about the heads of pedestrians. ... Chicago outside of a few buildings was nothing but veneering, sheet iron, pine planks, stucco, and in every variety of spurious architecture. ... Fear was in the hearts of thinking men. They wondered what a fire would do to these miles of wood, to these blocks of fragile metal, veneer, stucco and plaster. ... Great blocks of business houses also confronted wooden structures going to decay, dry as powder from the winds.* 99

Yearly, the strong winds blowing from the prairies in the southwest were notorious fire rousers, yet year after year the city council had refused to pass needed fire regulations. Existing laws failed to be enforced. The rapidity of building everywhere in town made close inspection difficult if not impossible. Also, graft enabled unscrupulous property owners to put up or keep flimsy structures that were clearly tinderboxes.

Chicago at least did have a professional fire department with a substantial amount of equipment and men. It also had a fire-alarm box system by which citizens could alert city hall to the exact location of a fire. The fire bell was in the famous Cook County Courthouse, erected in 1853, which contained at its center a bell tower. Its huge bell rang out the district number in strokes and signaled a widespread or general fire by continuously tolling.

The city suffered long dry spells in both the summer and early fall of 1871. The prairies had seen little rainfall at all. A major conflagration seemed almost inevitable in Chicago. On Saturday, October 7th, a blaze broke out, destroying four blocks in the area where Union Station now stands. It was not extinguished until the next afternoon.

Only five and a half hours after the first fire was extinguished at 9:30 p.m. on Sunday, October 8, in a barn owned by Patrick and Kate O'Leary in an area tenanted by cheap cottages, sheds, and shacks, another fire started. The location, on the north side of DeKoven Street, was a few blocks west of the river. Historical rehashing has never determined whether Mrs. O'Leary was in the cow shed or her bed when an oil lamp kicked by her cow started the fire. One hostile version days later implied she might have set it as revenge for being

Facing page, top: Chicago touted the stockyards as a tourist attraction, rather than apologize for the unpleasant odors that emanated from them. This chromolithograph by Charles Ratcher is innaccurate in its depiction of the area. The river, for example, was further north than portrayed here and was connected to the yards by "Bubbly Creek." Courtesy, Chicago Historical Society

Bottom: Many Chicagoans focused their antagonism on Mrs. O'Leary immediately after the fire. This illustration was sketched and copyrighted within weeks of the conflagration. A newspaper reported a rumor that she had been on the dole and had promised revenge on the city because she had been caught cheating. It was not true. From the author's collection

The Burning of Chicago—Firemen at Work appeared in the British newspaper *The Graphic* on October 21, 1871. One of the adverse factors in fighting the Great Fire was that the firemen were worn out from a major 24-hour blaze that had ended just hours before. From the author's collection

dropped from the city dole. Another tale, supposedly verbatim, had her going out with the lamp to check on her cow, deciding that it needed a salt lick, and returning to find that the lamp had exploded. Still another story involved a party of young neighbors who needed milk for their punch and tried to get it from Mrs. O'Leary's cow, who proved truculent and smashed their lamp. One way or another, the cow and the lamp were implicated.

The fire alert was quickly sounded by a neighbor, "Peg Leg" Sullivan. He even managed to save a calf from the barn but lost his wooden leg in the effort. He escaped by hanging onto the calf for support. The alarm system in the city, however, somehow failed to register properly in the central office. Nor did the fire-watcher in the bell tower pinpoint the locale. Fire engines rushed to the wrong spot. Although Chicago's fire department was one of the best in the country, the men had been worn down from fighting the 24-hour blaze the night before. Once they got to the shanty-town conflagration, some of their equipment malfunctioned. They lost precious time on an evening when the dreaded, dry, southwest wind was whipping through the city.

The district that had burned the night before was in the direct path of the fire, which should have stopped the flames. The wind, however, altered the fire's course and cut a swath around the already burnt blocks. Everyone expected the fire to stop at the South Branch of the river as it had the night before. But superheated drafts of wind and a pinching action by columns of fire suddenly shot the flames across the river in two places, igniting the gasworks (which terminated the city's lighting throughout town), Parmalee's stables (which served Chicago's omnibus company), and the flammable "Conley's Patch" (the shanty, vice-ridden district). With these areas aflame, all of downtown Chicago was clearly threatened.

By midnight it seemed certain that only a miracle could save the city. Wetting down roofs and wooden sidewalks didn't work. Nor did blasting powder, used to blow up buildings in the path of the fire. And the terrible fire, creating its own strong wind, blew flaming objects—mattresses, boards, hay bales—far ahead of itself to start up hundreds of new fires. The gigantic flank of flames swept across the central part of the city, obliterating whole blocks at a time.

Fortunately, the direction of the wind confined the great blaze to Harrison Street on the south, but not before burning a long row of mansions along Michigan Avenue. But there was no salvation for the North Side. As many thousands of refugees fled northward across the bridges, fire balls were already relentlessly vaulting the Chicago River. By early Monday morning the great wall of fire was consuming the homes and businesses, churches and breweries, factories and lumberyards, that a few hours before had seemed completely safe. Even the famed waterworks, with its pump covered by a wooden roof, was rendered inoperable, cutting off the city's water supply so that now firefighting became impossible. (The crenelated water tower next to it, made of Joliet limestone, survived the blaze.)

The city's residents scurried to save themselves, their children, money, pets, furniture, and whatever they had time to put on, or throw into wagons, or drag down the street. Saloon keepers rolled barrels of whiskey along. One mortician even managed to save his supply of coffins. Others, in their desperation to grab something to take, ended up carrying utterly valueless objects.

Alexander Frear, a New York state assemblyman who had been staying at the Sherman House, afterwards portrayed scenes taking place in the business section of the city as the fire approached it: 66 *Lake Street was rich with treasure, and hordes of thieves forced their way into the stores and flung out the merchandise to their fellows in the street. ... I went through to Wabash Avenue, and here the thoroughfare was utterly choked with all manner of goods and people. ... Most of them, in their panic, abandoned their burdens, so that the streets and sidewalks presented the most astonishing wreck. Valuable oil-paintings, books, pet animals, musical instruments, toys, mirrors, and bedding, were trampled under foot. Added to this, the goods from the stores had been hauled out and had taken fire, and the crowd, breaking into a liquor establishment, were yelling with the fury of demons, as they brandished champagne and brandy bottles.*

In this chaos were hundreds of children, wailing and crying for their parents. One little girl, in particular, I saw, whose golden hair was loose down her back and caught afire. She ran screaming past me, and somebody threw a glass of liquor upon her, which flared up and covered her with a blue flame. 99

Joseph Edger Chamberlain, a 20-year-old reporter for the *Chicago Evening Post* who had covered the fire almost from its inception, watched the crowds as they, and he, watched and heard the fire: 66 *As large as was the number of people who were flying from the fire, the number of passive spectators was still larger. Their eyes were all diverted from the skurrying mass of people around them to the spectacle of appalling grandeur before them. They stood transfixed, with a mingled feeling of horror and admiration, and while they often exclaimed at the beauty of the scene, they all devoutly prayed that they might never see such another.*

The noise of the conflagration was terrific. To the roar which the simple process of combustion always makes, magnified here to so grand an extent, was added the crash of falling buildings and the constant explosions of stores of oil and other like material. The noise of the crowd was nothing compared with this chaos of sound. 99

Chicagoans fled to the lake and drenched themselves in its cold waters to avoid the blast of the fire that ranged temperatures somewhere between 750 and 3,000 degrees Fahrenheit. Men buried wives and children in wet sand, leaving breathing holes for them. Others on the North Side crossed the river's North Branch to seek refuge westward on the prairie. Many thousands moved into the open green safety of Lincoln Park, where rich and poor alike were

Right: The Water Tower quickly became a symbol of post-fire Chicago. While the waterworks itself was burned, leaving only the building's walls and three burnt and broken engines, the crenellated Water Tower sustained only minor damage. From Andreas, *History of Chicago*, 1885

Below: People grabbed whatever possessions they could and raced through the streets by foot or on wagons to escape the fast-moving flames. This pencil sketch is by A.R. Waud. Courtesy, Chicago Historical Society (ICHi-02984)

homeless and near-possessionless.

Early Tuesday morning the fire finally abated in the area of Clark Street and Fullerton Avenue in a light drizzling rain. For days afterward there were smouldering remains. Buildings that had contained large quantities of metal were reduced to deposits of hot, contorted masses that had to be "mined" for removal.

The grandson of John Kinzie, Arthur M. Kinzie, wended his way southward through the burnt-out city on the way to his sister's house on the South Side. "It was a strange sight as we passed through the burned district that night," he remembered. "All squares formerly built up solidly were now so many black excavations, while the streets had the appearance of raised turnpikes intersecting each other on a level prairie. All the coalyards were still burning, and gave light enough to travel without difficulty."

The *Tribune's* William Bross, having lost his own home and his place of work, went out to survey Chicago on Tuesday: *The next morning I was out early, and found the streets thronged with people moving in all directions. To me the sight of the ruin, though so sad, was wonderful—giving one a most peculiar sensation, as it was wrought in so short a space of time. It was the destruction of the entire business portion of one of the greatest cities in the world! ... Desolation stared me in the face at every step, and yet I was much struck with the tone and temper of the people. On all sides I saw evidences of true Chicago spirit, and men said to one another, "Cheer up; we'll be all right again before long," and many other plucky things. Their courage was wonderful. Everyone was bright, cheerful, pleasant, and even inclined to be jolly, in spite of the misery and destitution which surrounded them, and which they shared. One and all said, "Chicago must and shall be rebuilt at once."*

Chicago life, both personal and commercial, had to go on. A first necessity was to sound a clarion call for the "Chicago Spirit" to rise and convert the ashes of destruction to a city even more splendid than before. Joseph Medill, conscious of his role as a *Tribune* editor, had managed to secure a printing shop on Canal Street for the newspaper's temporary new office. The *Tribune* staff cleaned the place up and prepared to issue the paper on Wednesday morning—complete with people's advertisements asking the whereabouts of missing kin. In the days thereafter Medill's editorial voice would resound: *All is not lost. Though four hundred million dollars worth of property has been destroyed, Chicago still exists. She was not a mere collection of stones, and bricks, and lumber. ... We have lost money, but we have saved life, health, vigor and industry. ... Let the watchword henceforth be: Chicago Shall Rise Again.* To make certain this would happen, Medill accepted a draft for the office of mayor—and won with his Union "Fireproof" ticket.

There were lessons to be learned from the remains. For example, architect John Van Osdel had hurriedly buried his record books and blueprints in a pit dug in the basement of the new Palmer House and then covered the deposit with several inches of wet clay. The valuable papers survived intact, to inspire a new clay fire-brick industry. The relative non-combustibility of certain buildings were also studied, and architects were urged to come to Chicago in the post-Fire weeks to study its ruins for helpful information about construction techniques and materials.

The statistics of the Chicago Fire were staggering, but a major dimension of the event, apart from its huge financial losses, was simply the number of witnesses. Each of the 334,270 people had a story to tell. The same day, October 8, an even worse fire started a little over 200 miles north of Chicago near Peshtigo, Wisconsin. In that disaster 1,200 people were burned to death and more than one million acres of land were devastated in a single night. It was, by far, the worst tragedy of its kind in U.S. history. Yet it is the Chicago Fire, with only one-fourth as many deaths, that is remembered.

The burning of the huge grain elevators at the mouth of the Chicago River was one of the most breathtaking sights of the fire. Seven of the city's 17 elevators burned, while some of the largest survived. This tragic scene was published in *Harper's Weekly*, which devoted issue after issue to the conflagration. From the Windsor Archives

What was lost in Chicago and what was not? First of all lives were taken. The number of deaths was estimated at about 300, although only 75 bodies were found. The intense heat of the fire along with suffocation probably trapped many persons whose bodies were totally incinerated. Since hundreds of people fled the city immediately after the fire a final counting could not be made.

The fire covered an area of 3.32 square miles. The actual number of buildings burned was 17,450. Of these, 13,300 were on the North Side; 3,650 on the South Side, and 500 on the West Side. The total cost of the fire was later put at $200 million. Of this figure $88 million was covered by insurance, but only half of this amount was paid, as 70 out of the 250 insurance companies doing business in the city defaulted or failed.

Commercial Chicago faced near, if somewhat temporary, extinction. The city, for example, had 17 large grain elevators. All were located along the river and many (contents included) went up in smoke. All the city's banks and large hotels were in the path of the fire, as were its major stores, insurance company offices, and business headquarters. The only two structures surviving the fire in the central city were Lind Block and the unfinished Nixon Building, both of which would be swiftly fixed up for occupancy.

Residential Chicago did not fare as badly. About 100,000 were made homeless. Many of these people had lived in downtown rooming houses and hotels. Most West and South Side homes were little affected by the flames. But the North Side up to Fullerton Avenue and east of Orchard Street was destroyed; only two homes were saved in this area, one of them owned by Mahlon Ogden. His brother, William B. Ogden, the city's first mayor, received the shocking news in New York on October 9. One of Chicago's largest real estate owners, William Ogden was, ironically, also the largest investor in Peshtigo, Wisconsin. The double loss proved more challenging than devastating to him.

Most of the city's records were destroyed along with the Courthouse, whose bell, set to continue ringing the general alarm, tolled until 2:05 a.m. on Monday, when it came crashing down. The Chicago Historical Society was destroyed along with its records, including the priceless first draft of the Emancipation Proclamation presented to Chicago by Lincoln himself. Fortunately for property owners, an officer in a major title company had managed to remove the files containing copies of deeds and other legal documents which proved invaluable in the difficult months ahead when decisions had to be made on what belonged to whom, how much, and exactly where. Special laws were enacted promptly, thanks to the recommendations of Myra Bradshaw, publisher of *Chicago Legal News*.

On the wide economic level the losses caused by the Great Fire were incalculable. People left. Companies relocated. St. Louis believed it would easily displace Chicago and become again the commercial capital of the Midwest. But

The Crosby Opera House, regarded by most architectural critics as the most beautiful building west of the Alleghenies, was one of the few burned in the fire that was considered irreplaceable. From *Harper's Weekly,* October 28, 1871

Chicagoans would scarcely allow this to happen. Elderly John S. Wright, surveying the blackened ruins of his once proud city, predicted that within five years Chicago would be even bigger and better than before, thanks to the fire. And William Bross of the *Tribune* took the first available train to the East—even going off without clean underclothing—so that he could present personally the dramatic tale of the Great Chicago Fire to financiers who could help the city out in the months ahead. The Great Booster did his work well. Bankers and wholesalers in the East extended the essential credits and furnished goods. As the news of the Chicago Fire spread across the nation and to Europe, contributions poured in from generous and compassionate people and groups everywhere. A specially welcome gift came from England: 7,000 books, which would launch the city's first free public library. Right after the fire martial law was declared and troops were sent in from Fort Leavenworth to prevent looting and other crimes in the devastated city. General Philip Sheridan took command of them.

Chicago, or at least a substantial part of it, was in ashes. But not for long. Resurrection began on Tuesday morning when William D. Kerfoot erected a temporary shack as a real estate office at 89 Washington Street. His sign proclaimed, "All gone but wife, children and energy." A temporary city hall was improvised. Behind it was a large, rusty water tank which was converted into the city's library with skylights. Because birds got in and flew around, it became known as "the Rookery"—the name given to the famous building erected later on the site.

Even in the depressing days most of Chicago's business leaders retained their belief in Chicago's great potential. They counted their remaining assets—primarily the railroad lines, which were only affected where they covered the fire zone though most depots had been burned. Intact were the canal; the stockyards; a number of factories; and of course the prime location itself—Chicago's raison d'étre. Significant too was the grain harvest poised to come into Chicago from the hinterland. Chicago entrepreneurs depended upon fulfilling prior arrangements made through contracts at the Board of Trade to receive and deliver this grain by railroad, boat, and canal barge.

Of crucial economic importance to the city's future was the ongoing work to improve the Calumet River area as a port. It involved digging a wider and deeper channel so that Lake Calumet could be used as a protected harbor. From now on, much of the heavy industry—the steel making, metal manufacturing, brick and tile works, eventually oil refining, chemical plants, and even the grain storage facilities—would begin a southeastward migration toward the Indiana border.

The fire at least had "cleaned house" in much of Chicago, by ridding the city's heart of a good many old or poorly built structures, unfortunately along

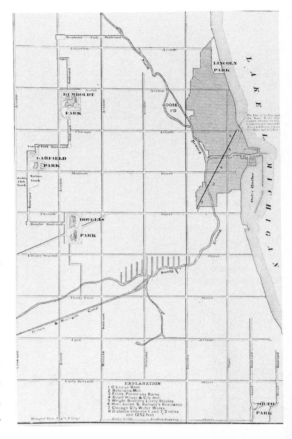

Above: The fire extended over a 3.32-square-mile area. This map shows not only what was burned, but also what was left unscathed. The numbered line indicates the basic path of the flames. Some of the area west of the river actually had burned the day before the Great Fire started. From Andreas, *History of Chicago,* 1885

Facing page, bottom: As soon as it was safe to sift through the charred remains, bank and jewelry store employees undertook the task of retrieving their safes and vaults. Note the soldiers (at right) standing guard. From the *Illustrated London News,* November 11, 1871

with the far better and costlier buildings erected in their midst. Now, everything had to be started anew. It was not a time for the faint-hearted. The loyal and determined Chicagoans remained—and built, mostly better then before. A week after the fire, over 5,000 temporary buildings were up, and in the next year a virtual army of 100,000 workers erected 10,000 structures. In order to accommodate business and residential needs, the city council conferred a strict one-year limit of existence on hastily erected wood buildings in the burnt-over area, but, this law was not always subsequently obeyed. Generally, however, new buildings met "fireproof" requirements with limestone, sandstone, or brick construction.

William A. Croffat, managing editor of the *Chicago Evening Post,* a few months later portrayed the rapidity with which the city's entrepreneurs, of every category, went back to business: " " *By far the most grotesque phase of the calamity is the manner in which the vast business of the city, suddenly driven into the street, instantly accommodated itself to new locations and conditions. When the crimson canopy of Monday night merged into the dawn of Tuesday morning, it was found that, besides personal property, some thousands of loads of merchandise had been saved—stowed away in tunnels, buried in back alleys, piled up all along the lake shore, strewn in front yards through the avenues, run out of the city in box cars, and even, in some instances, freighted upon the decks of schooners off the harbor. And, far more than this, five thousand merchants had saved their good name—that imperishable entity that carries an invisible treasury for him who wears its badge.* " "

One of the most astonishing transformations came in elegant residential areas just south and west of the fire's scope, which Croffat described with wry disdain: " " *Many a man who has done a business of half a million a year has invaded his own front parlor on the Avenue; has whisked the piano, the gorgeous sofas, the medallion carpet, and the clock of ormolu into capacious upper stories, and has sent his family to keep them company; while showcases have been arrayed through drawing and dining rooms, and clerks now serve customers with hats, furs, shoes, or jewelry, where they formerly spooned water ices at an evening party.* " "

In his survey of the makeshift arrangements housing Chicago's continuing business, editor Croffat paid a visit to the new location of "the largest dry goods store in the West," Field, Leiter and Company—burned out at its prime State Street property but ensconced now on 20th Street, selling merchandise. " " *Here are hundreds of clerks and thousands of patrons a day, busy along the spacious aisles and the vast vistas of ribbons and laces and cloaks and dress goods. This tells no story of a fire. The ladies jostle each other as impatiently as of old, and the boys run merrily to the incessant cry of "Cash." Yet, Madam, this immense bazaar was six weeks ago the horsebarn of the South Side Railroad! A strange*

Below: Soon after the fire, children took advantage of the demand for mementos of the conflagration by selling grotesque pieces of melted glass or iron found among the smoldering ruins. One adult entrepreneur remolded the fire bell in city hall into clappers for small bells. He then sold them with testimonial letters. From *Frank Leslie's Illustrated Newspaper,* November 11, 1871

Above: Even as the ruins of Chicago smoldered, people flocked to the city from all points ready to take away what little remained. To protect the area, the Fifth United States Infantry was called in to enforce martial law. This pencil sketch by Alfred R. Waud entitled *Who Goes There?* depicts the military presence in Chicago immediately after the fire. Courtesy, Chicago Historical Society (ICHi-02990)

Facing page: By noon on October 10, 1871, William D. Kerfoot had erected this 12-by-16-foot shanty on Washington between Dearborn and Clark streets, and was prepared to resume his real-estate business. He subsequently made millions of dollars in real estate. From *The Graphic,* November 25, 1871

metamorphosis!—yet it is but an extreme illustration of the sudden changes the city has undergone. "

Even the city's religious houses were taken over by business of one kind or another: " *The churches that are spared have been curiously appropriated— several of them by the Relief Societies, others by institutions that are of the earth ... . Here is one overrun and utterly deluged by Uncle Sam's mail—given up in all its parts to the exigencies of the city postal service. One is divided up for offices-a lawyer offers to defend your title ... an insurance man volunteers to save you from the next fire; and in the recess that used to hold the choir, a dentist holds the heads and examines the mouths of his victims.* "

Property owners, paying taxes on useless lots that had not diminished in value, *had* to build. Cellars were excavated, bricks were salvaged if possible, melted metal was extracted and sold cheap at foundries, and rubble was removed and dumped along the lakeshore, to help the Illinois Central raise its tracks and yards above the water and increase its girth of city land.

In the rush to build during the winter months, contractors discovered a technique that would alter construction schedules ever afterward. Croffat told of this too: " *It is December, but an artificial summer is created to keep the work from freezing up; a bonfire is blazing before the mortar bed, where the compound is prepared as the housewife prepares her dough; and other and smaller fires blaze briskly all around within the rising wall—a fire on every mortar-board, which keeps the mortar plastic and the blood of the bricklayer uncongealed. Thus is the smitten city rising again at New Year's-rising, as she fell, by fire.* "

In the 1870s the city expressed its strongest confidence by building new railroad terminals and hotels. Most notable among the latter were the "Big Four." The Tremont House rose once again. The Sherman House was rebuilt at a cost of $650,000. The Grand Pacific Hotel—designed by W.W. Boyington and burnt before it could open—was duplicated. Following Van Osdel's salvaged plans, the new Palmer House was resurrected. Costing one million dollars, it opened in 1875 and was considered the most fireproof hotel anywhere in the world—and one of the most elegant. The less grandiose commercial buildings were only beginning to use the hydraulic elevator that made taller buildings more possible. But in the 1870s architects had not yet developed the effective load-distributing steel skeletal structure that ushered in the true skyscrapers.

Architects found themselves in heavy demand to design new office buildings, churches, theaters, homes, and schools. Orders for work taxed the city's most popular and long-term architects, John Van Osdel, Augustus Bauer, and W.W. Boyington, as well as engineer William LeBaron Jenney, who had come to Chicago after the Civil War. They also attracted new designers, among them such future greats as John Wellborn Root, Dankmar Adler, Louis Sullivan, and

Daniel H. Burnham.

In 1872, in the midst of this frenetic building spree, a young man named Aaron Montgomery Ward set up business in Chicago, where he had previously been clerk for Field, Leiter and Company before going out on the road as a "drummer" or salesman for wholesale houses. While traveling, he had noticed that there might be a way to sell a variety of goods directly to people in towns and on farms across the Midwest—and who knew where else? By developing a list of such goods obtainable mainly in Chicago and then presenting them, along with descriptions and prices, in a catalog that could be sent through the mail directly to prospective customers, he would avoid middlemen and retailers and pass the savings from marked-up prices onto the individual buyers. He could also slowly build up a far larger stock of offerings than any small town dry goods merchant would be able to keep on hand.

Ward rented a loft in the McCormick Block and prepared his first "catalog." It was only a large printed sheet but he sent it to whomever requested it after reading small advertisements in out-of-town periodicals. He made a special connection with the farmers' Grange organization. With each season his catalog and the number of kinds of goods he offered expanded. So did the number of his customers, who ranged farther and farther afield from his Chicago headquarters. He expected cash in advance or arranged to get cash on delivery (C.O.D.) through rural delivery services, thereby avoiding unpaid bills. These catalogs understandably threatened the livelihoods of local merchants, who sometimes attempted to get them intercepted at post offices, causing Ward to mail them out for a time in plain brown paper envelopes, as though they were lurid books.

The 1870s, then, saw the start of the huge direct mail merchandising business through the spread of "wish books"—catalogs that rural families pored over for several generations. Ward's dominance would be challenged two decades later by Sears, Roebuck and Company, which later also made its headquarters in Chicago in the 1890s. Clearly the city was the most central and convenient buying and shipping location for this vigorous enterprise.

After the Great Fire the new suburban community of Riverside began attracting Chicagoans away from the dangers of combustion and disease and the unpleasantness of urban congestion. Frederick Law Olmsted, when asked in 1869 to plan a forward-looking park and boulevard complex for Chicago itself, was also enlisted to design an idyllic housing tract along the Des Plaines River. Architect William LeBaron Jenney, selected to implement Olmstead's ideas, contrived curving roads, parklands and recreation areas, a woodland, a boating pond, and a hotel. Industrial plants were confined to one area, and their buildings, as well as Riverside's homes, were required to have trees planted around them to ensure a pleasant appearance overall. A nine-mile boulevard for car-

Facing page, top: Horse-drawn streetcars conveyed sightseers around the ruins of the city. This view shows the area around State and Madison. Courtesy, Chicago Historical Society (ICHi-02811)

Bottom left: Not even one guest was able to experience the comfort of the Bigelow Hotel since it burned down just as it was preparing to open for business. The hotel's grand entrance was virtually the only part of the Dearborn Street building left standing after the fire. Photo by Jex Bardwell. Courtesy, Chicago Historical Society

Bottom right: Workmen equipped with shovels begin the monumental task of removing the rubble piled up throughout the burned area. Photo by Jex Bardwell. Courtesy, Chicago Historical Society

riages was planned to stretch directly to Chicago for commuters' rapid transit. But this early turnpike was never built because the construction corporation went bankrupt. Still, Riverside was notable as one of the nation's first carefully planned, "greenbelt" suburbs on the outskirts of a major city.

The rebuilding of the commercial city seemed the proper occasion for a fair—at which Chicago had excelled in the past. Confident that the city would be suitably presentable by 1873, town merchants obtained the Illinois legislators' approval of staging an Inter-State Industrial Exposition. They set to work at once. Architect W.W. Boyington designed and supervised the construction of a huge "Crystal Palace" fashioned after the iron and glass showcase in Victorian London. It was placed on the east side of Michigan Avenue, on public land that according to an old city edict could never be used for commercial purposes.

The Inter-State Industrial Exposition proved popular. At least 60,000 people passed through its doorway during the year to view the assemblage of the latest technological marvels used and produced in the state—but particularly, of course, in Chicago itself. The display, which was updated and given annually, became a tourist attraction. The large building itself was used for concerts and political conventions until it was torn down in 1891 to make way for the splendid new Art Institute of Chicago.

In 1876 William "Deacon" Bross published his *History of Chicago,* a collection of his speeches and writings on the city. Bross pointed to the accuracy of his past predictions for Chicago. Using that credibility he now predicted the population of the city for 1976. Chicago had an estimated 450,000 residents in 1876. As to next century he wrote: "With my eye upon the vast country tributary to the city, I estimate Chicago will then contain at least 3,000,000 people and I would sooner say 4,000,000 than any less than 3,000,000." Bross hit it on the button. Chicago's population in 1976 was estimated to be 3.25 million.

Bross and other Chicago boosters always kept their aims high. For others success did not come so readily. Workers, especially from Europe, came to Chicago to join in the rebuilding of the city, but they did not always find work. Poor housing and sanitary conditions for working-class families swelled the 1872 mortality rate to a higher figure than for 1871, the year of all the fire deaths. Two business recessions in Chicago during the 1870s—one caused by the nationwide Panic of 1873, the other by a grasshopper plague that destroyed the Midwest's grain crops—hit workers hard, especially the hordes out of work

Above: In 1872 Aaron Montgomery Ward established a mail-order dry goods business in Chicago primarily to sell goods to farmers who previously had to pay very high prices for a quite limited selection of low-quality goods. Ward's first catalog, only one page, offered 30 items. Within 16 years Montgomery Ward and Company's annual sales totaled one million dollars. From *Historical Encyclopedia of Illinois*. Courtesy, Chicago Historical Society (ICHi-12788)

Above right: The Field, Leiter and Company's retail building at Washington and State streets, finished in 1873, was one of the crowning commercial glories of Chicago after the fire. Unfortunately, it lasted only a short time. In 1877 another fire destroyed it. From Wing, *Illustrations of Greater Chicago,* 1875

Above, far right: In a town short on architects just after the fire, Potter Palmer decided to reuse John Van Osdel's plans for the old Palmer House. Adding to the plans, Palmer spent $2.5 million on what he claimed to be the world's "first fireproof hotel." Six hundred tons of Belgium iron and 34 varieties of marble were used to construct the hotel. Pictured here are workmen laboring on the Palmer House at night using calcium light. From Wing, *Rebuilt Chicago: Illustrated,* 1873

after the post-Fire building boom. People froze or died from hunger in the winter of 1872-1873. "Bread or blood!" protest signs declared. Although this economic depression passed, severe social unrest lay ahead.

In 1877 another recession hit the country. Labor anger that began with a strike of locomotive firemen in the East resulted in riots that swept westward and reached Chicago in July 1877. Mobs formed in the city, and to the business interests revolution seemed imminent. The newly founded *Chicago Daily News*—a "penny paper" that reintroduced the small-denomination coin by persuading its merchant advertisers to sell goods at 99 cents instead of one dollar, leaving customers a penny for buying a copy of the *Daily News*—sent squads of reporters into the street to talk with the people. The paper, mostly sympathetic toward laborers, published extras detailing the succession of events in "The Great Railroad Strike of 1877." A pitched battle was fought at the new McCormick Reaper Works along Blue Island Avenue. The police and nonstriking "scabs" were ranged on one side and the workers and radical supporters on the other. For the most part Workingmen's party leaders such as Albert Parsons tried to hold down the violence and to focus the workers' demands on higher wages and on attaining the eight-hour work day.

The *Chicago Daily News* meanwhile spoke on some of the causes of the rioting: " For years the railroads of this country have been wholly run outside of the United States Constitution ...

The people have no sympathy with the rioters, but they have as little for the Vanderbilts, the Jay Goulds, and the Jim Fisks who have been running the property until they have ruined one of the most expensive and finest the world had ever known.

The frightful evils we now endure were brought upon us by a course of legislation in the interest of capital and against industry. It is simply nonsense to say there are not two sides to the question. "

The demonstrations died down after awhile when an upswing in prosperity pushed discontent to the back of Chicagoans' attention. But the memory of grievances against America's "robber baron" class and its "railroad kings" would remain, to reassert itself among the workers and their articulate, radical spokesmen in years to come.

In 1879 the Calumet Club had held a reception for the city's old-timer fathers inviting the men who had settled in Chicago before 1840. And 149 came. Prominent in their midst was stout "Long John" Wentworth, who always loved an opportunity to recount his memories of early Chicago history,

Facing page: On July 26, 1877, an angry mob of railroad workers, frustrated by rolled-back wages, clashed with police and regular army reinforcements near the Halsted Street viaduct at 16th Street. The encounter was less bloody than portrayed in this *Harper's Weekly* illustration. From the author's collection

Below: Robert Fergus, who has been called ''the father of the printing industry in Chicago'' and ''perhaps the most thorough of practical printers,'' attended the 1879 Calumet Club reception for the city's old-timers. His firm, Ellis and Fergus, printed early Chicago documents such as the 1844 city directory. In 1876 he started reissuing early historical pamphlets as the Fergus Historical Series. By 1890 he had published 34 of them. From Gilbert and Bryson, *Chicago and Its Makers*, 1929

giving special emphasis on his terms in Congress and as mayor. Gurdon Saltonstall Hubbard—fur trader, pioneer, legislator, businessman, and meat-packing magnate—came too. Now blind and still stunned by the Chicago Fire, he would live seven more years. Silas Cobb, who had arrived in 1833, had started out in business by operating a ferry across the Chicago River at Dearborn Street, for an outlay of $9.60. Now, 46 years later, he was president of the Chicago City Railway. Present too was J. Young Scammon. William B. Ogden's partner in the first railroad, he had handled Abe Lincoln's law cases in Chicago, and had fought to establish the city's common schools. Even Mark Beaubien was there, recalling how as a youth in Detroit he had heard of the Fort Dearborn Massacre. The city's first schoolmaster, John Watkins, could not attend, but he wrote a letter mentioning that he had come to Chicago in 1832.

The reunion of elderly Chicagoans was also attended by Robert Fergus, one of the city's first printers, whose Chicago years began in 1839. In 1876 he had begun reprinting early Chicago documents, eventually compiling a 34-part series that became the bedrock on which much subsequent Chicago historical research has rested. Conspicuously missing, though, was the city's prophetical booster, John Stephen Wright. He had died in 1874.

The decade of the 1870s closed with the election of Carter Henry Harrison I as mayor of the city. In the years to come, this colorful, endearing, larger than life-size ''man of people'' would help to steer the city through times that saw tragedies as well as triumphs—different from the period of the Great Chicago Fire but equally full of drama.

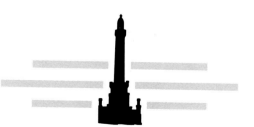

CHAPTER EIGHT

GROWING TOWARD THE SKY

THE 1880s

Built between 1883 and 1885, the Board of Trade building was located on Jackson Boulevard facing LaSalle. Though many Chicagoans were proud of the edifice, 2,000 others paraded in front of the building protesting that it was "a grand temple of Usury, Gambling and Cut-Throatism." For most, the structure became a rather awesome Chicago landmark. From *A History of the City of Chicago*, 1900

In the 1880s Chicago discovered all the pleasures and pains of maturing—socially, economically, and politically. The city saw itself as the rest of the country did: a giant railroad center, meatpacker, lumber dealer, and grain trader. It was also undergoing a metamorphosis from a commercial to a manufacturing center, building a towering kingdom of skyscrapers, and unknowingly preparing an arena for a bloody clash between anarchists and the establishment.

All through the 1880s the city experienced a major growth spurt. It would find, in due course, that its municipal supports—the streets, buildings, schools, water supply, sewers, and police, and fire departments—no longer matched its size.

A mark of the city's maturity was a prideful consciousness of its past. In 1883 Chicago celebrated its 50th birthday. In the half-century since its incorporation as a village, the number of residents had zoomed from 300 to 650,000. In addition, 75 suburbs had populations varying from 50 to 10,000. Of this increasingly fabled town the German statesman Bismarck said, "I wish I could go to America if only to see that Chicago." Niagara Falls and Chicago were mentioned as the nation's most astounding attractions.

The city, often quoting Bismarck's remark, was taking itself seriously. Authors wrote a number of books about Chicago on the occasion of its golden anniversary. In one, *Chicago Illustrated,* a short paragraph summarized the city's 1883 credo and experience: " *Chicago does not yet compare with New York in wealth or Boston in letters; but its commerce is large and growing—now more rapid than at any time in its history—and commerce begets wealth; wealth begets culture, refinement, and such blessings as make a happy and contented people.* "

Chicago did boast of many blessings. The nation's railroads, 90 percent of which were controlled by New Yorkers, were not all successful in 1883. But "those dependent almost entirely upon the trade of Chicago for their traffic" were successful, according to *Chicago Illustrated*. Each day 350 trains passed through Chicago conveying 40,000 passengers in and out of the city. Railroads brought 500 boxcars per hour into the city and carried 64 billion tons of freight annually, making it a rail center without equal in the world.

By 1879 Gustavus Swift, who had worked for more than a decade to perfect the insulated and ice-packed refrigerator car, was significantly increasing the distribution of fresh or "dressed" meat. Swift was soon to be joined by a competitor—Armour. Chicago's stockyards (still outside the city limits) were expanded but had to strain to keep up with the increased demand. Livestock shippers like Nelson Morris and Samuel Allerton gained new wealth. In 1883 the city was amazed as more than 40,000 cattle were slaughtered each week for seven straight weeks in the stockyards. Messrs. Armour and Swift also developed the idea of local branch outlets. Independent butchers fought vigorously against this kind of mass-marketing by requiring states or cities to inspect meat within 24 hours of slaughtering.

As the volume of the stockyards' output increased, the use of its by-products created more new industries than ever before. At this the two rival meatpackers especially excelled. Apart from the making of products from fat rendering, there were glue factories and pharmaceutical laboratories producing pepsin and pancreatin. Parts of horns, hooves, bones, and offal all spawned other Chicago enterprises. Referring to the main and subsidiary industries, Philip D. Armour declared, "Through the wages I disburse and the provisions I supply, I give more people food than any other man alive."

Finley Peter Dunne, the Chicago humorist, got good mileage out of gentle pokes at the city's meatpackers. His Mr. Dooley character commented:

> *A cow goes lowin' softly in to Armours' an' comes out glue, gelatine, fertylizer, celooloid, joolry, sofy cushions, hair restorer, washin' sody, littrachoor an' bedsprings so quick that while aft she's stilla cow, for'ard she may be anything fr'm buttons to pannyma hats.*

Indeed, Chicago's Union Stock Yards were world-renowned for their efficiency—and certainly notorious for the sounds, smells, and sights that assailed visitors. The stout-hearted and curious made grand tours of the premises within the city nicknamed, to its dismay, "Porkopolis!"

The industrial and retail growth was not confined to Chicago's meatpacking industry. Many passengers riding the trains out of Chicago were salesmen who offered an amazing variety of goods, including popular new contraptions such as bicycles and telephones. The firms that deployed these "drummers" across the countryside were beginning to find themselves the old "veterans." McCormick had been shipping reapers from Chicago since 1848. (In 1884—the year Cyrus

Facing page, top: South Water Street, now Wacker Drive, was a produce market where vendors with open-air stands competed with established wholesale grocers in the 1880s. This view of horse-and-cart-lined South Water looks east from Franklin. From Andreas, *History of Chicago,* 1886

Bottom left: By 1880 the Chicago, Alton and St. Louis Railroad had finally connected the industrial cities of Chicago, Kansas City, and St. Louis. During the early 1880s railroads carried 500 boxcars into Chicago every hour. From *Merchants and Manufacturers,* 1880

Bottom right: The Chicago and North Western Railway Company located its general offices on Kinzie Street between Franklin and Market. From Wing, *Illustrations of Greater Chicago,* 1875

died, 55,000 of them were sold to farmers.) Brunswick, Balke had been exporting billiard tables from Chicago for an equally long time. Crane and Company were manufacturing valves from 1855 on. W.W. Kimball had been making pianos and organs in the city since 1857. In that year C.A. Taylor began constructing trunks. Edson Keith was creating ladies' hats in 1858 and B. Kuppenheimer was offering men's ready-made clothes in 1863. Lyon and Healy had been publishing music since 1864—the same year N.K. Fairbank started making soap. Franklin MacVeagh's wholesale grocery trade dated to 1866. The department store of Carson, Pirie and Company (the Scott was added in 1892) and John M. Smyth's furniture factory both began in 1867.

Both local and exporting firms increasingly used novel ambulatory or showcase advertising to bring the people's attention to their wares. Visiting Italian writer Giuseppe Giacosa provides vivid examples of the parade of commercialism (not always in the best of taste): 66 *A military band passes on the street, followed by a troop of generals in imposing uniforms; the flag which accompanies them announces a new grain machine. Those imperial coaches, shining white with rays of gold, which are drawn by four gigantic white horses, decked with plumes and flowers, carry slabs of meat dripping blood from the butchers' knives; 'Armour and Co.' I can still see, right in the middle of the sidewalk, placed somewhere on a half column, a crystal goblet which my arms could not reach around, filled to the brim with anglo-saxon teeth. 'The set of twenty lower jaws all extracted by Dr. _____,' the sign said; 'one visit makes a customer.' Then you heard of the beautiful idea of that Chicago upholsterer: those promises to decorate with the most ornate furnishings the nuptial suite of the couple who would consent to be married in his shop window. The couple was found, the scene was made ready, a pastor happened along, and the knot was tied.* 99

Heavy-machinery production stimulated by the Union's urgent demands in the 1860s continued to increase. By the 1880s there were numerous blast and open-hearth furnaces and Bessemer steel works clustered in the Lake Calumet area. George Pullman relocated his plant there, partly because he used much metal in the working parts of the wooden railroad cars' rolling stock.

Not all of Chicago's major industries fared equally well in the 1880s. Chicago had held a virtual monopoly in the wholesaling of lumber until the 1880s; the railroads, however, had decentralized the industry, meaning that raw lumber no longer had to stop in Chicago to be processed. Chicago lumber dealers were able at first to use their powerful position to retard this development by enforcing tariffs on shipping from other lumber centers. The new Interstate Commerce Commission, however, assisted in abrogating these tariffs. Chicago nevertheless remained the greatest lumber center in the U.S. for a while longer. But as Michigan and Wisconsin forests yielded less first-rate timber, lumbermen began to turn to Minnesota, the South, and even California, making the city a

Facing page, top left: Philip Danforth Armour, who moved to Chicago in 1875, was responsible for making it the nation's major pork-packing city. Armour canned meat and exported it to Europe and shipped fresh beef on refrigerated cars to the East. Courtesy, Illinois Institute of Technology. From Cirker, *Dictionary of American Portraits*, 1967

Top middle: Chicago's Fairbank Canning Company "revised and improved" Aesop's fable "The Huntsman and the Lion" for use in this advertisement for the company's Lion brand of canned meats. From the Windsor Archives

Top right: Meatpacker Gustavus Franklin Swift became the first to use the refrigerator car to ship dressed beef to the East on a regular basis. To outdo his competitors, who soon began to ship dressed meat, Swift made use of all beef by-products. In 1885 he incorporated his business as Swift and Company. Courtesy, Swift and Company. From *Cirker, Dictionary of American Portraits*, 1967

Bottom: The Wilson Packing Company was organized in 1874 for the express purpose of utilizing a newly discovered process of preserving meat (a can invented by the Wilsons). Wilson's specialities included game, poultry, corned beef, and ham and beef tongues. This advertising card states the dire consequences of running out of Wilson's Beef. From the Windsor Archives

THE HUNTSMAN AND THE LION.

A man who was very skilled with his rifle, went up into the mountains to hunt. At his approach the wild beasts ran away as fast as possible, the Lion alone showing any determination to fight. When the Huntsman saw this, he said to himself, "That is the brand of meat I like, but I think I had rather get it out of the Fairbank Canning Co's package." Moral: Keep on hand a supply of our "Lion" brand of Canned Meats, and be happy.

USE FAIRBANK CANNING COMPANY'S "COOKED CORNED BEEF."

ÆSOP'S FABLES
REVISED AND IMPROVED BY THE
FAIRBANK CANNING CO.
CHICAGO.

No! Skobeleff. Our rifles were the best, we had plenty of ammunition, but we had used our last can of WILSON'S BEEF—and Plevna fell!!—*Osman Pasha.*

WILSON
CORNED BEEF

less important lumber shipping point. Chicago was still its own best customer for the product—98,838 buildings of all types were erected in the city between 1871 and 1893.

Among the most prominent lumbermen in the city was Samuel K. "Skinny" Martin. Associated with him in the 1880s was Edward Hines, who formed his own firm in 1892. Hines, whose name still appears on lumberyards in Chicago and its suburbs, later used wood to build a car racing track in suburban Maywood. The track was disassembled and used to build a veterans' hospital which today bears the name of his son killed in World War I.

New inventions in printing presses and techniques as well as new processes that used woodpulp in papermaking helped make Chicago, with its availability of heavy machinery and lumber, a leader in the publishing industry. Its central location aided in the distribution of books, magazines, foreign-language newspapers, pulp novels, and religious and propaganda tracts. There were also those increasingly popular mail-order catalogs. Printing became a highly developed art among some firms, who competed with each other in printing highly ornate, finely engraved stationery, business cards, advertisements, and invoices not only for Chicago firms but also for companies far away.

The 1882 *Chicago Business Directory* shows well over 200 job and book printers in the city. Donnelley, Gassette and Lloyd had not yet become R.R. Donnelley & Sons. William H. Rand and Andrew McNally were developing their firm of Rand, McNally and Company into one of the top publishers in the nation by printing maps, directories, and other useful publications. William Franklin Hall, one of the most successful master printers in Chicago's history, worked as a journeyman and then foreman for the Regan Printing House in the 1880s. In 1893 he organized the W.F. Hall Printing Company. A.C. McClurg, a bookseller since 1844, did a lucrative business not just in Chicago but also in outlying towns and cities where he was a book distributor.

Temperance and evangelism had found durable homes in Chicago. The Woman's Christian Temperance Union was led by the determined Frances Willard of Evanston, who also helped farm and small-town women stand up and fight for suffrage as part of her crusade. Dwight L. Moody made Chicago the headquarters of his evangelistic movement. Such reformers found in Chicago a central location, a good railroad stop, and a publishing center for their myriad tracts.

Yet the temperance people surely found it discomfiting to have agents of Satan in their midst. During the latter part of the 19th century Chicago contained a few distilleries and a good many breweries—most of the latter founded, and funded, by the German population in the city. Useful in the brewing and distilling processes, of course, were the grain varieties that came into the city. Busy as Chicago was with brewing beer, though, it still had to import more from

Facing page, top left: Edward Hines established a lumberyard in Chicago in the late 19th century. His name can still be seen on lumberyards in the city and surrounding areas. From Gilbert and Bryson, *Chicago and Its Makers,* 1929

Top middle: In 1855 Richard Teller Crane established the R.T. Crane Brass and Bell Foundry. His firm's manufacturing of malleable and cast-iron fittings made him a giant in industry, and respected as an enlightened businessman. From Gilbert and Bryson, *Chicago and Its Makers,* 1929

Top right: Frances Willard of Evanston was president of the Woman's Christian Temperance Union and founder of the world organization of the same name. At a time when the woman's suffrage movement was splintered and discouraged, she swelled its ranks with well organized, normally conservative church members and temperance advocates. From Cirker, *Dictionary of American Portraits,* 1967

Bottom: Peter Schuttler constructed this hub and spoke factory, sawmill, and lumberyard on the South Branch of the Chicago River in 1880. The location near both water and rail allowed logs to be delivered by schooner and finished products to be shipped by train. From *Merchants and Manufacturers,* 1880

Facing page, left: During the last two decades of the 19th century, printing became a highly developed art, and Chicago became a leader in the publishing industry. Among the city's prominent printers were George H. Benedict and Company (top) and the Franklin Engraving and Electrotyping Company (bottom). To catch the eye of prospective customers, both firms included pictures of comely women in these advertisements. Courtesy, Chicago Historical Society (ICHI-06561, 06566)

Right: On the Board of Trade, 1888 may be characterized as "the Hutchinson year." Benjamin P. "Old Hutch" Hutchinson, pictured here on the cover of *Harper's Weekly,* was the dominant trader throughout the 12 months. He cornered September wheat. From the author's collection

Milwaukee.

As a primary grain-transfer market, Chicago still had no peer. The city's two dozen grain elevators in 1883 could store 26.2 million bushels. The type of grain stored depended on the crops and the market. Between 1874 and 1883, for example, the amount of wheat shipped by Chicago dropped substantially (from 27.6 to 11.7 million bushels) while corn shipments more than doubled (32.7 to 71 million bushels). As for other grains, the oats shipped in those years jumped from 10.5 to 33.1 million bushels; the leap in rye was even greater, from 335,077 bushels to 3.9 million; and barley increased from 2.4 million in 1874 to 7.7 million bushels in 1883.

The Chicago Board of Trade, formed in 1848, had once offered free lunches to induce members to attend sessions, but the increase in speculation during the Civil War had changed all that. By 1875 membership was made transferable and seats acquired a market value. In the 1880s traders had to pay an initiation fee of $10,000 to acquire a seat on the board. In 1885 there were 1,933 members. The Board of Trade occupied its new building at Jackson and La Salle streets on April 30, 1885. An impressive structure, it looked more like a Midwest church than a business edifice.

A London *Times* correspondent described the human action within this new Chicago Board of Trade: *Upon the broad floor, between 9 and 1 o'clock each day, assemble the wheat and corn and pork and lard and railway kings of the town, in a typical American life scene of concentrated and boiling energy, feeding the furnace in which Chicago's high-pressure enterprise glows and roars. These gladiators have their respective 'pits,' or amphitheatres, upon the floor, so that they gather in three great groups, around which hundreds run and jostle ... This Chicago 'Board of Trade' has witnessed some of the wildest excitements of America, as its shouting and at times almost frenzied groups of speculative dealers in the 'pits' may make or break a 'corner'; and here in fitful fever beats the pulse of the great city whose exalted province it is to feed the world.*

But angry resentment against these mercantile "kings" was growing among workers and the Chicago unemployed. The year 1884, in CBOT President E. Nelson Blake's report, had "dragged its slow length along." At the opening ceremonies of the Board of Trade Building, 2,000 had marched to protest the erection of the "Board of Thieves" structure which they described as a "grand temple of Usury, Gambling, and Cut-Throatism." They carried black and red flags—the one symbolizing starvation, the other the blood of humanity. One of their leaders shouted, "How long will you sit down to fifteen-cent meals when those fellows inside are sitting down to a banquet at twenty dollars a plate?" Losing patience, the policemen chased the throng away. But they and others would come back again and elsewhere in the years ahead.

The two hallmarks of the 1880s certainly were the surge in commercial architecture and the start of radical labor protests. Each can be symbolized in a single event: the construction of the world's first skyscraper, the Home Insurance Building, and the notorious Haymarket Affair.

In the 1880s, according to Frank Lloyd Wright in his autobiography, Chicago was at first the center of the "united fundamentalistic ugliness" known as "General Grant Gothic." Structures such as the famed new gingerbread Palmer mansion on Lake Shore Drive were still Chicago, he wrote, as were the Palmer House and the Board of Trade Building. The city mushroomed with a hodgepodge of architecture. Trends, however, were becoming apparent. In contrast to the buildings going up in the major Eastern cities, Chicago showed a tendency toward leanness and a lack of ornate decoration. The solidly linear buildings by Eastern architect H.H. Richardson, and by John Wellborn Root were starting to appear. There were also innovative structures by William LeBaron Jenny and by the architect partners William Holabird and Martin Roche. They were joined by buildings designed by Wright's "Master," Louis Sullivan, and his partner Dankmar Adler, to whose firm Wright became apprenticed. A whole phalanx of Chicago architects were going to introduce a radical approach for designing and constructing the first tall buildings to reach for the skies of the world.

Chicago demanded more space and structures for its business establishments. The post-Fire construction had used up available building sites. A particularly desirable section was the central city area within "The Loop." Chicago's downtown acquired this permanent nickname in the 1880s because a cable car, the city's first, replacing horsecars on tracks, circled an area bound by Lake, State, Madison, and Wells streets. This loop-shaped route was later expanded to the present elevated train route of Lake, Wabash, Van Buren, and Wells.

Downtown was the place where successful firms wanted to be headquartered, along with retail stores and wholesaling houses. Here were the banks, the Board of Trade, the Stock Exchange, the insurance offices—almost the whole financial capital of the Midwest. Here were railroad stations and almost all of the elegant hotels, as well as theaters and other cultural and entertainment places. And here beat the rapid pulse of commerce in the great city of Chicago.

Real estate value rose disproportionately as people competed for space. Each square foot of Loop property became dearer. The only way to make it "pay" was to create vertical space by placing larger structures upon it that would accommodate more renters. By the 1880s, the five- or six-story brick or stone buildings put up after the Fire were no longer practical. Few professionals wanted to lease offices in the higher reaches of elevatorless buildings, since their clients would have to walk up the stairs. Many older downtown buildings therefore rented out living space in their top floors. Property owners, however, knew that better profits and fewer tenant problems came with office rentals.

Chicago's grain elevators acted as standpipes evening out fluctuations in the flow of grain shipped through Chicago. Vincent Nelson and Company's National Elevator, shown here, could hold one million bushels. By 1893 there were 27 elevators with a total capacity of 32.8 million bushels. From Wing, *Illustrations of Greater Chicago,* 1875

Above: Chicago's photographers utilized the ornate artwork provided by local printers in their advertisements, which usually appeared on the reverse side of each photograph. Thus, each portrait was also a business card. From the Windsor Archives

Above right: According to the advertisement on the back of this family portrait, the sitters posed at the ''photographic studio of Oscar Schmidt—Art Photographer.'' Schmidt's business was located at 237 North Clark Street. From the Windsor Archives

Banks and other business firms that had invested in Loop property, needing only the ground floor for their transactions, could appreciably increase their income by building a tall structure providing space for other businesses. Somehow, the city of Chicago *had* to build upward. And the new architects began devising ways to do so, always taking into account the problems peculiar to the Chicago terrain.

The best of the Chicago architects, once they had mastered the available technologies of the day, invented some of their own, generally adhering to the dictum later stated by Louis Sullivan: ''Form follows function.'' The businessman who was primarily concerned with function entrusted the form largely to the expertise of the architectural firm—a business enterprise too, after all, which depended on satisfying its clients and turning a profit.

Architectural critic Montgomery Schuyler wrote in 1895 of this dynamic interrelationship of architect and client: " " *Elsewhere, the designer of a business building commonly attempts to persuade or to hoodwink his client into sacrificing something of utility to art and, when he succeeds ... the sacrifice has been in vain and the building would have been better for its artistic purpose if it had been better for its practical purpose.*

Commercial architecture in Chicago is long past that stage, and that it is so is due rather to the businessman than to the architect. In this way and to this extent it is the architecture of the people and by the people as well as for the people. " "

By the 1890s visitors to Chicago would almost invariably comment upon the skyline developing there, as did James Fullerton Muirhead while collecting information for a Baedeker guidebook: " " *He who states that exigency of*

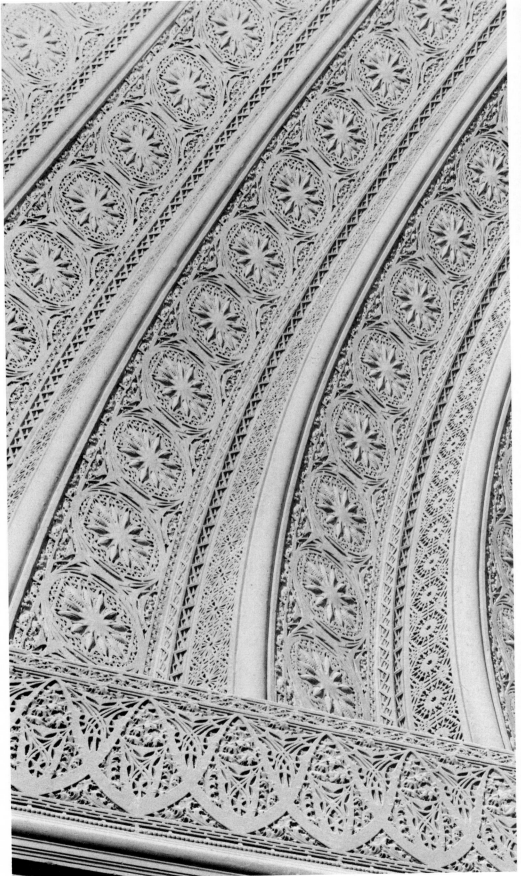

Facing page, left: Richard Nickel photographed architect Louis Sullivan's ornamental fantasy arched above the Schiller Theater stage. Courtesy, Institute of Design, IIT

Right, top: William Holabird, who had been a draftsman with the architectural firm of William LeBaron Jenney, formed his own firm with Martin Roche in the 1880s. They helped pioneer the use of skeletal steel construction with the firm's Tacoma Building (1888). Painting by William P. Welsh. Courtesy, Chicago Historical Society. From Cirker, *Dictionary of American Portraits,* 1967

Right, middle: Located at 209 South LaSalle, the 11-story Rookery Building (1886) stands as a monument to the innovative partnership of John Root and Daniel Burnham. From *Notable Men of Chicago and Their City,* 1910

Right, bottom: Louis Henri Sullivan, like William Holabird, had worked for William LeBaron Jenney before going into business for himself. In 1881 he formed a partnership with Dankmar Adler, and their Auditorium Theater building (1889) brought worldwide acclaim to the firm. His architectural concept of "form follows function" was the basis for the "Chicago School" of architecture. From the author's collection

site gives some excuse for 'elevator architecture' will find a good deal to interest him in its practice at Chicago. Indeed, no one can fail to wonder at the marvelous skill of architectural engineering which can run up a building of twenty stories ... and the observer might unreservedly admire the general effect were it not for a proper estimate of the proportions. 99

Apart from the burgeoning of Chicago's commercial architecture in the 1880s and the decades following them, there was also domestic architecture in its two main forms: institutions, such as churches and museums, which tended to follow traditional forms; and homes, whether single-family residences or luxurious apartments built for the wealthy, middle-class row houses often combining several families, or the tenement houses of the working class and the poor. (The word "tenement" originally meant a multiple-apartment residential building but acquired a pejorative connotation because of increasing placement among the underemployed and overpopulated.)

Sometimes the well-to-do broke new ground and tradition. In the early 1880s Potter Palmer started to develop a tract of land he had bought along the lakeshore. The North Side, the hardest-hit residential area in the Great Fire, was not a prime location for the wealthy class, but here was a highly visible representative expressing his intention to build a mansion upon a soggy remote site reachable only by a badly rutted dirt road. If Palmer and his young wife, Bertha Honoré, had not gone mad, they were at the very least behaving unstylishly. However, they drained a frog pond, used sand dredged from the lake as landfill to raise the property level, improved Lake Shore Drive, and proceeded to put up the most elaborate mansion ever erected in the city. Even before the Palmers' "Castle" started going up, other well-endowed citizens began buying into the area, making it a choice place for elite society in the coming years.

The well-to-do Chicagoans would continue to group themselves in exclusive neighborhoods such as Prairie Avenue, Washington Boulevard, and the new Gold Coast region on the Near North Side. Crenellated and convoluted, Old-European-style residential architecture, however, would soon be on the way out. Ostentatious to the point of garishness, it was both costly and impractical. The new commercial architecture in Chicago had created a revolution with its attention to simple verticals and horizontals, to discrete details, to a wider use of materials like glass, concrete, tile, and building stone, and to the suitability of the structure itself not only for its owners, but also for the surrounding land or cityscape. The business people who spent long hours conferring with architects acquired new tastes and knowledge. A radical departure from the traditional became more frequent in the design of their own houses, in which comfort and convenience took precedence over "show." In Chicago and its surrounding suburbs in the last part of the 19th century the first revolutionary "modern-

istic" homes and churches in America were built as early samples of the "Prairie House" style, with its Japanese-derived wide, low-hanging eaves and sharply rectangular facets introduced by Frank Lloyd Wright.

The wide-open spaces of the old West—at least the part of it called Chicago—were being filled in. As in the older cities, residential property became ever more scarce and expensive. Some people chose suburban living, made possible as commuter transit developed. In-town solutions to gain space were to cut down lot sizes, place homes closer together, and build upward. Apartment hotels became popular solutions for many who liked being relieved of responsibilities for upkeep of buildings and grounds.

Land scarcity also affected residents in undesirable quarters of the city. Wood-frame houses were pushed to the back of lots to make room for tenements. In such areas health and safety hazards grew with congestion. This was worsened by poor sanitation facilities, irregular refuse collection, lack of fire inspection, inadequate police protection, and inattention by residents unacquainted with basic principles of hygiene.

Increasingly, blighted urban areas contained the independent "cottage" industries carried on by immigrant women doing piecework for the garment industry. And here too were located dreaded "sweatshops"—cramped, unheated, ill-ventilated premises run by notorious "sweaters," clothing contractors who arranged for the stitching and finishing of apparel to be sold at Chicago's department stores or through mail order and wholesaling firms.

George Pullman believed he was doing thousands of his employees a large favor by creating a company town south of the city, on the shore of Lake Calumet, where he had erected his new factory that produced all sorts of

Frank Lloyd Wright called Sullivan's Getty Tomb in Graceland Cemetery a "requiem in architecture." The ornamentation on the bronze doors (pictured here), like that above the entrance to Carson, Pirie, Scott and Company, represents the organic forms Wright felt should come from nature. This photograph is by Richard Nickel, who was killed in 1972 while photographing Sullivan's Stock Exchange as it was being torn down. Courtesy, Institute of Design, IIT

Above: George Mortimer Pullman, who developed and manufactured the railroad sleeping car, created the town of Pullman, Illinois, for his factory and employees. Unhappy with the restrictions imposed on them by Pullman, such as no saloons and no private home ownership, the employee/citizens voted to annex their town to Chicago. Later, the state forced Pullman to relinquish control of the town. From Cirker, *Dictionary of American Portraits*, 1967

Above right: The Palmer mansion on North Lake Shore Drive, an imitation Rhenish castle, was constructed in 1882. It had no doorknobs or outside locks and visitors had to be admitted by the servants. Even close friends had to write for an appointment. With its turrets, balconies, and minarets, the residence stood for over 70 years until it was torn down to make room for a 22-story high-rise building. From the author's collection

railroad equipment in an efficient assembly-line way. Architect Solon S. Beman designed Pullman as a practical, self-sufficient paradise for workers, and in some aspects it resembled Olmsted and Jenney's "planned community" of Riverside of the previous decade. George Pullman pointed out that the endeavor was not really charitable because through its operations it was to pay for itself, even though it might not turn a tidy profit for the company's stockholders. This imaginative sideline of an ambitious entrepreneur captured the attention of people around the world, especially enlightened businessmen and reformers increasingly concerned with the quality of workers' lives. For a time, the town he had built was *the* place for out-of-towners to visit.

Pullman had obviously intended to apply engineering principles to regulating the well-being of Pullman workers who settled in his community. Frenchman Paul de Rousiers interviewed him and went away impressed. " *Mr. Pullman's endeavor has been as follows: To mould not only a body of employees, but a whole population of workmen and their families to ways of living which would raise their moral, intellectual and social level. Strongly imbued with the Anglo-Saxon idea that exterior respectability aids true self-respect, he wished to test his theory on his workmen, and conceived the great plan which many treated as that of a madman ten years ago, and which everybody admires today in its realized form. This scheme was nothing less than to build a new town according to sanitary, healthy principles; to make it not only elegant, but convenient; and to transfer thither the workshops of the Pullman Car Company, and to lodge some of the workmen in it.* "

Many visitors, impressed with the order and cleanliness of his town, thought perhaps the higher-than-city rents were justified. But Pullman's paternalism approached dictatorship. No saloons were permitted in or close to the town, and there were other restrictions as well. Workers were not allowed to buy their own houses and could remain in Pullman only so long as they remained in the company's good graces. (Littering the streets might be cause for expulsion.)

"It is not the American ideal," Professor Richard T. Ely wrote about the town of Pullman in an 1885 *Harper's Magazine* article. "It is benevolent well-wishing feudalism, which desires the happiness of the people, but in such a way as shall please the authorities."

In the late 1880s the employee-citizens of Pullman voted to annex their community to Chicago, along with nearby Hyde Park, in a move disappointing to George Pullman. The company, however, still owned the houses, the hotel, and all other premises. Trouble would follow, first in the great Pullman Strike of 1894 and later from a state supreme court ruling that company ownership and management of a town was illegal. Pullman had to divest himself of all nonfactory buildings. So well had they been built that many of them remain today.

The dynamics of an expanding Chicago did not always confer peace between entrepreneurs and workers. Confronted with two irrevocably opposed groups, Chicago occasionally seemed pulled apart in an attempt to find the right solution to some grave social or economic problem. This happened in 1886 with the Haymarket Affair.

By the late 1880s more than 75 percent of the city's population was foreign-born. Chicago's native-born citizens looked down on them, calling them "ignorant working men." Many immigrants, however, were anything but ignorant. Having come to America with an ability to read and write in their own languages, they now used many periodicals published in Chicago to learn how to read and write English. And the many foreign-language newspapers kept up with the swirling political and economic issues in the city.

Since the mid-1860s, Chicago workers had fought for the eight hour work day, but their dream was forever frustrated by a new recession or a new wave of job-seeking immigrants willing to work longer hours for less money. There were pay cuts that employers imposed in order to economize. And worse yet were layoffs, especially if followed by hirings of less-demanding new workers. (A firm in which workers threatened to form a union or strike might run an advertisement for several hundred jobs, bringing several thousand applicants, making their workers feel fortunate to hold jobs at all.)

One effect of the industrial revolution of the 19th century was that craftsmen and other skilled workers had now to perform mind-numbing tasks. Boredom resulting from repetitive labor added to the problems of already-dangerous factories, for it led to inattention or carelessness, which in turn could cause injuries or the production of defective goods. Few employers in the 19th century carried accident insurance for their workers, nor did many feel obligated to pay medical treatments or compensation. A man permanently disabled would simply be dis-

On July 10, 1886, Captain George Wellington "Cap" Streeter's steamboat, The *Reutan,* was beached on the sands just north of the mouth of the Chicago River. While repairing the boat, Streeter filled in the area around it with rocks, built a 180-acre shantytown along the shore of the lake, and called it the District of Lake Michigan. For years he claimed squatters' rights, but eventually the courts ruled against him and his heirs. Pictured here is Cap with his wife Maria, or "Ma." Courtesy, Chicago Historical Society (ICHI-12592)

missed unless suitable work could be found elsewhere for him in a plant. Workers' grievance committees were often ignored, and sometimes their spokesmen would be dismissed. The "Pinkertons"—Allan Pinkerton's private force of detectives and uniformed guards—were hired to protect big business. The municipal "coppers" (a Chicago coined word based on an early police superintendent's interest in copper-mine stocks) were also expected to defend aggressively the status quo when threatened by attack. Should a strike occur, all participants might be jailed.

Many immigrants, especially those from Germany, had been highly politicized by events in their homelands. Many workers were impressed with the class-struggle theories of Marx and Engels, which paralleled, yet countered, the Social Darwinist philosophy espoused by the entrepreneurs. Chicago developed its own brand of anarchism and socialism.

Dynamite had just been invented by Sweden's Alfred Nobel. Some radicals hailed it as the great "equalizer." Little wonder that members of Chicago's business establishment became nervous after reading inflammatory letters to the editor, like this one written by T.Lizius and published in a radical newspaper, *The Alarm:* " *Dynamite! Of all the good stuff, this is the stuff. Stuff several pounds of this sublime stuff into an inch pipe (gas or water pipe), plug up both ends, insert a cap with a fuse attached, place this in the immediate neighborhood of a lot of rich men who live by the sweat of other people's brows and light the fuse. A most cheerful and gratifying result will follow. In giving dynamite to the downtrodden millions of the globe, science has done its best work. The dear stuff can be carried around in the pocket without danger, while it is a formidable weapon against any force of militia, police or detectives that may want to stifle the cry for justice that goes forth from the plundered slaves ...* "

For once, at least, it was not just rhetoric. Some Chicagoans had secretly started to make dynamite bombs in 1885, and several had been placed but not detonated in strategic spots as political statements. The first dynamite bomb ever used in protest in the United States exploded in Chicago on May 4, 1886, in Haymarket Square, a wide area between Desplaines and Halsted close to where Randolph Street now crosses the John F. Kennedy Expressway.

A clash had occurred at the McCormick plant on Monday, May 3, between police and a crowd protesting the firm's use of scabs during a long strike. Speaking nearby in front of some 5,000 people had been August Spies, one of the city's leading anarchist editors. He had tried to dissuade a mob from storming the reaper works, and in the melee supposedly six men had been killed. (In fact, only one died.) Having witnessed the clash personally, Spies returned to the office of the *Arbeiter-Zeitung,* where he or somebody else (he disclaimed authorship afterward) penned an inflammatory circular urging "Revenge! Workingmen, to arms!!!" Printed in both English and German, some 2,500 copies were

Mayor Carter Harrison I was greatly loved by his constituents. He served from 1879 to 1887 and was selected again to be the mayor and official host of the city for the World's Columbian Exposition in 1893. Harrison was castigated for his objective response to the Haymarket affair and for tolerating open vice districts. He was assassinated by a would-be office seeker. From the author's collection

distributed in working-class neighborhoods.

The newspaper itself on Tuesday morning carried an editorial written by August Spies informing its readers of a protest meeting to be held that night at Haymarket Square. It also asked workers to "rise in your might and level the existing robber rule with the dust." Meanwhile, Chicago's daily press roused the citizenry against the anarchists in their midst with such headlines as "Ten Thousand Men Storm McCormick's Harvester Works" and "Riot Reigns."

But Carter Harrison I, the dapper mayor of Chicago, was ever unflappable in the presence of free speech. He attended the Haymarket gathering, lighting up his cigar often so that the assemblage could see his face. He found the meeting of some 800 people long-winded but peaceable. Going home before the speeches were over, he stopped at the nearby police station and told Inspector John Bonfield that his men would not be needed that night. But Bonfield later became angry when one of his informants quoted a speaker's incendiary statements. He charged out into the square with about 170 of his men to break up the rally. Right after he ordered the crowd to disperse, an unknown hand threw a bomb at the policemen. Police officer Mathias J. Degan and a civilian were killed outright and many policemen were wounded (seven fatally). The police shot into the crowd, and an unknown number of bodies were subsequently carried away.

The newspapers and many of the city's most powerful men called for revenge. Spies was arrested, as was Louis Lingg. Several radical and socialist leaders were also rounded up. Albert Parsons went into hiding but subsequently turned himself in. Finally, eight persons were tried for murder. Besides Spies, Lingg, and Parsons, these also included Michael Schwab, Samuel Fielden, Adolph Fischer, George Engel, and Oscar Neebe. The *Chicago Tribune* made its position clear by printing a cartoon of the accused men hanging even before the trial.

Many at first did not expect a conviction, much less the death penalty. The bailiff, it was revealed later when he bragged about it, had packed the jury, and Judge Joseph E. Gary approved it. The latter's conduct of the trial seemed more the work of prosecutor than judge. Some of the time, however, as the proceedings went on he sat at his high bench working puzzles. In a magazine article published in 1890 he boasted about his part in the convictions.

The case against the defendants was established on the grounds that they had formed a conspiracy through their efforts to incite the populace of Chicago to overthrow the social order through violent means. Evidence supposedly gathered in raids indicated that the anarchists were trying to create a climate for revolution. Much of the voluminous material was brought in by Police Captain Michael Schaack. (Both he and Bonfield were subsequently suspended for taking bribes in a matter wholly unconnected with the Haymarket Affair.)

Not one of the defendants was ever proven to have actually thrown the bomb. It mattered not, the prosecutors argued, who actually threw the bomb. On August 19, 1886, having failed in various appeals, seven of the eight men were sentenced to die. On the eve of execution, Lingg committed suicide in jail. Parsons, Spies, Engel, and Fischer were hanged on November 11, 1887. Two others had their death sentences commuted but received life imprisonment. Standing on the gallows, the four condemned men had given brief messages. "There will be a time," said Spies, "when our silence will be more powerful than the voices you hear today." And Parsons declared, "Let the voice of the people be heard!"

In 1893 the new governor, John Peter Altgeld, who had once been a judge, was asked to review the Haymarket case. After a painstaking scrutiny of the proceedings, he decided that the men had not received a fair trial. He pardoned the two in jail. Altgeld's action horrified many. The business community has often been portrayed collectively as sighing with relief that the Haymarket trial and its executions ended serious threats to the exercise of free enterprise in the city. But in fact a number of important Chicago business leaders doubted that this lethal scapegoating had been wise or ethical. They included the First National Bank's president, Lyman Judson Gage, hotel and real estate magnate Potter

Attention Workingmen!

GREAT

MASS-MEETING

TO-NIGHT, at 7.30 o'clock,

AT THE

HAYMARKET, Randolph St., Bet. Desplaines and Halsted.

Good Speakers will be present to denounce the latest atrocious act of the police, the shooting of our fellow-workmen yesterday afternoon.

THE EXECUTIVE COMMITTEE.

Achtung Arbeiter!

Große

Massen-Versammlung

Heute Abend, halb 8 Uhr, auf dem

Heumarkt, Randolph-Straße, zwischen Desplaines- u. Halsted-Str.

☞ Gute Redner werden den neuesten Schurkenstreich der Polizei, indem sie gestern Nachmittag unsere Brüder erschoß, geißeln.

Das Executiv-Comite.

Left: After witnessing violent treatment of strikers by police at the McCormick plant on May 3, 1886, anarchist editor August Spies supposedly composed this handbill and had about 2,500 copies of it distributed to workingmen in the Chicago area. Courtesy, Chicago Historical Society (ICHI-06214)

Bottom: Though at first sentenced to life imprisonment for their alleged part in the Haymarket conspiracy, Samuel Fielden (bottom left), Michael Schwab (bottom, second from left), and Oscar Neebe (bottom, second from right) were pardoned by Governor John Peter Altgeld in 1893. From Lucy Parsons, *The Life of Albert R. Parsons*, 1903

Below: Convicted Haymarket conspirator Louis Lingg was among those sentenced to death. The night before the scheduled hanging, however, Lingg committed suicide in his cell. From Lucy Parsons, *The Life of Albert R. Parsons*, 1903

Above and right: John Bonfield (right) joined the Chicago police force in 1878 and by 1885 he had been promoted to inspector. On May 4, 1886, he commanded the police detachment that went to disperse the crowd in Haymarket Square, contrary to Mayor Harrison's warning. A bomb was thrown at the police, and they retaliated by shooting into the crowd. Both incidents comprising the ''Haymarket Massacre'' are depicted here (above). From McLean, *The Rise and Fall of Anarchy in America,* 1890

Far right and bottom: August Vincenz Theodor Spies (bottom left), Adolph Fischer (bottom middle), George Engel (bottom right), and Albert R. Parsons (far right) were all hanged on November 11, 1887, for conspiracy to incite Chicagoans to violently overthrow the social order. From Lucy Parsons, *The Life of Albert R. Parsons,* 1903

BALLOON PARK (GABRIEL YON BALLOON C°)

COTTAGE GROVE AVENUE AND 50TH STREET
(WEATHER PERMITTING)
DAILY CAPTIVE ASCENSIONS (1300 FEET HIGH)
FROM → 10 AM TO 10 PM ←

EVERY AFTERNOON AND EVENING GRAND CONCERTS BY A LADIES ORCHESTRA

CAPTAIN JULHES AERONAUT

BEST SELECT AMUSEMENT PLACE IN CHICAGO.

JULES GOURIER ENGINEER AERONAUT

GABRIEL YON BALLOON CO.

THE ONLY ENTERPRISE OF THIS KIND IN AMERICA.

Balloon ascensions became popular in Chicago shortly after the Civil War. During the 1880s Chicagoans could visit Gabriel Yon Balloon Company's Balloon Park at Cottage Grove Avenue and 50th Street and ascend to heights of 1300 feet in hot-air balloons. Entertainment was provided twice a day by a female orchestra. Lithograph by Shober and Carqueville. Courtesy, Chicago Historical Society (ICHI-14897)

Palmer, former Illinois Senator Lyman Trumbull, Marvin Hughitt of the Chicago and North Western Railroad, and Rabbi Emil Hirsch. They and others had actively worked either for clemency or a reversal of the verdict. Lyman Gage became so concerned about the lack of dialogue between capital and labor that he presided over the Civic Federation, a group that sponsored a series of forum meetings in which anybody could speak out about anything.

Frustration over the trial and its outcome helped other Chicagoans channel their concern for the workers, the poor, and the large immigrant population into productive avenues. These included Jane Addams, who with Ellen Gates Starr founded the Hull House settlement in 1889; "attorney for the damned" Clarence Darrow; and the polemic exposer of the abuses of wealth, Henry Demarest Lloyd, a former editorial writer for the Chicago *Tribune*. Lloyd, whose life became haunted by the hangings of men whom he believed innocent, wrote the pioneering study of capitalism's abuses, *Wealth Against Commonwealth,* in 1893. His father-in-law, William "Deacon" Bross disowned Lloyd over his views on the Haymarket Affair.

The Haymarket bomb was not the only explosion in Chicago during the late 1880s. The city's population growth continued to explode. In 1889 many of Chicago's suburbs, including Lake View, Hyde Park, Pullman, Jefferson Park, and part of Cicero voted to annex themselves to the city. Chicago grew in that year from 36 to 168 square miles. It built a new intake crib in Lake Michigan to provide a larger and fresher water supply. After an 1889 epidemic the Metropolitan Sanitary District was also formed to protect the area's water and to help dispose of its domestic and industrial wastes. Almost immediately the district initiated the plan that would eventually save Chicago from its own waste: the famed reversal of the Chicago River.

There was much work to be done in the decade ahead. One of the biggest jobs Chicagoans would truly enjoy doing involved putting on a grand show to display itself before the entire world.

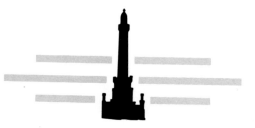

CHAPTER NINE

THE WHITE CITY AND THE BLACK CITY

THE 1890s

The World's Columbian Exposition was held to commemorate the 400th anniversary of Columbus' discovery of America (even though it actually opened in 1893). Some 200 buildings, ponds, basins, statuary, exhibits, and entertainment covering 633 acres (now Jackson Park) drew over 27 million visitors to the fair. From the author's collection

In the nation the 1890s began with a smile of self-esteem. For the most part businesses were succeeding and expanding. Education was turning toward pragmatism and the scientific method. Art and culture were prospering as never before among a people who seemed to be shaking loose from an overemphasis on the Protestant work ethic.

Chicagoans felt exhilarated. They could boast of such successes as the most powerful electric lighting plant in the world (Edison Electric Lighting Co.), the largest apartment-flat building (the Mecca), and the biggest show windows in the world (John M. Smyth Company on West Madison Street).

Chicago also had one of the finest orchestras in the country, was building a richly endowed new university (the University of Chicago), and was preparing to tear down its post-Fire "crystal palace," the Inter-State Industrial Exposition Building at Monroe Street and Michigan Avenue, to make way for an imposing new structure to house the Art Institute of Chicago, which had been founded in 1866 as the Academy of Design.

The touchstone for the 1890s Chicago, however, was not bigness, growth, success, or even trends. It was one event—an international fair held in 1893, the World's Columbian Exposition. Whenever a city holds this kind of celebration, the planning and execution tend to be overwhelming. The 1890s belonged in an era when people did not even know how others spoke on the opposite side of the country, let alone the world. Regions were insular in their inventions and aesthetics, especially if they were far from the commerce and communication in big cities. An earlier age, without convenient railroad transportation, could not have held a true world's fair; a later age would find the task far easier.

Chicago's determination to hold a world's fair to commemorate the 400th anniversary of Columbus' entry in the Americas formally began in 1885 when the board of directors of the Inter-State Industrial Exposition passed a resolution stating their willingness to support such a venture. Later on in the decade the idea built to a point where the quest for the world's fair became an obsession. Describing this phenomenon in a popular magazine, *The Chautauquan,* James P. Holland later wrote: " " *Turn where you might in those days, you were sure to be confronted with the little starshaped stickers bearing the legend "Chicago World's Fair 1892." Business firms bought these labels by the thousands and every letter, package, or newspaper sent out by them carried with it the little messenger announcing Chicago's determination to hold the World's Fair. Missionaries in every walk of life, ministers of the Gospel, politicians, commercial travelers, newspaper correspondents, and a hundred others traveled the country over preaching the gospel of "Chicago and the World's Fair." The two names became so invariably linked together on people's tongues that eastern men visiting Chicago to sell goods to Chicago merchants soon found it necessary to confess their faith in Chicago and the World's Fair before they could hope to obtain a patient hearing.* " "

The national debate over a location for the fair was highly tinged with sectionalism, brought to a pitch in 1889 when a special committee considered the various bids. Congress was to settle the matter. The leading contenders besides Chicago were New York, St. Louis, and Washington, D.C. Increasingly the debate focused on national purpose. Chicago, its boosters said, was America—attuned to the language, thought, and aspirations of rural and small-town life. Successful Chicago was a commercial venture done right. But the opposition declared that "Porkopolis" was not cosmopolitan, did not understand the fine arts, and was lacking sophistication. And Chicago was accused of lacking a soul, specifically a Fundamentalist Christian soul. The city represented blatant commercialism and materialism, and paraded open vice—which its mayor, Carter Henry Harrison, tolerated. (True enough, since he believed that a certain amount of vice was expectable in humans and that trying to outlaw it entirely, caused worse problems.)

The struggle to land the fair was formidable. A number of Chicagoans even sailed across the Atlantic in 1889 to inspect the Paris World's Fair, aiming to outdo the French in their own exposition—if Chicago got it. An extra boost was given to Chicago's cause in the Congressional proceedings when Lyman Gage of the First National Bank arrived to represent his city, which guaranteed an outlay of $10 million, twice as much as New York had been willing to spend. During this acrimonious auction period Chicago acquired one of its best-known epithets. Charles A. Dana of the *New York Sun* told his readers to disregard "the nonsensical claims of that windy city. Its people could not build a World's Fair even if they won it." ("Windy" in those days was the slang equivalent to "hot air," which was often present in the city's boostering exercises, familiar to Dana from a past stint as a Chicago newspaperman.)

On February 24, 1899, the House of Representatives selected Chicago as the fair site. Now the real work had to begin, if the city was going to disprove

Facing page: The Chicago architectural firm of Daniel H. Burnham (top) and John Wellborn Root (bottom) was selected to plan and supervise the design of the exposition. They had already built the Montauk Block (1881-1882) and the Rookery (1885-1886) and were engaged in constructing the Monadnock Building when they were hired for the fair. At first Root handled most of the design aspects and Burnham concerned himself more with the business and organization. Then in January of 1891 Root died of pneumonia and Burnham became Director of Works, assuming the design and construction responsibilities. From Cirker, *Dictionary of American Portraits,* 1967

Dana's disparaging contention. The monumental and intricate planning for the fair was assigned primarily to the well-established Chicago architectural firm run by Daniel H. Burnham and John Wellborn Root. To save time and money, they decided to bypass competitive designs and instead choose architects for specific assignments. The overall scheme, however, had to be approved by a national commission. The firms selected to design the major buildings were located on the East Coast. Famed landscape architect Frederick L. Olmsted was summoned to create a suitably elegant setting in the dismal site; Jackson Park at the time was a marshy place containing scrubby vegetation. Olmsted commenced a huge landmoving project that involved the creation of lake inlets, lagoons, and a large basin for the main "Court of Honor."

In the meantime, Burnham and Root met with visiting architects, as well as with local engineers and contractors. Noted sculptor Augustus Saint-Gaudens was persuaded to supervise the creation and placement of statuary on the Exposition grounds and to use his influence in hiring other artists. After one exciting convocation he remarked that Chicago had assembled the greatest collection of creative people since the Renaissance period.

Unfortunately, Burnham's partner and close friend John Root died from pneumonia in January of 1891, probably from overexposure to the damp and chilly fair site. Burnham continued resolutely on without him. A whole tradition of scorn has been heaped upon him for his execution of the Exposition grounds. Critics (including Louis Sullivan, Frank Lloyd Wright, and Root's sister-in-law, poet and architectural critic Harriet Monroe) blamed him for the domination of the derivative, frivolously decorative Roman Empire, Neoclassical, and Beaux Arts styles in the main Court of Honor buildings and other major structures. They maintained that had Root lived, he would have done things differently. They also expressed annoyance that Burnham had vetoed the use of color on the buildings. Their criticism was that the architecture was designed to overawe rather than serve or involve people. Such a concept of art, they felt, was a total violation of the sense and spirit of democracy for which America and Chicago stood.

The basic material overlaying wood and iron frameworks of buildings was "staff," a durable yet lightweight stucco-like combination of jute fibers with cement and plaster. Before hardening, it could be applied easily and quickly. It was also capable of being modeled into shapes for decorative touches, and even statues could be ready-made by applying staff over wire mesh forms.

Italian writer Giuseppe Ciacosa, coming to Chicago in early 1892, hoped to be able to see the "colossal frame" of the exposition-to-be that had been so widely publicized: *Alas, the foundations for the Exposition were scarcely started, and the boasted park and gardens seemed to me an abject and unpretentious thing ... Beautiful on the map, I thought, but the work of ten years. I perceived very*

To ensure the uniform appearance of each of the exposition buildings, Burnham decided to assign the design of the individual structures to one architect or architectural firm rather than have a number of architects work on one building. This resulted in a variety of architectural styles. When all the construction was completed there were about 12 major buildings, 19 built by foreign governments, 38 constructed by different states, and about 130 smaller structures. According to accounts of the time, one would need to spend three weeks and walk over 150 miles just to see everything the exposition had to offer.

Left: Sculptor Daniel Chester French, who is known for his statue of Abraham Lincoln in Washington, D.C.'s Lincoln Memorial, created the tallest sculpture at the World's Columbian Exposition—the 65-foot-high *Republic.* The gilded statue stood in the northeastern corner of the Grand Basin. Photo copyright 1893 by Charles Dudley Arnold

Left, bottom: The Transportation Building was designed by Louis Sullivan. Harriet Monroe, John Root's sister-in-law, praised Sullivan's door as "the best example on the Fair grounds of Root's ideas of Fair architecture." From Davis, *Picturesque World Fair,* 1894

Above: Chicago architect Henry Ives Cobb designed the Fisheries Building, which housed in its East Pavilion a double tier of aquariums filled with a wide variety of fish, crustaceans, and other aquatic creatures. Photo copyright 1893 by Charles Dudley Arnold

Right: George B. Post fashioned the 1,687-foot-long Manufactures Building, the largest man-made structure in the world at the time of its construction. Chicagoan Frank Agnew, an ex-sheriff, was the contractor for the woodwork. Photo copyright 1893 by Charles Dudley Arnold

Right, bottom: A young visitor to the fair gazes northward from the eastern veranda of the Woman's Building, the first structure of national importance to be designed and run by women. The Italian Renaissance-style structure was designed by Boston architect Sophia Hayden. Photo copyright 1893 by Charles Dudley Arnold

soon how, in Chicago, a thing is no sooner said than done. 🎧🎧

Significantly, Chicago's new motto, *"I will!,"* originated in a determined-looking female sculpture at the Exposition. The undertaking, however, was so grandiose that it became obvious that the city would be unable to mount the fair by October of 1892, precisely four centuries after Columbus' first trip to the New World, although a dedication ceremony (featuring a long ode written by Harriet Monroe) took place at that time. The grand opening itself had to be delayed until the following year; even then the Exposition's builders were hard-pressed to finish up. The winter of 1892-1893 was especially nasty, hindering work and causing setbacks. There were thousands of construction workers employed at the site, entailing hundreds of injuries and about two dozen fatalities. In the main buildings alone, 30,000 tons of staff were used, 70 million feet of lumber, and 20,000 tons of iron and steel. Throughout the long preparation, curious visitors came into the grounds to watch the ongoing work, sometimes as many as 5,000 a day. This gawking was finally made profitable by charging a $.50 admission fee.

Altogether on the 633 acres devoted to the World's Columbian Exposition some 200 buildings were going up. A dozen presented major themes, such as Manufacture (said to be the most immense exhibition hall ever built), Agriculture, Machinery, Electricity, Mines, Transportation, and Horticulture. The Palace of Fine Arts was to be an international art gallery. The Woman's Building, under the competent guidance of Mrs. Potter (Bertha Honoré) Palmer, would contain strictly the products of women's work in many forms. (The building itself had also been designed by a woman architect, Sophia Hayden.) Next to it a small Children's Building would serve as a child-care center. At the head of the basin and dominating the entire scene was the domed Administration Building. Other exhibitions found space in smaller structures. Additionally, there were 19 pavilions prepared by foreign governments and 38 by American states, plus a number of individual halls put up by U.S. and foreign firms. Then there were annexes, service buildings, warehouses, and numerous eating places. Transportation to and from the huge premises came in varied forms, such as an elevated, electrified railway, street railways, or steamboats and electric launches. Italian gondolas within the fair's waterways were plied by authentic Venetian gondoliers, "rolling chairs" could be rented at $6 a day with a guide's services attached; the cost decreased with fewer features. So enormous was the Exposition, outdoors and in, that it was estimated that one would have to walk 150 miles to see everything—and to do so properly would take at least three weeks.

By Opening Day, May 1, 1893, the World's Columbian Exposition was ready to receive President Grover Cleveland and a throng of half a million celebrants. As the thousands of spectators jamming the Court of Honor rushed

The entrance of the Midway Plaisance was located one mile west of Jackson Park. As exposition visitors walked along the midway, barkers called to them in all languages, imploring them to come see their attraction or show. The Captive Balloon, Chinese Theatre, and the Ferris Wheel are visible from left to right. Photo copyright 1893 by Charles Dudley Arnold

Bertha Honoré Palmer was queen of Chicago society and president of the Board of Lady Managers of the Columbian Exposition. In her speech delivered at the opening ceremony for the Woman's Building she espoused feminist tenets: "The women of today ... having had a taste of independence, will never willingly relinquish it. They have no desire to be helpless and dependent. Having the full use of their faculties, they rejoice in exercising them." Painting by Anders Leonard Zorn. Courtesy, Art Institute of Chicago

forward to see and hear their President, panic took place in which women and children were crushed and trampled, but fortunately the leaders on the platform and the special Columbian Guards calmed the multitude. After speaking to the vast crowd in front of the Administration Building, the President pressed a button that miraculously, and electrically, turned on fountains, unfurled flags, and lit electric lights.

The big show began—to last five months, during which time there were 27.5 million admissions, with receipts totaling $32.75 million. Since the total expenditures were about $30.5 million, the exposition turned a profit—one of the few such fairs to do so. And it came at a time when people were worrying about money. The Panic of 1893, brought on by a stock market crash, commenced while the fair opened. A large number of total admissions involved Chicagoans—there were over one million of them by now—who made repeated visits. But many were the out-of-towners who came to see both the exposition and Chicago. The effect on visitors from rural and small-town America was recalled by writer Hamlin Garland in his autobiography, *A Son of the Middle Border:* " *Stunned by the majesty of the (exposition) my mother sat in her chair, visioning it all yet comprehending little of its meaning. Her life had been spent among homely small things, and these gorgeous scenes dazzled her, overwhelmed her, letting in upon her in one mighty flood a thousand stupefying suggestions of the art and history and poetry of the world.* "

Mrs. Garland would have been further amazed had she attended the opening ceremony at the Woman's Building, in which Bertha Palmer delivered an extraordinary speech sharply criticising the Industrial Revolution and the status quo, in particular the lot of womenfolk.

The fair, then, was far more than its architecture and exhibits. People exchanged ideas about literature, art, manufacturing, religion, women's rights, inventions, agriculture, and world politics. And special congresses on these and other topics were held at the new Art Institute building to the north.

Gasoline engines were exhibited at the fair, and Henry Ford came to study them. Electricity and its applications to streetcars, lighting, and manufacturing were promoted. Edison demonstrated phonographs as well as his kinetoscope. The American Bell Telephone exhibit offered long-distance phone calls. The New York exhibit even demonstrated the use of the world's first electric chair.

There were events such as parades and athletic contests; special days honoring particular places, professions, and ethnic groups. On Poet's Day *As You Like It* was performed in an amphitheater. On Chicago Day—commemorating the Great Fire of October 9, 1871—over 700,000 visitors attended. August 25 was Colored People's Day, during which orator-statesman Frederick Douglass gave a speech on "The Race Problem in America," Paul Laurence read a poem written expressly for the fair, and spirituals were sung.

The World's Columbian Exposition also lavishly entertained, particularly at the Midway Plaisance. This narrow rectangular walkway located west of the fairgrounds featured displays, shows, and structures mostly in a carnival atmosphere. In Cairo Street exotic dancer "Little Egypt" demonstrated belly dancing. Nearby there were miniature foreign "settlements"—German, Javanese, Bedouin, West African, Turkish. There was an ostrich farm. And the greatly popular Natatorium was open for public swimming.

Within the Midway Plaisance and standing tall above all the fun and fascination was the Ferris Wheel, the world's first and most enormous. Stretching 264 feet into the air, it provided passengers with a panoramic view of the whole Exposition and of the University of Chicago campus rising to the northwest. Each car on the wheel could carry 60 passengers and there were 36 cars. George W. Ferris had built it in Pittsburgh at a cost of $380,000, in the exposition's fling at outdoing Paris' Eiffel Tower.

Chicago's outside additions to the fair's entertainments that season included Chicago-born Lillian Russell, Florenz Ziegfeld's troupe, Buffalo Bill's "Wild West Show," piano virtuoso Paderewski, and the great Italian tragedienne Eleonora Duse.

October 31, 1893, was scheduled to be the last day of the fair. Its closing ceremonies, planned to be triumphant, instead were subdued since they lacked the ebullient presence of Chicago's all-time favorite mayor, Carter Henry Harrison. Three days earlier he had been killed in the doorway of his own home by a deranged office-seeker.

Once the closing was official, crowds began swarming over the Midway area to snatch souvenirs by ripping the premises apart. They were halted by the Exposition guards. In later months, however, there were few protections for the grounds and its buildings, even though many of the latter still contained exhibits. Fires were lit either by vandals or by vagrants who took up residence around the buildings. By July 1894 most structures had been destroyed, and remain only as photographs, illustrations, and memories.

The only major surviving building on the site was the Palace of Fine Arts, which was separated from the Court of Honor area. Because it would house valuable paintings and sculptures from around the world, it had been constructed of brick rather than of the more flammable staff. Now familiar to Chicago as the Museum of Science and Industry, the building was used in post-fair years as the Field Columbian Museum, which largely contained natural history collections. After the Field Museum moved to its new building, the old Fine Arts building was rebuilt for its present use. Retaining primarily the original architectural exoskeleton, it at least gives visitors an impression of the White City's architecture. But according to an angry Louis Sullivan, the White City was a "miasma with the white shadow of a higher culture," causing

Above and facing page, left: When the exposition opened, among the foreign "settlements" to be found along the Midway Plaisance were those of Algeria, Austria, China, Dahomey, Holland, Germany, Hungary, Ireland, Japan, Java, Lapland, Tunisia, and Turkey. Later on more "villages" were added to the midway, including a Samoan settlement and a Bedouin one. Pictured here are two 18-year-old Samoan women (right) and a Bedouin chief and his family from Syria (above). The baby in the latter photo was born in Chicago and named "Chicago Columbus." Photos copyright 1893 by Charles Dudley Arnold

Facing page, right: To the delight of many fair visitors and to the dismay of not a few others were the foreign dancers' performances which could be viewed along the Midway Plaisance. In the Hungarian Cafe Chantant a visitor could enjoy a dancer performing to Listz's music (top), while on the street of Cairo one could watch a performer of the danse du ventre move "her shoulders and body rhythmically to the sharp beats of the tambour" (bottom). Photos copyright 1893 by Charles Dudley Arnold

widespread damage that "will last a half century from its date, if not longer." Courthouses, churches, libraries, stores, banks, and commercial structures were indeed erected around the nation to imitate the Exposition's buildings. Sullivan and other critics pointed out that the designs effectually separated people from the buildings' intended functions. Since their purpose, they said, was to overawe rather than serve people, they were actually deep-rooted but subtle attacks on democracy and the common man or woman, who so readily embraced them as "beautiful."

Whatever one thought of its architecture, the World's Columbian Exposition made an astounding cultural impact not only upon the city that built and hosted it but also on the nation. Its deliberate internationalism conferred upon Chicago, a cosmopolitan status.

The World's Columbian Exposition, a city unto itself, was often compared with the far larger city of Chicago surrounding it. "The White City" remained clean-looking because the burning of soft coal was prohibited nearby. The outer city, however, had been blackened through the years by the cumulative soot of coal-burning trains, factories, and homes. It was called, by contrast, "The Black City."

Because the fair was a financial success, and provided employment to thousands, it helped the economy of Chicago immeasurably. But, the nation had plummeted into a deep depression. In Illinois alone during 1893 more than 16,000 firms went bankrupt, including 50 companies each with capital of a half-million dollars. Wholesale prices continued to drop sharply, taking wages, farm prices, and profits with them. When the fair closed down, the grim reality of the nationwide economy hit the city hard.

Hunger became well known in Chicago during the winter of 1893-94. English reformer and editor William T. Stead visited the city just at this time. Considering it almost a microcosm of the United States, he spent almost the entire four months of his American stay in Chicago.

Out of Stead's observations came his book *If Christ Came to Chicago.* Among its intriguing passages was this description of the city's unique means of relieving hunger: 66 *The suffering in the city was very great and would have been very much greater had it not been for the help given by the labor unions to their members and for an agency which without pretending to be of much account from a charitable point of view, nevertheless fed more hungry people this winter in Chicago than all the other agencies, religious, charitable and municipal, put together. I refer to the Free Lunch of the Saloons. This institution, which is quite unknown in the Old World, is one of the features of the feeding of the hungry in Chicago which most amazes a stranger. There are from six to seven thousand saloons in Chicago. In one half of these a free lunch is provided every day in the week. And in many cases the free lunch is really a free lunch. That is to say, in many saloons, notably in my friend*

Facing page, left: On the cover of its February 5, 1898, issue, *Harper's Weekly* lambasted Chicago for its open graft and corrpution. From the Windsor Archives

Right, top: Stationer George E. Cole fought for governmental reforms in his battle against crooked politicians and crime. In 1896 he became the head of the newly formed Municipal Voters League (MVL) and succeeded in ousting corrupt aldermen from office. Courtesy, Chicago Historical Society

Right, bottom: Charles Yerkes, who virtually monopolized the traction industry in Chicago, supposedly bribed his way to the top. When he tried to buy the city council into granting him a 50-year franchise for his street railway, the Municipal Voters League managed to defeat the corrupt council members, thereby destroying Yerkes' chances for the extended franchise. From *A History of the City of Chicago*, 1900

Hank North's in Clark Street, scores of people were fed every day and are being fed at this moment without fee, or reward or any payment for drink with which to wash down the more solid viands. In Hank North's saloon throughout the winter he has given away on an average about thirty-six gallons of soup and seventy-two loaves of bread every day. 🙶🙶

Stead attempted a major reform movement in Chicago with his lectures, his articles, and his help in strengthening the Civic Federation begun by people like Lyman Gage in the 1880s. In 1896 this organization, determined to reform the city council, spawned the Municipal Voters League (MVL). Graft-taking aldermen—who supposedly included 57 of the 68 members—were termed "the Gray Wolves" because of their rapaciousness. The MVL selected a stationery shopowner by the name of George E. Cole to head the new organization.

The reform was business-oriented. The new political figures were often well-known commercial figures or their sons. Among them were William E. Dever (later mayor); Honoré Palmer (son of Potter and Bertha Honoré Palmer); and a wolf in sheep's clothing "Big Bill" Thompson (son of a wealthy Chicagoan and later, a corrupt if colorful mayor of Chicago).

In the first year of its dedicated attack on the city's boodlers, the reform group replaced 12 of the "Gray Wolf" aldermen and broke the two-thirds majority that had been able to pass whatever it wanted over the veto of Mayor George B. Swift. By the year 1900 the league had forged a true reform council and had ably defeated traction magnate Charles T. Yerkes, the most prolific provider of boodle in the city's history.

Complex questions and heated debates swirled around the city's transit system. In 1897 the Illinois legislature passed the Allen Bill, which allowed cities to grant 50-year street railway franchises instead of the 20-year ones provided by its general traction law.

The Allen Bill at once became a crucial issue in Chicago because Yerkes was behind it. In the past he had successfully bribed the city council into granting him extension after extension of his street railway franchises. Indignation meetings were held in 1898 when Yerkes attempted to get the Chicago city council to give him a 50-year franchise. There were threats of hanging the aldermen who voted for Yerkes. The Municipal Voters League managed to help eliminate a significant number of the more corrupt council members in the new election. Yerkes lost the battle and afterwards the state legislature repealed the Allen Bill. Yerkes reorganized his company and sold it at great profit. He took $10 million and left town permanently to reside in London, where he took charge of building an early subway. (He supposedly had managed to get the contract because he astutely impressed an astronomy-loving city councilor with his generosity in promising a one-million dollar telescope to the University of Chicago. Hence the origin of the famed Yerkes Observatory.)

In the 1890s Chicago had to renew a basic artery. The city had been chosen as the best location for a canal from Lake Michigan to the Illinois River, and its prosperity was not assured until that waterway was completed in 1848. A half-century later, however, the Illinois and Michigan Canal could not contribute much lifeblood to a city almost 100 times bigger than when the canal was constructed. Only 18 feet wide, its locks could not handle the larger steamboats and barges. Furthermore, although the depth of the canal had been increased by several feet, it still was sluggish. An attempt had been made earlier to deepen the channel sufficiently to make it possible to have Lake Michigan water flow into the Chicago River, rather than vice versa, thus using a boundless supply of water to help move crafts through the canal toward the Illinois.

Chicago had an allied problem: its sewage. Because Chicago is located on an old shelf of the Lake Michigan basin, it drains naturally into the lake. In the 19th century this also meant that its stockyards discharged tons of effluvia daily into streams and sewers which ultimately poured into the lake. Vast as its waters were, the lake area close to Chicago could not handle the waste adequately. An additional problem had been created when property owners, such as Ogden and Wentworth, of the swampy land just south of the city began creating ditches to drain off the excess water in order to improve its value. This action raised the water flow in the South Branch of the river but also added silt to the system, virtually undoing some of the dredging work. In 1871 $3 million had been spent to improve the pumps at Bridgeport so as to push the city sewage eastward through the canal and down the Des Plaines River. It was not enough. The number of cattle slaughtered in Chicago increased from 532,964 in 1870 to 1,382,477 in 1880. The waste from the stockyards and packing plants still emptied into the Chicago River and most of it got out into Lake Michigan. The intake cribs for the water supply simply could not be built far enough out into

Chicago's character and characters have been portrayed in many ways ranging from the fine portraits painted by G.P.A. Healy to the lightly veiled personalities in the many novels set in Chicago. No one, however, has provided us with a better portrayal of Chicago's street people than did photographer Sigmund Krauz. For his book *Street Types of Chicago*, Krauz carried his camera into the city's streets and persuaded people to pose for him. Here we see some of Krauz's portraits. From Krauz, *Street Types of Chicago*, 1891

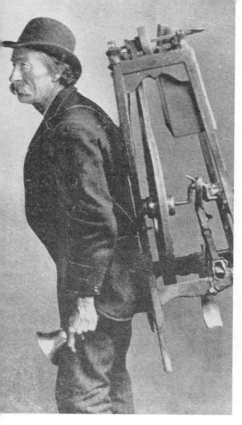

the lake to avoid the increased pollution.

By the early 1890s Chicago's sewage was almost strangling the city. In 1891 the town's typhoid death rate reached 174 per 100,000 people. Newspapers in the 1890s printed maps of the city that regularly showed little flags to alert its readers as to which sections had to boil their drinking water that day.

If the problem was distinct to Chicago, so was its solution. Biochemists had recently proven that running water and the process of oxidation broke down sewage to safe levels for downstream communities. Chicago therefore determined to construct a canal wide enough to carry Chicago waste across the drainage divide to the Mississippi basin. To carry this out, the Illinois state legislature in 1889 created the Metropolitan Sanitary District. On September 3, 1892, it began work on the Chicago Sanitary and Ship Canal that was designed to be 164 feet wide in the rock sections and 300 feet in the earth portions. A high-level Basin was created in Chicago's harbor with a lock entrance to the lake. In the process the flow of the Chicago River was completely and successfully reversed. On January 2, 1900, the Beartrap Dam at Lockport was opened and Chicago began to flush its wastes into the Illinois River. The *Chicago Inter-Ocean* called it "the greatest and most important municipal undertaking in modern time."

People in St. Louis and downstate Illinois, however, were scarcely enthusiastic about the flow of Chicago's sewage. They attempted to get an injunction to prohibit the dam from being opened. But Sanitary District officials started the water flowing early, before the judge could issue one.

As for the famous, or infamous, Union Stock Yards that brought in a considerable portion of the city's revenues while causing certain unwelcome problems like befouling the air and the lake water, it continued to be a favored place to take out-of-towners.

One of the less tolerant stockyards spectators was the Anglo-Indian poet, storyteller, and essayist Rudyard Kipling. Little or nothing about his brief stay in Chicago pleased him—except for providing him with ample material to launch marvelously barbed complaints in his account of "How I Struck Chicago, and How Chicago Struck Me. Of Religion, Politics, and Pig-Sticking, and the Incarnation of the City Among Shambles." For him the Union Stock Yards epitomized the monstrous barbarism of the entire city. " " *I went off to see cattle killed by way of clearing my head. They say every Englishman goes to the Chicago stock-yards. You shall find them about six miles from the city; and once having seen them you will never forget the sight. As far as the eye can reach stretches a township of cattle-pens, cunningly divided into blocks so that the animals of any pen can be speedily driven out close to an inclined timber path which leads to an elevated covered way straddling high above the pens. These viaducts are two-storied. On the upper storey tramp the doomed cattle, stolidly for the most part. On the lower, with a schuffling of sharp hoofs and multitudinous yells, run the pigs ... It was to the pigs I first addressed myself. Selecting a viaduct which was full of them, as I could hear though I could not see, I marked a sombre building whereto it ran, and went there, not unalarmed by stray cattle who had managed to escape from their proper quarters. A pleasant smell of brine warned me of what was coming. I entered the factory and found it full of pork in barrels, and on another storey more pork unbarrelled, and in a huge room the halves of swine, for whose use great lumps of ice were being pitched in at the window. The room was the mortuary chamber where the pigs lie for a little while in state ere they begin their progress through such passages as kings may sometimes travel. Turning a corner and not noting an overhead arrangement of greased rail, wheel, and pulley, I ran into the arms of four eviscerated carcasses, all pure white and of a human aspect, being pushed by a man clad in vehement red. When I leaped aside, the floor was slippery under me. There was a flavour of farmyard in my nostrils and the shouting of a multitude in my ears. But there was no joy in that shouting. Twelve men stood in two lines—six a side. Between them and overhead ran the railway of death that had nearly shunted me through the window. Each man carried a knife, the sleeves of his shirt were cut off at the elbows, and from bosom to heel he was blood-red. The atmosphere was stifling as a night in the Rains, by reason of the steam and the crowd.* " "*

The national economic depression hung on. George Pullman proved a hard-nosed businessman as he aimed to keep his company paying its stockholders the eight percent dividend they had received since 1867. To do so, wages were cut and layoffs were heavy. The squeeze was especially difficult at Pullman City, where rents, gas prices, and other expenses were not commensurately cut.

The frustrated workers attempted to negotiate but the plant owner refused to talk with their representatives. Angry, they struck the Pullman plant on May 11, 1894. Three thousand left their jobs, and the remaining 300 were laid off by

Facing page, top: Chicago was the biggest horse market in the world by the late 1890s with the average daily sale at 300. Auctions, such as the one portrayed here, were held every day except Sunday. Every horse sold was guaranteed to be sound and to work or else it could be returned by noon the following day. From Grand, *Illustrated History of the Union Stockyards,* 1896

Bottom: Because Chicago was the center of the horse trade, it was only natural that businesses related to horses would emerge. From Grand, *Illustrated History of the Union Stockyards,* 1896

LOUIS GELDER,
Harness. Saddlery. etc.

Facing page, top: This photograph of the Illinois Central passenger station at Randolph Street, taken on May 21, 1895, gives no indication that it was a time of economic depression in Chicago. In a little over a month, railroad workers would be voting to refuse to handle trains with Pullman cars. Courtesy, David R. Phillips, Chicago Architectural Photographing Company

Bottom: Three thousand Pullman workers protesting wage cuts and heavy layoffs went on strike on May 11, 1894. They then joined the American Railway Union, which in turn voted to refuse moving any Pullman railroad cars. Soon 25,000 more railroad workers across the nation went on strike. To get the trains moving, President Grover Cleveland sent troops to Chicago. This illustration depicts the U.S. Cavalry escorting the first meat train out of Chicago on July 10, 1894. Courtesy, Chicago Historical Society

the company. Pullman workers joined the American Railway Union, newly founded by Eugene V. Debs. Before the ARU, unions had only represented skilled tradesmen. The ARU, however, attempted to organize the great number of nonskilled workers connected with railroading.

Debs' union now tried to deal directly with Pullman, but the entrepreneur fired the strike leaders and argued there was "nothing to arbitrate." Against Debs' advice the ARU voted to boycott moving any Pullman cars on the nation's railroads. The boycott meant, in effect, refusal by workers to move almost every train in the nation unless the railroad companies first removed the Pullman cars. This they refused to do, in part because their managers backed George Pullman's anti-union stand.

A showdown quickly ensued. Nationwide, some 25,000 railroad workers went on strike. "The struggle with the Pullman Company," according to Debs, "has developed into a contest between the producing classes and the money power of the country." The union had no control over the crowds that tried to block the movement of the nation's trains. In several cases, angry workers grouped together to stand in the paths of oncoming trains. Mobs—often made up of the unemployed, whether or not their work had to do with railroads—furiously wrecked railway property.

The Pullman Strike—or "Debs Rebellion," as the papers liked to call it—was short. The Attorney General of the United States, a former counsel for the railroads, appointed Edwin Walker as a special assistant attorney general for Chicago. (Walker at the time was the lawyer for the General Managers Association, the organization representing the railroads in the dispute.) He went to court and got an injunction against the union. Over the protests of Mayor John Hopkins (a former paymaster at Pullman) and Illinois Governor John Peter Altgeld, President Grover Cleveland sent federal troops to Chicago to move the trains, using the argument that they carried the interstate U.S. mails.

The strike was aborted. The injunction, more than the troops, squelched it. The leaders of the Pullman strike permanently lost their jobs. Clarence Darrow quit his position as attorney for the Chicago and North Western Railroad so he could represent the workers. His client, Debs, was sentenced to jail for contempt by the same federal judge who had issued the injunction.

By his actions Cleveland had committed political suicide; he would see himself publicly repudiated in 1896 by the Altgeld-influenced Democratic party at its national convention in Chicago. There the politicians sought a different kind of candidate to offer the nation in the troubled times.

In the mid-1890s there was "deflation." Wages and prices spiraled downward, but debts and mortgages did not. Frequently businessman, homeowner, or farmer did not have the income to pay off loans or mortgages contracted years before. The results were often bankruptcy or eviction. For those who wanted to avoid either one, it was a strenuous struggle. The Populist movement gained its largest following in the Midwest, especially in rural areas. Responsive to the mood of the times and to various Populist ideas, the Democrats argued in the summer of 1896 that the country should renounce its tight money policies, which were caused, at least in part, by the nation's adherence to the gold standard.

At the Democrats' convention held at the Coliseum on the South Side presidential hopeful William Jennings Bryan, alluding to gold standard advocates, won the party's nomination with a stirring speech that ended, "You shall not press down upon the brow of labor this crown of thorns, you shall not crucify mankind upon a cross of gold." But in spite of Bryan's eloquence and popularity, he lost out to the Republicans' William McKinley. The voters, it seemed, partly blamed the Democratic administration for the economic setbacks and for not ending them soon enough.

Chicago, along with the nation, gradually worked its way out of the depression years in the mid-1890s. Not surprisingly, the Spanish-American War invigorated the city's economy.

On January 9, 1898, the *Chicago Tribune* summed up the city's commercial success by elaborately proving that the town in its last half-century was a richer gold mine than the Klondike. The *Tribune* writer described the people who had become millionaires through the commerce of Chicago. "You do not need a pick and shovel to get your gold in Chicago," the article advised. "What you do need is an outfit of good sense, sobriety, industry, economy and stick-to-it-iveness." The proof was in the pudding: "Today there live in Chicago over 200 men whose fortunes reach or pass the million mark. Every great fortune was made here."

As its prime Chicago rags-to-riches example, the *Tribune* account chose Silas B. Cobb, whose fortune-making "furnishes a whole sermon." Arriving in Chicago at the age of 21, Cobb went on to find work as an auctioneer; within a year bought half-interest in a harness shop, and a year later owned the building. He invested in real estate, weathered the city's depression, and at the age of 55 became the wealthiest man in Chicago.

By 1898 a few others had caught up with or surpassed Cobb, but he was still one of the 10 wealthiest. The article said admiringly of Cobb, who had become head of the Chicago City Railroad Company: "He never received a cent from his father, never borrowed a cent except once ... never paid a lawyer or a doctor a cent. He has no extravagances and no dissipations." These clearly were virtues to be emulated.

Other wealthy Chicagoans had also made their fortunes through real estate, banking, manufacturing, merchandising, the trading of grain and other commodities, and meatpacking. The *Tribune* listed 175 of the city's millionaires and

William Jennings Bryan, who graduated from Chicago's Union College of Law in 1883, served as a delegate to the Democratic national convention of 1896. There Bryan delivered his "Cross of Gold" speech and won the nomination, though he lost the election. From the author's collection

Leander J. McCormick (top) and Samuel Waters Allerton (above) were among the top 10 millionaires residing in Chicago in 1898. Both had net worths of $20 million. Marshall Field, the wealthiest man in Chicago at the time, had $75 million. From the Windsor Archives

their worth, but because many people had money in unknown holdings the writer believed that the actual figure in Chicago was closer to 300.

CHICAGO'S MILLIONAIRES, 1898

Marshall Field	$75 million
Philip D. Armour	$40
Nelson Morris	$25
Levi Z. Leiter	$20
Leander McCormick	$20
Samuel Allerton	$20
Potter Palmer	$15
Silas B. Cobb	$15
Charles T. Yerkes	$15
Samuel Nickerson	$15
Mrs. Frank Lowden (nee Florence Pullman)	$10
Gustavus Swift	$10
Mrs. Cyrus Hall McCormick	$10
Cyrus McCormick, Jr.	$10
Mrs. George Pullman	$10
Ernest J. Lehmann	$10
C.K.G. Billings	$10
Richard T. Crane	$10
William Deering	$10
Mrs. Joseph T. Bowen	$ 5
Andrew Crawford	$ 5
H.N. Higinbotham	$ 5
Joseph Spaulding	$ 5
John R. Walsh	$ 5

And the article ended on an inspirational message: *Stop right here and make your Klondike and probably 25 or 30 years hence you will be written up in* The Sunday Tribune *as one of the millionaires who have helped make latter-day Chicago and whom latter-day Chicago has made possible.*

As in any list of wealthy Chicagoans, there now appeared the names of women who had inherited wealth from their fathers or husbands. Sometimes, as in the case of Mrs. Cyrus McCormick, they actually directed the family business. Through adroit money management an inheritor could also increase the fortune, as Mrs. Potter Palmer would do.

Many of the "merchant princes" and "captains of industry" dabbled in commodity speculation as a chancy but challenging way of augmenting their wealth. The most dramatic occurrence came in 1897, when young Joseph Leiter tried to corner the wheat market. His father, Field's ex-partner Levi Z. Leiter, had given him money to make a grand tour of Europe. Instead, Joseph

Facing page, top: A family poses on the stoop of a variety store in the late 1890s. Note that *The Tribune,* "Chicago's Greatest Daily," is advertised for one cent. Chicago's newspapers, with the exception of *The Daily News,* had only reluctantly sought mass circulation. Instead, they wanted customers who would patronize their more expensive advertisers. In 1895, however, *The Tribune* lowered its price from two cents to a penny a copy in order to reach less affluent readers. It helped cause a significant change in journalism. Courtesy, Chicago Tribune

Bottom left: In 1892 John Peter Altgeld became Illinois' first Democratic governor since the Civil War. Though a rich man himself, Altgeld advocated individual rights but believed in limited enterprise. He was defeated for reelection in 1896. From Cirker, *Dictionary of American Portraits,* 1967

Bottom right: Richard W. Sears, the founder of Sears, Roebuck and Company, was one of the most successful salesmen ever in the United States. It was said that he could sell anything, and he did. In this case he sold a stereoscopic card showing himself seated at his desk with a copy of the Sear's catalogue. Actually, customers could purchase an entire set of cards showing his firm in operation. Courtesy, Sears, Roebuck and Company

took it and began buying up wheat and future contracts for wheat, involving millions of bushels—a good portion of the just harvested crop in the Midwest. He intended to make millions by forcing "short" speculators to pay artificially inflated prices in order to cancel out their contracts to deliver wheat that would be unobtainable.

By early December it was evident that Leiter could control the price of wheat worldwide, since there was a crop failure in Europe. Yet much of the actual wheat remained in the hinterland, not yet belonging to Leiter himself, who mainly had "bought" contracts for wheat.

Philip D. Armour, an inveterate speculator, had gone "short" on wheat that year in a large amount. Starting a fierce drive to break Leiter's corner, he sent his agents throughout the grain-producing regions to buy up real wheat, using his powerful connections, money, and transportation network. Employing ice-breakers and dynamite, boats heavily laden with grain began moving through canals and lakes. Wheat began to arrive in long trains ready to deliver to Armour. Soon the grain elevators were stuffed, and surplus was stored in box-cars, in warehouses, in every available space, finally even in piles on the ground. On December 31 Armour notified Leiter that the 8 million bushels of wheat he contractually owed him were now ready for delivery. When wheat became a glut on the market, the cash price dipped low. Sixty-five-year-old Armour made a gross profit calculated at $2.5 million. And he had thwarted a greedy scheme by an upstart young man who had lost not only his own competence but also $7.5 million of his father's fortune.

Chicago's early entrepreneurs were clearly imbued with work ethic. Skilled at saving pennies and stretching dollars, they were adept at persuading others to part with theirs. They had shrewd and practical intelligence and worked hard to start and expand their business enterprises.

The vital connections among transportation, industry, and commerce were forged early, and each improvement in one worked to benefit another. Businessmen who had close dealings in all three major forms of business activity, also exercised political influence and obtained legislation beneficial to Chicago business, often running for public office themselves.

Not only did meatpackers, merchants, railroad magnates, and grain traders socialize, they also intermarried. They bought shares in each other's companies and sat on boards of directors, and often used the same legal counselors, bankers, and ministers. And whether they were notably Republican or Democratic in their voting habits, and whether they subscribed to the *Tribune* or the *Times* or the *Daily News* (or actually owned them themselves), they were, above all, men who believed that the furtherance of their own business interests would strengthen their city. And they believed that they possessed a far wider perspective in economic matters than their workers.

One of the important figures of the time was John Peter Altgeld, a lawyer who had grown wealthy through real estate investments in Chicago. When he became the governor of Illinois during the last decade of the 19th century, he offended many associates with his liberal ideas, harking back to the common-sense idealism and principled realism of his role model, Abraham Lincoln. A man of money who defended the common man, Altgeld advised steering a median course in society that allowed for strong ambitions yet set definite limits upon enterprise that recognized the virtue of commonality but judged it impracticable.

The making of and spending money to help Chicago grow physically and economically had been the primary activities of the city's 19th century entrepreneurs. An always important sideline of their role, however, was the enrichment of Chicago culture. In the first decade of the 20th century the partnership between the business community and the growing number of intellectuals, creators, educators, and reformers would be visibly close. Not without discordances, this financial and even spiritual association nevertheless would forge strong permanent values and institutions to propel Chicago forward in the decades to come.

Business leaders would have to recognize that they had responsibilities to the community at large, whether as fund-giving philanthropists or shirt-sleeve humanitarians. And if they did not already sense it themselves, they were going to become aware that the new era ahead of them would begin to do things differently. Disappearing now was the single, dynamic "strong man" who had launched and dominated his company while it expanded. Increasingly, corporations would find their drive, intelligence, and strengths in effective combinations of differing executive talents and in a growing, cooperative dialogue between management and workers.

In 1899 Chicagoans were inclined to look back upon the century about to close. One hundred years ago there had not even been a Fort Dearborn. Now there was a pyramid of culture, industry, and other human achievements that proclaimed, "No, Rome wasn't built in a day, but this city of Chicago was built in less than a century."

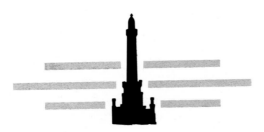

Chicago, as it appeared in 1881, is depicted in this engraving. Note the triple-turreted Inter-State Industrial Exposition building on the left along the lake. In 1820 at that spot the river (having curved) entered the lake. Thirty-six years later the site was in the bay that separated the Illinois Central Railroad from the shoreline. It is now the location of the Art Institute, erected in 1892. From the author's collection

No 21

LICENSE

IS
HEREBY GIVEN

BY AUTHORITY OF THE
CITY OF CHICAGO.

To Wm Wintermeyer   to keep a

SALOON

OR GROCERY,

FOR THE SALE OF MALT LIQUORS ONLY.

At No 149 West Chicago Avenue

IN THE CITY OF CHICAGO,

AND to sell, barter, give away, or deliver MALT LIQUORS ONLY, in quantities less than one gallon, in the place above designated, from the date hereof until the 30th day of April 188 , bonds having been filed pursuant to the Laws of the State of Illinois, and the ordinances of the City of Chicago, in such cases made and provided, to be subject to such ordinances of the said City of Chicago as now or hereafter may be in force, and the laws of said State now or hereafter in force, in regard to the sale of Liquors. No vagrant, no keeper of house of ill-fame, no prostitute, no drunken or disorderly person, shall be allowed in or about the premises ; nor shall the premises be kept open on any days of election. No concert, exhibition, ball, dance or play shall be given or performed in the same room where the liquors are sold. No playing for money, liquor or anything else, upon any table of any kind, or with cards or dice, (or pigeon holes,) or upon or with any articles or thing whatever, shall be allowed. In case said Licensee shall sell or convey said premises, he and his sureties shall be holden for a faithful and exact observance of all the conditions of the bonds accompanying this License, until any transfer made of it shall be duly recorded on the books of the City. NEVERTHELESS, this License, with all its rights under it, is subject to revocation at the discretion of the Mayor, and this License, with all the rights under it, shall terminate absolutely upon the notice of said revocation being left at the bar, and the person to whom it is issued shall stand in the same position as if he had not taken out any License.

Given under the hand of the Mayor of said City, and the corporate seal thereof, this 14th day of April A.D., 1884

Carter H. Harrison Mayor.

Attest   City Clerk.

Chicago &
North Western
Railway

Dining Car.

Facing page, left: In 1884, under the pressure of temperance reformers, the cost of a saloon license in Chicago rose to $500. Nevertheless, the city had over 5,000 taverns. The brewers often helped saloon owners pay for their licenses or owned an interest in the taverns. In the latter case the brewer's emblem would often be part of the saloon building's masonry. Courtesy, Chicago Historical Society

Right: The Chicago and North Western Railway offered good, substantial meals in their dining cars in the 1880s. The supper menu on which these illustrations appeared offered tea or coffee; bread, toast, biscuits, or pancakes; choice of roast beef, ham, beef tongue, steak, mutton chops, fish, chicken, or eggs; potatoes, and cake for 75 cents. Lithography by Shober and Carqueville. From the Windsor Archives

This page: In the 1890s Montgomery Ward and Company moved into this large "Beehive" structure on Michigan Avenue between Madison and Washington streets. The mail-order house had grown larger than any other in history and had to establish assembly lines to fill orders. Courtesy, Chicago Historical Society

HAGENBECK'S TRAINED ANIMALS.

MIDWAY PLAISANCE — WORLD'S FAIR. — MUSEUM AND MENAGERIE OPEN DAY AND EVENIN — THREE GRAND PERFORMANCES DAILY.

THE CRUEL WAR IS OVER.

FATHER KNICKERBOCKER.—I congratulate you, Madam, and I hope you won't be in '92 where I am now.

Facing page, top: The midway at the World's Columbian Exposition was alive with various forms of entertainment, including Hagenbeck's trained animals. The Hagenbeck-Wallace Museum and Menagerie toured the country from 1890 to 1929. Courtesy, Chicago Historical Society

Bottom: The New York-based publication *Puck* showed good sportsmanship when Chicago, in 1890, won the battle to host the World's Columbian Exposition. During the wordy war another New York publication, Charles Dana's *Sun,* nicknamed Chicago the "Windy City" because of its confident claims about being able to handle the world's fair. From the author's collection

This page: The first Ferris wheel ever built was located at the World's Columbian Exposition. Conceived of by George Washington Gale Ferris, the wheel contained 36 cars and would stop six times in the first revolution to load before turning another revolution without stopping. The wheel, which had cost $380,000 to construct, had earned its entire cost back by September 1, 1893, at which time it paid the exposition $25,000 in royalties. Courtesy, Chicago Historical Society

Facing page, top: In the 1870s and 1880s expanding industries liked to show the multiplicity of operations involved in manufacturing or processing goods. This chromolithograph by Shober and Carqueville entitled *A Modern First Class Pork Packing & Canning Establishment* depicts all departments of such a company including, interestingly enough, a fire department of its own. Courtesy, Chicago Historical Society

Bottom left: Cotosuet, a cooking fat made from beef suet and cottonseed oil, was a new product offered by Swift and Company beginning in 1893. According to Swift, Cotosuet was "the best cheap cooking fat offered to the public ... a wholesome substitute for lard ... unequaled for frying ... excellent for shortening pastry." From the Windsor Archives

Bottom right: Armour's Extract of Beef "gives to soups a zest and flavor attainable in no other way. Always ready, never spoils, convenient, economical" according to this advertisement dating from about 1895. From the Windsor Archives

This page: With better methods of canning available, Chicago meatpackers reached out for the world market beginning in the 1880s. A decade later Armour and Company decided to appeal to the French market with the artistic poster. Courtesy, Chicago Historical Society

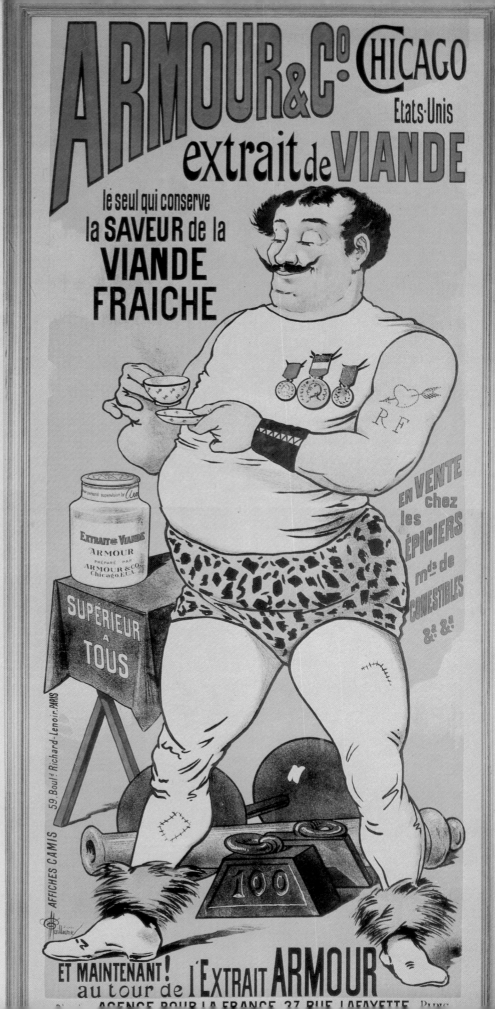

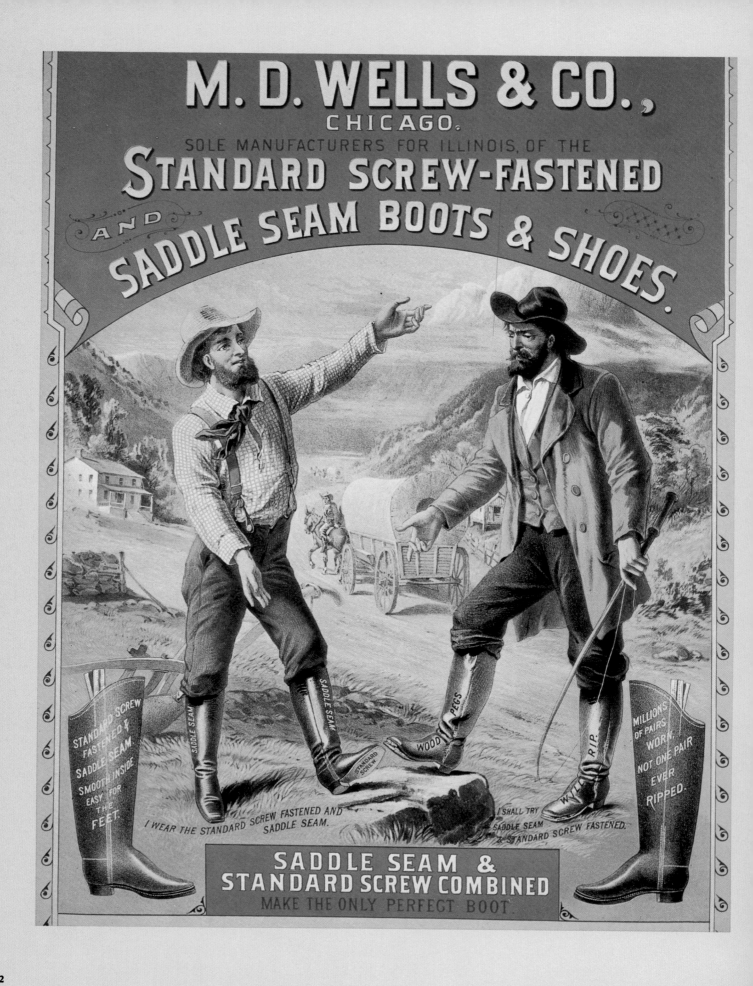

Facing page: This advertisement from M.D. Wells and Company proclaims the superiority of ''standard screw-fastened shoes and boots.'' By the late 1870s the factory production of shoes and boots in Chicago superceded hand labor in many of Chicago's leather-working shops. By 1889 Chicago stood fifth among the 13 leading shoe centers in the country. Courtesy, Chicago Historical Society

This page, top: Phelps, Dodge and Palmer manufactured boots, shoes, and rubbers for all ages. The company was located at Adams Street and Fifth Avenue. From the Windsor Archives

Bottom: Chicagoans who wanted to purchase wigs in the early 1880s could visit J. Hall's State Street establishment. From the Windsor Archives

Facing page, top left: Singer Adelina Patti, who stayed at Chicago's Grand Pacific Hotel while on a tour of the United States, ordered eight of the Chicago Corset Company's Ball's Corsets before she returned to Europe. To the company she wrote: "I can understand physicians recommending Ball's Corsets. I have tried them and regret not having known of them before." From the Windsor Archives

Bottom left: A sample of Queen Bess Triple Perfume was once attached to this 1884 advertising card put out by B.D. Baldwin and Company. The firm was located on Wabash Avenue. From the Windsor Archives

Facing page, right and this page: These illustrations appeared on a broadside printed by the Chicago firm of Shober and Carqueville. In the 1870s and 1880s businesses were discovering that Chicago had a printing industry with the ability to depict their products in graphic color. Courtesy, Chicago Historical Society

Left: G.A. Hyers' Big Bonanza Stove Polish was made from pure Ceylon Plumbago and according to this whimsical advertisement each package came with a cooking stove. From the Windsor Archives

Below left: The Thomson and Taylor Spice Company listed four reasons for using its Red Cross brand of powdered or granulated lye instead of other brands: 1. only a portion of the can could be used at a time; 2. its absolute purity; 3. its economy; 4. its convenience. From the Windsor Archives

Below: Dr. Price's Cream Baking Powder, manufactured by Steele and Price, was "comprised of pure material and free from amonia, alum, or adulteration of any kind, as well as from anything in the least injurious or objectionable." This idyllic advertising card dates from 1883. From the Windsor Archives

QUAKER
OATS
—
EASY TO BUY
EASY TO COOK
EASY TO EAT
EASY TO DIGEST
—
THE EASY FOOD

THE WORLD'S BREAKFAST.
Copy of Booklet for 2 cts on application
THE AMERICAN CEREAL CO., CHICAGO.

QUAKER
Oats.

This act, my friends, completes the 'hopper show;
Step up and try our oats, before you go!

Above and above right: Beginning in the 1890s Chicago's American Cereal Company was producing Quaker Oats, which it billed as "the easy food" and "the world's breakfast." In 1901 the Quaker Oats Company became the name of the holding company that owned most of the stock in the American Cereal Company. Finally, American Cereal became the Quaker Oats Company. It is headquartered in the Merchandise Mart. From the Windsor Archives

Right: James S. Kirk and Company at 352 North Water Street was the largest soap manufacturer in the world in 1880. The business produced 3 million pounds of soap per week, ranging from "the very finest toiletries to the more common quality." The company's "White Ceylon" soap, one of its finer products, is advertised here. From the Windsor Archives

JAS. S. KIRK & CO. SOAP MAKERS
CHICAGO.

"WHITE CEYLON"

197

REPRESENTING THE
STORY & CLARK ORGAN CO.
CHICAGO.

MANUFACTURED BY
NEWMAN BROS., CHICAGO.

Facing page, top left: Salesmen working for the Story and Clark Organ Company distributed advertising cards such as this one. The company was located at Canal and 16th streets. From the Windsor Archives

Bottom left: Newman Brothers manufactured organs for the parlor and chapel. It is interesting to note that a drum, not an organ, is used in this advertisement from the 1880s. From the Windsor Archives

Right: The one-cent *Chicago Daily News* had a daily readership of over 200,000 in 1881, the date of this poster. Two years later humorist Eugene Field began writing his "Sharps and Flats" column for the paper. Courtesy, Chicago Historical Society

This page: In 1895 Chicago newspapers aggressively competed for circulation among the city's growing population. Several papers, including the *Tribune*, cut prices for the first time ever to a penny a copy. The *Times-Herald* utilized artist Will W. Denslow to create this poster. Denslow later achieved fame for his spritely illustrations of the *Wizard of Oz* books. Courtesy, Chicago Historical Society

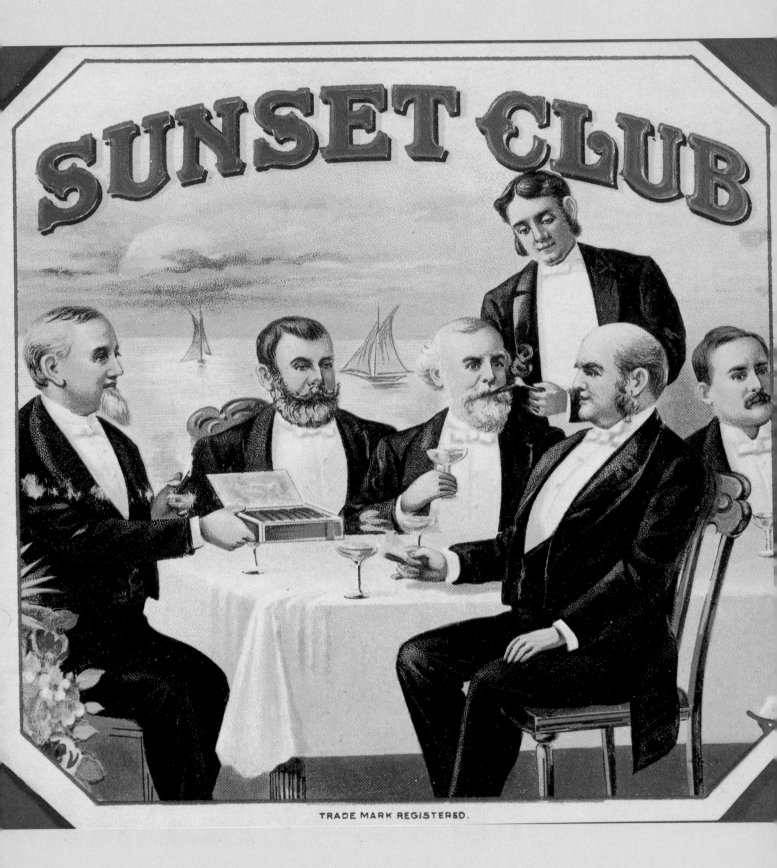

SUNSET CLUB

TRADE MARK REGISTERED.

200

CHAPTER TEN

PARTNERS IN PROGRESS

Chicago millionaires George Pullman, Levi Z. Leiter, Lyman Gage, Philip D. Armour, and Alfred Baker are depicted on this cigar label from the 1890s. The Sunset Club was actually a civic, freewheeling debate club rather than one for millionaires. From the author's collection

Make no little plans; they have no magic to stir men's blood," said city planner Daniel H. Burnham, one of Chicago's foremost architects. He uttered those words long after the city had risen from the drab lowlands around the southern rim of Lake Michigan.

In the beginning there seemed little promise for the midwestern trading and military outpost called Fort Dearborn. By 1848, though, inklings of what the future would hold came when Chicago acquired a canal to the Mississippi River, a railroad, a telegraph line, and plank roads that stretched into some of the world's richest farmland.

In the 19th century, as the nation's population moved inexorably westward, the rapidly developing hinterlands needed a conduit through which goods from the East Coast might flow. They also needed a terminus for shipping out the raw materials and abundant produce for trade. By virtue of its geographical features and citizens' will, Chicago became conduit and terminus.

Soon everyone was making great plans, especially those early heroes of Chicago business—Cyrus McCormick, William B. Ogden, George Pullman, Potter Palmer, Marshall Field, Gustavus Swift, Philip D. Armour, and Joseph Medill—individuals who stand out today in the metaphorical cityscape of Chicago history as strong structures unrivaled in their majesty.

Business did well because Chicago's explosive growth had been properly nourished. And Chicago did well because business flourished. In the first 60 years of the city's existence the population increased from 4,000 to more than one million people. These rough-and-tumble years drew a host of unique entrepreneurs eager for speculative ventures and economic challenges. Businessmen played important roles in developing services and structures needed by the expanding community. They also enriched its social and cultural life.

Fortunes were made from basic economic functions like merchandising, real estate, railroads, grain handling, meatpacking, and lumber. But as the economy matured and the Industrial Revolution gained momentum, Chicago demonstrated capabilities in manufacturing, as with making clothes, shoes, soap, chemicals, furniture, and musical instruments. There were printing plants, breweries, steelmaking firms, metal-fabricating factories, oil refineries, power generators, and food processors.

Close to both raw material sources and markets for finished goods, Chicago experienced an amazing prosperity for decades, interrupted occasionally by business slumps. The city's dramatic recovery from the Great Fire of 1871 proved its business community's mettle. Two decades later the city staged the most impressive world's fair ever seen.

Many Chicago firms have beginnings in the 19th century. But all Chicago companies, whether young or old, have been influenced in profound ways by the forces that shaped the formative years of the business community.

BUSINESS BIOGRAPHERS: DONNA GILL BUKRO • MICHAEL EDGERTON • CHARLES CHI HALEVI • EDWARD HAWLEY • FRITZ K. PLOUS • JAMES L. STOTT •

ALLSTATE INSURANCE COMPANIES

On May 18, 1931, William A. Lehnertz, a machinist living in Aurora, Illinois, wrote a check payable to Allstate Insurance Company for $41.60 and received an insurance policy covering his 1930 four-door Studebaker sedan for one year. Lehnertz was the firm's first policyholder.

The origin of Allstate lies behind the foresight of Robert E. Wood, a retired general of the U.S. Army. Although only 51 years old in 1930, he already had several sizable careers behind him: first as chief assistant to the exacting General Goethals, in the building of the Panama Canal; later as acting quartermaster general during World War I; and then as president and chief executive officer of Sears, Roebuck and Co.

In 1930 General Wood regularly rode the 7:28 commuter train from his home in Highland Park to his office in Chicago. Occasionally he played bridge with other commuters while en route. One day, during a bridge game, Carl L. Odell (an insurance broker and neighbor) suggested, "Why don't you fellows over at Sears start an auto insurance company?"

General Wood realized the increased mobility the auto provided would enable people to move out from the shadow of the city smokestacks into suburban areas. For these reasons, in the closing years of the 1920s, he had established the new Sears retail stores around the perimeter of larger cities and in small towns, where they were to become the first outlying shopping centers as we now know them.

The insurance idea appealed to him as a way for Sears to market a total package for the all-important automobile. Experts were called in, and an exhaustive study of auto insurance was undertaken. Applying his own wide and varied background to the problem, General Wood saw that the whole business of selling and servicing insurance policies could be streamlined and simplified. He saw many similarities between the problem of insurance and the problems he had faced and conquered in the field of retail merchandising.

He knew that a modern insurance company would have to keep overhead costs down and sell quality services to the public at the lowest possible prices. Until then the expense of attracting new policyholders had contributed sizably to the cost of a policy. He planned to save expenses by offering his insurance directly to the public, and expected rates to be about 20 percent less than those charged by other firms.

In October 1930 a proposal for the organization of an insurance company was presented to a meeting of the Sears' board of directors in New York City. The board was against any type of insurance operation; only the general's firm support of his plan forced the acquiescence of the members. In April 1931, when the insurance company evolved, the Allstate name was borrowed from the Sears tire trademark.

In its first year, the fledgling company recorded $118,000 in premiums written from 4,217 policies, most of which were ordered through "cut-and-mail" coupons in Sears catalogs. As a contrast, auto premiums alone for 1981 totaled more than $3.7 billion.

Allstate began with a staff of 20 people in a one-room, sixth-floor office adjacent to the Sears administration building on Chicago's West Side. In 1933, when Chicago was celebrating its "Century of Progress," Allstate opened

New employees visit the firm's historical exhibit to see 10-foot-high pictures of Allstate's founder, General Robert E. Wood (left), and William A. Lehnertz, first policyholder. Allstate's name was borrowed from Sears' tires.

Pictures of Allstate's early home offices are described by a personnel representative during new-employee orientation. The first one-room office was in Sears' Chicago West Side headquarters, upper photo.

Elected Allstate chairman and chief executive officer in March 1982, Donald F. Craib, Jr., is pictured with the first car insured by the company, a 1930 Studebaker renovated to occupy this place of honor in Allstate's 50th anniversary display at the home office. Craib, who joined Allstate in March 1950 as a claim adjuster, became vice-chairman in 1978 and vice-chairman/administration of Sears in 1980.

a booth in the Sears building on the midway at the World's Fair; here the Allstate agent made his debut. In 1934 a permanent sales-service office was opened in a Sears, Roebuck store in Chicago. The company expanded rapidly in its early days and was soon licensed in every state.

In 1950 one of the best-known slogans and symbols in the insurance advertising business was born. Davis W. Ellis, then Allstate's general sales manager, was among those planning the company's ad program for the coming year. He recalled a conversation he had with his wife during their daughter's serious illness: "Our family doctor says not to worry, we're in good hands with Dr. Cummings." From that came the slogan: "You're in Good Hands with Allstate." The slogan was illustrated with a drawing of a pair of hands cradling a car. (A home and people were added later.)

Four critical factors shaped Allstate's growth. Two can be seen early in its history, the others not until after World War II. The Sears stores provided the first factor. Their use substantially reduced overhead so that Allstate could continue charging lower rates than the standard bureau rates. It also gave the company access to a loyal following of satisfied Sears customers. The second ingredient was Allstate's corporate style. Its young management was willing to take chances and to do things in a way unique in

the insurance industry. The early personalities important at the company were General Wood, Calvin Fentress, Jr., and Judson B. Branch. The third component in Allstate's success was a substantial piece of luck. After the war, passage of financial responsibility laws created a heavy consumer demand for auto insurance. Finally, Allstate management had the foresight to reorganize the organization after the war—decentralizing to handle the growth generated by financial responsibility laws.

Allstate's growth from 1945 to 1956 was staggering. By taking advantage of the financial responsibility laws, Allstate nearly doubled its size every two years, through 1956. But, thanks to those laws, new-sales potential had dwindled significantly. And it was estimated that by 1956, some 80 percent of all car owners had insurance. Before then, companies writing auto insurance were going after part of a growing market. After that, growth could only be achieved at the expense of someone else, or by growth in public demand for more cars.

NBC-TV "Today" show tapes "Intercom," Allstate's employee television network.

Allstate had a little over 6 percent of the private auto market in 1956. Throughout the firm, people felt the days of dramatic growth were over; but a minority of Allstate's management, chiefly Calvin Fentress, Jr., Judson B. Branch, Archie R. Boe, and the planning department, could not believe the Allstate spirit had been stilled. In 1957 they compiled a report called "A New Era for Allstate." It was one of the earliest, full-scale strategic plans for an insurance company.

Employees of Northbrook Property and Casualty Insurance Company, an Allstate commercial insurance subsidiary, learn to process material using electronic video display terminals.

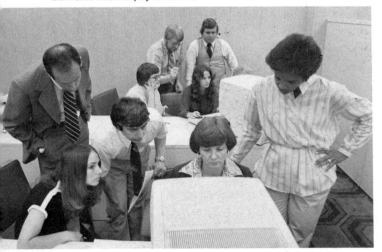

Elected president and chief executive officer in February 1957, Branch used "A New Era" as his personal statement of what the company should achieve under his administration. He agreed that Allstate's auto market was not going to grow dramatically in the future; he did not believe that this spelled the end of Allstate's rapid growth. The solution was to increase writings in other insurance lines.

Branch announced his intention of seeing Allstate become a writer of one billion dollars in premiums by 1965. The plan laid out the products Allstate needed to become a full, multi-line carrier. Thirteen personal and 29 commercial and reinsurance products would augment the existing automobile coverages making up the bulk of the company's sales. The report included a detailed study of the organization necessary to carry out such grandiose plans. Field autonomy was sacrosanct, but home office and zones added and reorganized staff to accommodate new product development and new sales and marketing needs. The firm was organized not by product, but by function. And agents were expected to sell all Allstate products, not just personal auto.

"A New Era for Allstate" rekindled enthusiasm at all levels of the business. Allstate continues to place very heavy emphasis on planning. In the 1940s the company had begun using monthly profit-and-loss statements, rather than quarterly, to see where it was at any given moment, and to deal with an adverse development in some location or with some product immediately. With use of such numbers, careful market positioning, and continued reliance on an exceptional agency force, Allstate hit its sales targets consistently.

The face of insurance is far different today than it was in 1931; the industry is more aggressive and competitive. Many changes and innovations Allstate initiated seem commonplace now—tailored rating plans for auto insurance, good-driver discounts, driver-training discounts, the guaranteed renewable feature, new-home discounts, payment-in-advance claim settlement programs, and drive-in claim offices, just to cite a few. Changes are copied quickly and innovations don't stay noticeable long.

Allstate's major future expansion lies in commercial insurance, and the firm is gearing up with five relatively new Northbrook Insurance companies. Wholly owned subsidiaries of Allstate, they are entering the market on a professional basis. The commercial insurance market amounts to an estimated $50 billion in annual premiums, compared with about $44 billion in the personal insurance lines.

Foreign operations and reinsurance on a worldwide basis will also provide interesting challenges. Canada was the proving ground for expansion outside the United States when Allstate started selling auto insurance there in 1953. Today the company is not only one of the leaders in that field, but sells life and commercial lines there as well.

Allstate also now operates in Switzerland, the Netherlands, England, Mexico, and Japan.

Most recently, a reorganization related to new acquisitions of Sears puts some of Allstate's pioneering efforts in separate Sears groups. Sears' Coldwell Banker Real Estate Group includes Allstate's PMI Mortgage Insurance Company, PMI Mortgage Corporation, and Allstate Enterprises Mortgage Corporation. Sears' Dean Witter Financial Services Group includes the Allstate Savings and Loan Association in California, with over $3 billion in assets. Sears is building these two groups into major arms of the corporation alongside of the Sears Merchandise Group and the Allstate Insurance Group.

Allstate, the sixth largest insurance group in the United States, now has some 20 million policies in force, pays out more than $16 million in claims on an average working day, and employs 40,500 people. The Allstate Insurance Group in 1981 recorded $6.8 billion in revenues, $406 million in net income, $11.5 billion in assets, and $2.9 billion in capital.

For the past 50 years the "Good Hands" people have adhered to the philosophy that the good of the company revolves around its benefit to the customer, to the nation, and to society.

About 4,000 of Allstate's 40,500 people work at the home office, Allstate Plaza, in Northbrook, Illinois. Nine buildings, comprising 1.32 million square feet of space, are located on a campus-like setting of 122 acres.

AMERICAN NATIONAL BANK AND TRUST COMPANY OF CHICAGO

American National Bank and Trust Company of Chicago is the fifth largest bank in Chicago. That is remarkable because it attained this position in the relatively short span of only 53 years.

American National began life on June 27, 1928, as a wholly owned subsidiary of S.W. Straus and Company, a Chicago mortgage-banking firm. The bank functioned as the commercial banking arm of S.W. Straus, and was called Straus National Bank and Trust Company of Chicago.

It seemed like a good time to start a bank, and Straus National's statement of condition at the end of 1928 must have borne out that feeling. Deposits had risen to $14,637,444 and capital funds to $1,479,568, reflecting the unprecedented prosperity in which the country was basking.

That all changed with the onset of the Great Depression, which eventually put that bank's parent out of business and landed control of the institution in the hands of a New York bank that was holding stock as collateral for a loan to Straus. A group of Chicago businessmen, headed by prominent attorney Weymouth Kirkland, repurchased the stock and changed the name of the bank to its present one.

Chicago businessmen gather at American National Bank's opening day at the LaSalle and Washington location, December 4, 1933.

American National moved from headquarters at 306 South Michigan Avenue a few blocks away to its current location at LaSalle and Washington, opening its doors at the new site on December 4, 1933. The move attracted a great deal of attention at the time because it occasioned the use of six armored trucks to carry more than $200 million worth of currency, bullion, and securities through busy Loop traffic. Forty private Brinks guards—armed with machine guns—were on hand to safeguard the bank's assets.

The bank occupied the second through the fifth floors; depositors had to cross through several retail establishments to gain entry to the second-floor banking lobby.

In 1933 Laurance H. Armour, a member of the Chicago meat-packing family, was elected chairman of the executive committee and president. In 1940 Lawrence F. Stern replaced Armour as president and chief executive officer, holding the latter position for 23 years. By 1942 deposits exceeded $100 million for the first time, and by 1945 they exceeded $200 million.

As with many other businesses, women played a larger part during the war years. By the end of 1942, for example, the staff totaled 388 people (50 individuals were on leaves of absence with the armed services) and the majority of them were women.

Readjustment to peacetime production brought several years of no growth at all for the bank. Savings, which had grown as wartime wages soared, were withdrawn; the government's deposits, which had reached unprecedented levels during the years of all-out wartime manufacturing, also fell off. Year-end deposits of $228 million in 1945 fell to $220 million at the end of 1948. There was one bright spot, however. The bank's management, anticipating a huge expansion in foreign trade at war's end, established an international banking department in 1945; it had relations with banks in 33 countries by the end of 1952.

American National marked its 20th year on LaSalle Street by acquiring the first floor of its building. The remodeled first floor was officially opened to the public on December 20, 1954, a year when deposits reached the $300 million level.

The bank's entry to the era of modern banking was underscored by the conversion of its check processing to a completely automated electronic system in 1962, as the year's deposits surpassed the $500 million level. That was also the year that federal regulations first allowed payment of the unprecedented rate of 4 percent on savings deposits.

In 1963 Allen P. Stults, who had joined the bank as a pageboy 30 years before, was appointed president. Lawrence F. Stern relinquished his post as chairman, and

During the move to LaSalle and Washington, money and negotiable securities were transported through crowded downtown streets, as armed guards stood by.

Robert E. Straus was elected to that position.

By the end of 1964 the bank's $700 million in assets ranked it fifth in Illinois and 65th in the nation. Its staff had grown to a total of 861 employees, with 100 officers.

In the 1960s American National undertook a number of distinctive ventures. In 1966 it purchased Tel-A-Data Corporation, which provides on-line customer account services for savings and loan associations. To serve the growing on-line data processing needs of correspondent banks, American National Data was formed in 1976, and by 1980 it had become one of the largest private data processors in Chicago.

American National assumed a highly visible position in the student loan business by inaugurating its National Defense Education Act Student Loan Service Center, the forerunner of the American National Educational Corporation. The first in the nation, it quickly became one of the largest providers of automated billing and accounting services to the educational community.

In 1968 Allen Stults was elected chairman of the board of directors. Two years later the bank's assets exceeded one billion dollars. The final stages of a major renovation program completed the bank's transformation to a Williamsburg decor.

American National had established American National Corporation, a one-bank holding company, in 1969 in order to be in position to expand its services; but a far more significant restructuring took place in 1972 and 1973, when Walter E. Heller International Corporation purchased the bank holding company.

Heller's strengths in international commercial finance and factoring helped to fulfill the bank's commitment to Chicago's middle-market companies and professionals. It was also at this time that the bank earned its reputation as a pioneer in developing innovative investment management products and services, both for the institutional and individual user.

Allen Stults retired at the end of 1978; Michael E. Tobin was elected chairman of the board at that time. Keene H. Addington was elected president. It was the bank's 50th year in operation. Two years later deposits were $1.8 billion and total resources $2.5 billion, as the "bank for business" prepared to move into the decade of the 1980s and its new atmosphere of competitiveness amid the spirit of deregulation sweeping the banking industry.

The Commercial Banking Department after extensive remodeling to Williamsburg decor. The focal point (left), a 300-year-old Flemish tapestry, depicts life in the 17th century.

ARTHUR ANDERSEN & CO.

Arthur Andersen, a 28-year-old Northwestern University professor, knew that clients wanted accounting service that was constructive; he and his partner, Clarence DeLany, determined to provide that service.

In December 1913 they formed Andersen, DeLany & Co., at a time when few firms thought of hiring full-time accountants. Those in the accounting profession objected to a permanent staff, reasoning that the cost would chase away clients by making fees prohibitive. The new firm proved them wrong. Andersen's personnel were to be professionals, and the firm still knows that its people are responsible for its success.

The same year that Andersen and DeLany opened their offices at 111 West Monroe, the U.S. Income Tax Law

Arthur Edward Andersen (1885-1947), founder of Arthur Andersen & Co.

went into effect. It caused only mild reaction at first, but by 1920 people were seeking Andersen's professional tax advice and the firm's revenues had already risen sevenfold to $322,000. The founder attributed much of that increase to his firm's early leadership in federal taxation.

In addition to its Chicago world headquarters, the Arthur Andersen & Co. Societe Cooperative was recently established in Geneva, Switzerland, to form an entity to facilitate complying with the laws and professional regulations of each country and to expedite the rendering of worldwide accounting, auditing, tax, and consulting services. The structure is set so that each partner—there are currently 1,400 worldwide—shares in the results of operations in more than 40 countries, a true one-firm concept.

Because of the constant emphasis on uniform high quality and close, personal attention, Arthur Andersen places the highest priority on training. With that in mind, in 1970 the company took over a college in St. Charles, Illinois, which can house over 700 students for intensive one-day to three-week classes.

From two partners and six staff members, the firm has grown to 22,000 people in 142 offices today. Although it is one of the largest groups of professionals in existence, Arthur Andersen & Co. still provides personalized service to each client and its partners and employees strive to follow the advice of its founder, "Think straight—talk straight."

A reproduction of the U.S. Income Tax Law of 1913.

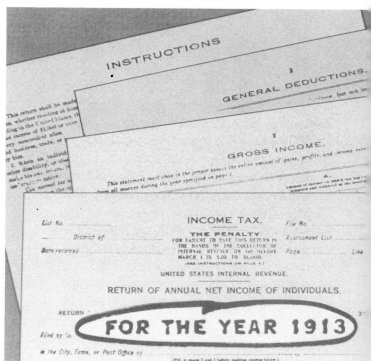

BINKS MANUFACTURING COMPANY

Joseph Binks didn't want to paint the town red in 1890—just the basement of Marshall Field's State Street store. But thanks to his invention millions of buildings and automobiles have been painted, enough to populate any town many times over.

Young Binks was a maintenance supervisor at Field's who periodically oversaw the whitewashing of the sub-basement walls, a tedious, time-consuming, costly, and chronic chore. Like Tom Sawyer, Binks did not appreciate the boredom of whitewashing.

Unlike Sawyer, however, Binks didn't just get someone else to do the job for him—he invented the spray paint machine. His first cold-water paint-spraying machine, crude as it was, was a vast improvement over the hand method. Unfortunately, few people beyond Field's basement ever heard of it. Then came the Columbian Exposition in 1893, with huge numbers of buildings going up almost overnight and not enough people or time to paint them before opening day. Binks put his machine to work and at the same time created a reputation for it.

His feat attracted the attention of the British import firm of Wallach Bros., Ltd., which became his primary customer for a number of years and distributed the machines in Europe and the United States.

Curiously, the machine was at first used mainly by American dairy farmers, who were required by health regulations to whitewash their barns—and disinfect their cattle. Then the auto industry began painting cars with Binks spray machines and the company's future was assured.

Binks' venture, at first called the Star Brass Works, was located at the northeast corner of LaSalle and Lake. Later the fledgling business moved and changed its name to Binks Spray Equipment Company. It grew steadily in the '20s, and in 1928 was sold to Neil Hurley and John F. Roche. Less than a year later the stock market collapsed.

John Roche guided Binks through the Depression and World War II, as well as the postwar industrial boom. Just before he died he passed the managerial reins to his son, Burke B. Roche, who still guides Binks today in its Franklin Park headquarters.

Burke Roche's experience as a naval officer enabled him to pilot Binks through such previously uncharted areas as automatic painting systems, which Binks pioneered, and electrostatic painting and airless spray painting, which use hydraulic pressure instead of compressed air.

Franklin Park headquarters of Binks Manufacturing Company.

Just as the spray gun replaced the paintbrush and established new levels of performance, so too can robots revolutionize the industry, with arms that can reach into crevices and angles that human arms cannot. Furthermore, robots can work 24 hours a day without taking coffee breaks or vacations, and can produce more for less cost. And they never get bored with whitewashing. Robotics is important to Binks' future; however, the company will continue to furnish all types of spray finishing equipment.

Tom Sawyer and Joseph Binks would have appreciated that.

Precision equipment at Binks Manufacturing Company.

AXIA INCORPORATED

These AXIA present-day products illustrate the company's concept of diversification.

Originally founded as a partnership in Harvey, Illinois, in 1891, AXIA, then known as Bliss & Laughlin, one of the first firms in this country to produce cold-finished steel bars, quickly forged into the forefront of the industry. Today, with six manufacturing plants located throughout the United States, AXIA's Bliss & Laughlin Steel Group produces steel bars in a broad range of sizes, shapes, finishes, and grades, for use by manufacturers of a variety of products, equipment, machinery, and appliances. The company is the leading independent producer of cold-finished steel bars in the United States.

The partnership was later organized as a publicly held corporation in 1919 as Bliss & Laughlin Steel Co. and today its stock is traded on the New York Stock Exchange. Following its organization as a publicly held corporation, AXIA rapidly embarked on a major and continuing program of expansion to keep pace with growing industry demands for high-quality steel bars. The first step was the enlargement of its manufacturing facilities in Harvey, Illinois, and the broadening of its sales reach beyond the

The executive offices of AXIA are located in the Chicago suburb of Oak Brook. The company maintains 39 manufacturing and distributing facilities in 16 states, Belgium, Canada, and Mexico.

Midwest.

In 1929 AXIA established its second manufacturing facility in Buffalo, New York, later adding facilities in Mansfield, Massachusetts; Detroit, Michigan; Los Angeles, California; Seattle, Washington; and Medina, Ohio. At the most recently established facility in Batavia, Illinois, the company has installed some of the most modern automatic machinery in the world for converting coil stock into cold-finished steel bars.

By 1961 AXIA's board of directors concluded that to assure continued growth and to provide its shareholders with a satisfactory return on their investment the firm would have to expand into new areas of operation. A concerted active program of diversification was commissioned. As a consequence of this plan, the Bliss & Laughlin Steel Group now represents but one of its three major operating groups. This deliberately executed break with the past constituted a major watershed decision for the company.

Assuming that the cost of labor would increase faster in the construction industry than other segments of the economy, this industry was selected as AXIA's initial target. The management also recognized that, with the high content of labor involved in the "joining of things," improved productivity in "joining" components in the construction industry represented a major opportunity. In addition, with its metallurgical experience, AXIA concluded it would pinpoint acquisitions whose product capabilities involved metal fabrication.

AXIA's first acquisition outside the steel business, concluded in 1962, involved the Ames Taping Tool Systems Company. Ames, the market leader in its field (the manufacture, rental, and service of drywall taping tools, labor-efficient devices used in the "joining" of gypsum wallboard), fits perfectly within the concept of AXIA's new expansion and diversification policy. Ames, which serves a select and discrete portion of the construction market, has remained less sensitive to recession than many other suppliers of construction tools and equipment and has served as the cornerstone of AXIA's Construction Tools Group.

In 1965 AXIA, recognizing its changing character, became Bliss & Laughlin Industries Incorporated. In February of that year, the company concluded the acquisition of the Faultless Caster Division, the initial building block of its Metal Products Group.

Since the initiation of its diversification program, AXIA has acquired or established such businesses as Goldblatt Tool Company (1965); Doerner Products Company Limited (1965), now Faultless-Doerner Manufacturing

Shown are the operations at AXIA's original facility in Harvey, Illinois, which consisted of a small building with an office arrangement on the second floor. Mostly confined to the manufacturing of shafting, its products were distributed primarily within a 300 mile radius.

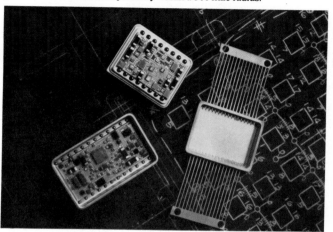

Acquisitions of new divisions and products has moved AXIA into space-age technology. The Tekform Products Company division produces packages for advanced micro-electronic circuits.

Inc.; Andamios Atlas, S.A. (1966), 49 percent-owned; Tekform Products Company (1968); Nestaway Division (1968); Marco Paper Products Company (1971); Jensen Tools Inc. (1974); Markson Science, Inc. (1975); Dave Fischbein Company and Compagnie Fischbein, S.A. (1977); Metalart Buckle Company (1979); and Amprix Electronics Company (1980). Consistent with Bliss & Laughlin's diversification concepts, each of these companies enjoys a distinctive niche in its respective industry.

In recognition of the profound diversification accomplished over the prior 20 years, the stockholders of the company approved the change of name to AXIA Incorporated. Today, with annual net sales in excess of $250 million, the company's three major operating groups are comprised of 15 subsidiaries and divisions and employ more than 3,200 employees, with facilities throughout the United States and in Belgium, Canada, and Mexico.

BALLY MANUFACTURING CORPORATION

In the Depression year of 1932, a Bally customer received 10 balls for a penny in "Ballyhoo," a pinball machine introduced in Chicago, and named for a contemporary satirical magazine.

Today, in recognition of the ways in which we style our leisure time, Bally customers are the family on a "mini-vacation" at Six Flags, the video game devotee at Bally's Aladdin's Castle, and the adult at Bally's Park Place Casino Hotel, in Atlantic City, New Jersey.

Ray Moloney, a principal of Lion Manufacturing Corporation, helped create the pinball industry with "Ballyhoo." The machine sold 50,000 units within seven months and fostered a separate division of Lion, Bally Manufacturing Company, the predecessor to the present Bally Manufacturing Corporation.

An inventive man, Moloney maintained leadership through new games which required skill and coordination of hand and eye. His machines were the most attractive and the most challenging. He brought electricity to the mechanical game board and lighted its vertical back glass with topical themes in a unique art form.

During World War II, Bally retooled for victory and won the coveted Army/Navy "E" Award three consecutive years. In the years after the war, Bally continued its leadership role through innovation, developing new game mechanisms and concepts.

After the death of Moloney in 1957, the firm declined

for several years and the estate's trustee bank considered liquidation. But an aggressive officer of the firm requested the opportunity to buy the assets. William T. O'Donnell successfully raised the funds and became president and chief executive officer in 1963. He had risen from purchasing department clerk, his first job with the company after his discharge from the Marines in 1946.

O'Donnell made Bally profitable—he introduced an entirely new, electric slot machine that captured the Nevada gaming market, established the firm's credibility in the European casinos, and made obsolete the totally mechanical machines. Within a few years Bally had become the leading manufacturer of slot machines in the world, having invented the "progressive" machine and the one-dollar machine for greater player appeal.

In 1968 Lion Manufacturing formally merged with Bally, forming Bally Manufacturing Corporation. Common stock was offered the public in 1969 and Bally was listed on the New York Stock Exchange in 1975.

Recognizing the broader dimension of the industry, Bally acquired Midway Mfg. Co. in 1969 to provide a myriad of arcade machines and games. Under O'Donnell's leadership Bally acquired an international network of ancillary firms—companies to provide materials such as quality cabinets, a German manufacturer of wall gaming machines, Great Lakes Acceptance Company to finance sales for Bally distributors, a chain of amusement centers, and a number of other acquisitions.

Acquired in 1974, Bally's Aladdin's Castle family centers have increased from 30 regional sites to some 400 locations in 45 states. These attractively decorated, well-lighted, and supervised facilities feature approximately 50

The pinball machine, innovated and engineered by Bally in Chicago, changed coin-operated games to adult pastimes requiring skill and concentration.

Through its development of the first electrical slot machine, Bally captured the Nevada gaming market, made mechanical machines obsolete, and became the leading manufacturer in its field.

The video game "Pac-Man" brought a new level of sophistication to individual amusement in 1980, combining intellectual challenge with the need for hand-eye coordination.

Bally's Aladdin's Castle game rooms offer a range of video games from all manufacturers. The Bally subsidiary has become the leading family amusement center operator in the country.

video and flipper-type pinball games in major enclosed shopping malls, sharing in their high traffic and attracting entire families. This subsidiary has become the leading family amusement center operator in the country.

The unprecedented popularity of video games has been predicated on the success of two new games—"Space Invaders," introduced in 1978, and "Pac-Man," in 1980; each quickly sold more than 70,000 units in an industry where 20,000 sales are significant. In 1981 electronic games and family amusement arcades provided 50 percent of Bally's revenue.

Under O'Donnell, Bally positioned itself to participate in the resurgence of Atlantic City as the eastern capital of adult gaming. Bally's Park Place Casino Hotel, an 83-percent owned subsidiary, opened in 1980. The $300-million facility, located on a nine-acre site on the Boardwalk, features 512 deluxe rooms, restaurants, meeting and exhibition space, and an opulent gaming area of 60,000 square feet. With future demand, the hotel could add a 750-room tower and the casino might expand to 100,000 square feet.

As one of the most modern casinos in the world, Bally's Park Place is a working demonstration for Bally's "Slot Data System II." With each pull of the handle, data is computerized, assuring an accurate operating history of each machine for the regulatory authority and the casino operator. Three installations of "SDS II" are being used in other casinos in the United States.

Upon O'Donnell's retirement, Robert E. Mullane became chairman and president of Bally Manufacturing in 1980. The Harvard Business School graduate, with Bally since 1972, set out to diversify the corporation in several

areas.

He sought to continue the change in Bally from basic manufacturer to major factor in the ownership and management of every segment of the growing leisure industry. With markets segmented and products for every age level, Bally would no longer be dependent on any one corporate division or product.

Bob Mullane's long-term goal is to generate the best return for stockholders. And his strategy is to make Bally the owner and operator of diverse entertainment facilities. With the acquisition of Six Flags, a chain of six family-oriented theme parks, Bally offers modern outdoor leisure-time activities. Bally purchased Barnaby's Family Inns, as the basis for its Bally's Tom Foolery chain of family restaurants with family amusement centers. To establish Bally in living rooms and dens closer to home, Bally has licensed games and programs to CBS, which will market Bally's games to the home games market.

Bally has also acquired the Scientific Games Development Corporation, the leading designer, producer, and supplier of instant and weekly lottery games.

In becoming an institutional-grade investment, the Chicago-based Bally has grown from manufacturer of a skill or chance game to full-range provider of entertainment itself.

With revenues in excess of one billion dollars, Bally Manufacturing Corporation has matured as an entertainment conglomerate, comparing favorably in the leisure industry with Disney and Warner.

BAXTER TRAVENOL LABORATORIES, INC.

Out of the prairie, just west of the Tri-State Tollway in suburban Deerfield, rises a striking building. Austere and white, long and low, it hangs suspended by cables from a pair of white pylons shooting straight up through a flat roof. The award-winning Skidmore, Owings & Merrill structure is the world headquarters of Baxter Travenol Laboratories, Inc.

The firm was founded as the Don Baxter Intravenous Products Corporation by two physicians, Dr. Donald Baxter of Los Angeles and Dr. Ralph Falk, a surgeon from Boise, Idaho. Dr. Falk's brother, Harry Falk, joined them in the establishment of the small enterprise.

Their motivation was simple—to simplify and mass-produce modern medical technology so that all doctors could use it. Intravenous (IV) restoration of lost bodily fluids was their starting point. The technique showed great promise as a method for building up the strength of weakened patients, but the technology of intravenous therapy remained primitive because its development had never been centralized or organized. Only a few large teaching hospitals were applying IV therapy, and each

hospital was experimenting with its own chemical formulas, glass bottles, and rubber tubing. Because of this fragmented effort, IV solutions were regularly being contaminated by "pyrogens," toxic residues of bacteria that had been killed by sterilization. The pyrogens caused severe chills and fevers in many patients. Unable to solve the pyrogen problem with their own limited resources, physicians either dismissed IV therapy altogether or reserved it only for the most desperate cases.

Dr. Baxter, the Falk brothers, and their six employees attacked the pyrogen problem with a one-two punch, combining scientific research and proven industrial-

World headquarters of Baxter Travenol Laboratories, Inc., located in Deerfield, Illinois. The building was completed in 1975.

Vernon R. Loucks, Jr., president and chief executive officer.

William B. Graham, chairman of the board

engineering principles. They produced IV fluids, containers, and administration equipment in large, uniform batches under constant monitoring for quality control. Contaminants were eliminated, adverse patient reactions stopped, and the medical profession at last had a series of effective, standardized products that could be used routinely by physicians in small hospitals as well as major medical centers. Later the line would be marketed under the name Travenol (from inTRAVENous sOLution), and in 1976 the term became part of the company's name.

In 1935 Dr. Falk purchased Dr. Baxter's interest in the firm and set up a permanent research arm within the organization. Within four years the effort yielded a stunning breakthrough in blood-preservation technology, the TRANSFUSO-VAC ®container. Where blood formerly could be stored only a few hours, the glass TRANSFUSO-VAC ®container allowed practical storage for up to 21 days, making blood banking possible. When World War II broke out, demand for the containers skyrocketed; temporary plant facilities had to be opened to produce them for the armed forces, where they saved untold thousands of American and Allied lives.

But the end of the war brought a collapse in military demand and a corresponding need for the company to cultivate the civilian market, in which its 1945 sales totaled only $1.6 million. A young patent lawyer named William B. Graham joined the firm that year as vice-president and manager. His leadership would guide the company through an exciting period of innovation and growth. By 1947 business had improved enough to dictate a move to larger quarters in Morton Grove.

In 1953 Graham became chief executive officer and began putting his ideas into effect on a wider scale. By 1955 the firm was clearly growing, as its IV products found markets in hospitals at home and abroad. Baxter Laboratories of Belgium was established in 1954 to serve this burgeoning overseas demand. Five years later the company acquired Flint Laboratories, with its line of pharmaceuticals for prescribing physicians, and Fenwal Laboratories, with its pioneering BLOOD-PACK ®unit that permitted separation of blood components within a closed system. Offered in conjunction with the company's growing line of blood-preservation and transfusion equipment, the Fenwal line made great strides in the marketplace.

But the project that was to thrust Baxter Travenol into the international limelight was still to come. In the early 1950s a Dutch physician named Willem Kolff came to Graham seeking assistance in perfecting an invention

The company's first manufacturing facility, a renovated automobile showroom in Glenview, Illinois, circa 1933.

whose theoretical success he had already demonstrated— an artificial kidney. Two major U.S. medical-supply laboratories had rejected Kolff's crude device, but Graham agreed to develop a working model—and by 1956 the U200A ®was a reality. Acceptance came slowly; as late as 1958 the company could not donate an artificial kidney to one leading research hospital. But persistent marketing and education efforts paid off as desperately ill victims of kidney failure demanded dialysis treatment, and additional improvements in the technique's performance made it even more widely accepted. Today some 160,000 persons worldwide are kept alive by this life-sustaining technological breakthrough.

The company's pioneering advances continued in many medical areas. In the 1960s it developed the first heart-lung system, helping to make open-heart surgery a commonplace lifesaving procedure. The first concentrate for treatment of hemophilia followed a few years later. Today the company's tradition of marketing innovative medical care products continues. An array of products and services for home care of kidney disease, nutrition problems, hemophilia, diabetes, and other disorders offer patients the opportunity for an improved quality of life, while controlling health care costs. The company is also building on its technological leadership in intravenous solution manufacture through a program to provide widely used intravenous drugs in a ready-to-use, premixed form.

Under the leadership of William B. Graham, now chairman of the board, and Vernon R. Loucks, Jr., president and chief executive officer, Baxter Travenol develops, manufactures, and markets a wide range of life-saving and life-supporting products that are used in 100 countries around the world. With revenues exceeding $1.5 billion and climbing, Baxter Travenol has proven to be an enterprise of extraordinary resourcefulness, producing a line of products so high in quality and so necessary to life and health that their utility scarcely needs to be demonstrated.

BEATRICE FOODS CO.

The southern view from the observation deck of the Sears Tower shows a vast stretch of former railroad property—most of it cleared for redevelopment during the 1970s. But one prominent building still stands—a huge insulated food warehouse at 1526 South State. Built in 1916-1917, it still bears a time-faded legend—"Meadow Gold Butter"—around its 10th and topmost story. But this unpretentious building, a combination creamery/cold-storage warehouse, was once the corporate headquarters of what is today a $9-billion multinational corporation: Beatrice Foods Co.

The enterprise began in the mind of a young Nebraskan with visions of "modernizing" the midwestern creamery business. The year was 1892; George Everett Haskell was 29 years old. And his employer, the Fremont, Nebraska, Butter and Egg Company, had just gone bankrupt.

In the 1890s business failure was common among the dairies and creameries of the Plains states. The problem, as Haskell saw it, was the uncoordinated handling and marketing of dairy products. As a result—and despite a growing demand for fresh milk, butter, and cream in the burgeoning eastern cities of the United States—most farmers concentrated on grain crops. Dairying was only a marginal sideline.

This lack of commitment to dairying was reflected in the seesaw fortunes of local creameries, some of which did little more than collect churned butter for resale. Since each farm wife had her own recipe for butter, product quality differed considerably from family to family; standardized branding and consistent quality control were impossible to achieve. The "independent" creameries, moreover, were too small to command reasonable freight rates from the railroads. And then there was the "seasonal" problem: Half of the annual milk output came in the three warmest months of the year.

Haskell's plan: coordinate the flow of dairy products from farmer to consumer. Essentially, his blueprint made local dairies and creameries more than mere processors of milk products; they also became central marketing agents. Success would mean coordinating a network of creameries—each making a product of uniform taste and appearance, and making enough of it to allow economical storage, handling, and rail rates.

In 1894 Haskell took a small nest egg and joined forces with a friend, William W. Bosworth. Quickly, the firm of "Haskell & Bosworth" acquired not one, but three

enterprises. In neighboring Beatrice, Nebraska, they bought a defunct operation of the Fremont Butter and Egg Company, leased the Beatrice Creamery Company's plant, and opened a new branch in Lincoln.

At first the new company did little more than follow the traditional "butter-collecting" system. But soon the firm began reblending the farm-churned butter at its plant. Fresh water flushed out excess salt and buttermilk, creating a uniform consistency, color, and sweetness acceptable in any market. Packed in 60-pound tubs, it then was shipped in refrigerated railroad cars to New York, Chicago, and other large distribution centers. The partners also began collecting fresh cream and making their own butter. Conveniently located cream-separation stations let farmers deliver their milk without excess travel. Later, separators were sold to the farmers, who paid for them on the installment plan from cream sales revenue. Between 1895 and 1905 Haskell & Bosworth sold 50,000 such separators.

This almost revolutionary innovation had an immediate effect: It made dairying more profitable. And that started a chain reaction: Farmers enlarged their dairy herds and improved herd management. As the cream supply increased, the firm expanded its distribution and secured a growing share of the market. The farmer, the creamery—and the consumer—shared the benefits.

The Beatrice Creamery Co. was incorporated on February 15, 1898, with Haskell & Bosworth contributing 85 percent of the capital. (It became Beatrice Foods Co. in 1946.) All churning operations were concentrated in a large new plant at Lincoln. In 1899 Bosworth withdrew from the partnership, which was then consolidated as Beatrice Creamery.

Early headquarters of Beatrice Creamery Co. in Lincoln, Nebraska.

Chicago was the hub of the nation's transportation system when Beatrice moved its headquarters to the city in 1913.

Success came quickly. In its first year, Beatrice Creamery sold 940,000 pounds of Lincoln Brand Separator Creamery Butter and more than 350 cream-separation stations were shipping to the Lincoln plant. To smooth out seasonal production peaks and valleys, cold-storage warehouses were built and butter stored in them for winter distribution.

The corporation began to expand both the number of its plant sites and the scope of its operations. Creameries were built in Chicago, Oklahoma City, and Pueblo, Colorado. Other companies—such as Lincoln Ice and Storage Company in Lincoln, Nebraska, and Chicago's Fox River Butter Company—were acquired. An ice cream plant

opened in Topeka in 1907, three years after ice cream cones took the nation by storm at the St. Louis Exposition. By 1910 the company was operating nine creameries and three ice plants, and had sales offices across the nation.

Beatrice established its headquarters in Chicago in 1913 and began planning the giant structure on South State Street. Opened in 1917, the new building's top floor accommodated the corporate office. Creamery operations were on another entire floor. The second floor, adjacent to the elevated right-of-way of the St. Charles Air Line Railroad, contained indoor sidings capable of holding 20 railroad refrigerator cars at once. In all, the warehouse could hold 3,500 railroad carloads of refrigerated foodstuffs.

Haskell died in 1919, and vice-president William Ferguson succeeded him. He presided over nine years of solid growth before retiring in 1928. Leadership of Beatrice then became the responsibility of Haskell's nephew, Clinton H. Haskell, a 22-year company veteran.

Clinton Haskell directed a surge in corporate growth that even the Great Depression could not seriously impede. Marketing opportunities in the East sparked a construction boom: a modern creamery in Brooklyn, ice cream plants in Baltimore and Washington, and a milk and ice cream facility in Pittsburgh. The company had only four milk plants in 1919; three years later it had 32. Between 1927 and 1932 its annual milk production leaped from less than one million gallons to 27 million. In the same period, ice cream production went from 1.5 million to 9.5 million gallons per year. The trade name "Meadow Gold" (created by employees of the Topeka creamery in 1901 and the country's first national retail brand name for butter) had become a nationwide household word.

Americans by now were demanding clean, sanitary, table-ready products available under the same brand name at comparable prices from coast to coast. Beatrice maintained its leadership position by introducing new technology and distribution methods.

For instance, the first Beatrice ice cream was produced in 40-gallon batches by a primitive revolving freezer. It differed only in size from the hand-cranked home unit. In 1931 the company introduced the Vogt continuous-freezing process. Almost overnight, reduced cost changed ice cream from a costly delicacy to America's favorite dessert.

It also was one of the first companies to package butter in sealed one-pound cartons and to pasteurize churning cream on a large scale.

Spurred by changing consumer buying patterns, growth through diversification became Beatrice's major thrust during the three decades following World War II. Most of this was accomplished under William G. Karnes, who became chief executive officer in 1952 following the death of Clinton Haskell.

Diversification came through mergers with companies in the convenience food field. Among these are LaChoy Oriental foods, Clark candy, Gebhardt and Rosarita Mexican foods, Fisher nuts, Martha White convenience corn meal and biscuit mixes, Tropicana orange juice, and soft drink bottling operations.

Manufacturing companies making machinery used in the food business also fit neatly into the early merger pattern. Included are Taylor soft ice cream freezers, Market Forge cooking equipment, Bloomfield restaurant equipment, and Wells commercial cookers.

Soon, well-known companies with products in other fields came into the Beatrice fold: Samsonite luggage and furniture, Stiffel lamps, Melnor lawn and garden tools, and Culligan water treatment equipment, to name a few.

Specialty chemical companies made Beatrice even more diversified. Stahl Finish and other suppliers of finishes for the apparel industry came first—followed by specialty ink, paint, waterproofing, and high-technology plastic molding firms.

International markets have beckoned since the early '60s. Beatrice's first overseas operation—a condensed milk plant in Malaysia—opened in 1961. In the next few years partnerships were developed with dairy, grocery, candy, and snack food companies in Europe, Asia, Australia, and Latin America. A major dairy operation was established in Canada.

Expansion into China is of special significance. Through a joint venture agreement signed in 1981, a partnership organization will develop for Chinese plants both export and domestic markets for Chinese-produced canned fruits and vegetables, soft drinks, and citrus juices. Other food and light industrial projects in China are also being evaluated.

Today Beatrice owns or has substantial interests in nearly 200 plants and branches in dozens of countries outside the United States, as well as franchises or some other presence in many more nations. Its products are in use on every continent.

In the early '80s, opportunities resulted in new growth strategies. Under James L. Dutt, who became chairman and chief executive officer in 1979, Beatrice began redeploying assets to reach longer-term corporate objectives: 18 percent return on equity, 16 percent net earnings growth, 5 percent real growth, market leadership, and continued diversification.

By 1981 operations with sales of one billion dollars annually had been divested. Proceeds were invested in more promising ventures. For instance, soft drink bottling operations around the country were sold; with money from the sale, Beatrice bought Coca-Cola of Los Angeles—the nation's number one soft drink brand in the nation's number one market. To foster growth, existing operations with high-growth potential obtained capital to expand.

Throughout the years, the primary management principle has continued unchanged: decentralization. At Beatrice, decentralization means that each plant manager has the responsibility—and the authority—to implement policies, procedures, and tactics that he feels are necessary to meet objectives.

The philosophy of Beatrice's senior management has stayed consistent: operations scattered throughout the

Beatrice Foods Co. and its products capture the attention of more than a quarter-million passers-by each day via this giant electronic sign facing Chicago's Kennedy Expressway.

world require sound on-site management—and minimal "interference" from headquarters.

Because of this policy, Beatrice is unusual among large and successful enterprises. Although fiscal 1982 sales were about nine billion dollars, the corporate headquarters staff is relatively small—about 300 persons. Still, Beatrice is a major employer in the Chicago area: 6,000 of its 80,000 employees worldwide work at 26 city and suburban locations.

It also is committed to another corporate objective: community involvement. In Chicago, Beatrice has a high profile as a civic benefactor through its sponsorship of America's Marathon/Chicago, one of the nation's largest amateur-athletic events. It underwrites major art exhibitions such as "The Search for Alexander" at the Art Institute and supports new dramatic works at the

Goodman Theatre. It sponsors all opening-night radio broadcasts of Lyric Opera performances, as well as their rebroadcast over more than 300 U.S. public radio stations and Canadian Broadcasting network stations.

And, as a contributor to the Local Initiative Support Corporation and Neighborhood Housing Services, Beatrice helps strengthen the economic and residential life of Chicago's older neighborhoods. Beatrice managers also are leaders in promoting the Second Harvest food bank organizations, and its companies are major donors throughout the United States.

In nearly 90 years since George Haskell planted the seed from which Beatrice Foods Co. grew, the fruits of his efforts—and of the leaders who have followed—far exceed what even that visionary entrepreneur could have imagined. Unsurpassed in its record of consistent growth, Beatrice today stands among the elite in American industry, ready to challenge the changing business environments of the coming decades.

BOOZ, ALLEN & HAMILTON INC.

Modern management consulting scarcely existed until Edwin G. Booz opened Business Research Service on LaSalle Street in 1914. Newly graduated with a master's degree in psychology from Northwestern University, young Booz was dissatisfied with the grim, stopwatch-laden "efficiency experts" who passed as management consultants in that era. He strongly suspected that business success could be unlocked by another approach—selection, organization, and motivation of the right people for each particular business.

An Evanston banker lent Booz the money to start his new venture. He also became Booz's first client. Neither man realized that what they started was not just a business but a whole new industry, and that Chicago was just the place to get it started.

Booz appreciated that the Chicago business environment would be receptive to unique ideas and approaches and would provide opportunities to test them. Booz was a student of Walter Dill Scott, often called the "father of industrial psychology," and had observed Dr. Scott's influence on the Chicago business community. He also witnessed the rapid emergence of major business firms and their need to sustain the vitality which fostered their growth. And he saw that his concepts of consultancy could contribute to the needs of business.

The business grew slowly at first. A sole proprietor, Booz had to interrupt his business to serve in World War I. When he returned at war's end, however, clients sought him out, not only to solve their organizational and

A 1915 photograph of Edwin Booz.

Partners of Booz, Allen & Hamilton in 1944 are seated from left: James Allen, Edwin Booz, and Carl Hamilton; standing from left, Edward J. Burnell, James C. Olson, Harold F. Smiddy, and Dr. John L. Burns.

personnel problems, but for research and statistical work as well. Nonprofit organizations, even communities, joined commercial firms as his clients. An associate was added in 1925, and in 1929 another Northwestern alumnus, James L. Allen, joined up. The client roster now listed 100 names.

The Great Depression, far from injuring the young firm's business, actually strengthened it, for Booz's firm had valuable analytical expertise to offer managements battling with the economic turmoil of the 1930s.

By 1936 the original proprietorship had become impractical; Ed Booz, George Fry, and Jim Allen—the original "staff"—were joined by Carl Hamilton, an experienced executive, to form the four-man partnership of Booz, Fry, Allen & Hamilton. Full-time staff now numbered 10, and the client list read like a *Who's Who* of the midwestern corporate elite.

What were the clients coming for? Essentially, Booz, Fry, Allen & Hamilton had evolved an entirely new approach to business consulting: Executive appraisal and development, executive recruiting, principles of organization and organizational behavior—later to become standard services with most management consultants—were exclusives with these innovative Chicagoans. Executive recruiting was an especially attractive service when Booz, Fry, Allen & Hamilton pioneered it.

World War II created a demand for management consulting even more urgent than that experienced in the Depression, and Booz, Fry, Allen & Hamilton's record immediately brought the company into the international spotlight. President Roosevelt's Secretary of the Navy, Frank Knox, had benefited from the firm's counsel when he was publisher of the Chicago *Daily News.* Now he asked some of the firm's partners to serve as "dollar-a-year men," volunteering their expertise to help the Navy establish a Bureau of Management to study and improve its own managerial technique. By 1942 the organization was deeply involved in both military and civilian aspects of the war, as civilian clients joined the armed services in demanding productivity improvements to meet the rigors of a two-front campaign. It was at this time that George Fry left the partnership to organize his own firm and the current name of Booz, Allen & Hamilton Inc. came into use.

The postwar economic boom created a continuing need for professional management services, and the firm expanded from its hub in Chicago and its offices in New York into Cleveland, Los Angeles, San Francisco, and overseas. In Italy Booz, Allen & Hamilton was called in to help rebuild the steel industry; in the Philippines it developed a land-title system and in Egypt it established management standards in the state-owned textile industry.

Increasing business complexity in the 1950s led Booz, Allen & Hamilton to develop a scientific and technical research-development arm, as well as its first international subsidiary. The company pioneered PERT, the Program Evaluation and Review Technique now accepted worldwide as the way to pace and manage large-scale industrial projects. And the firm's landmark new-product management study has helped literally hundreds of client companies to develop and market new products successfully, while stimulating some 200 doctoral dissertations on the various elements entering into evolution of new products.

During the '50s and '60s Booz, Allen & Hamilton broadened and deepened its research into new approaches to managerial science. Out of this corporate effort came new services never before offered by management consultants: distribution economics, research-and-

development management, R&D organization, executive assessment and succession planning, sales-territory analysis, and the management of new products.

Today Booz, Allen & Hamilton stands as a unique resource to management worldwide because of its ability to combine general managerial expertise with broad experience in particular industries and comprehensive technological and implementation skills. Since its founding in 1914 the company has conducted some 50,000 assignments for over 10,500 organizations around the world. Now a private corporation owned by its 170 officer-partners, it has a staff of more than 2,500 directed from a headquarters in New York. Offices outside the United States are in Europe, Latin America, the Middle East, Africa, and Asia.

But the firm's roots remain in Chicago, anchored not only by commercial and industrial clients but also by Booz, Allen & Hamilton's assistance to such local institutions as the Chicago Urban League, Chicago United, the Lyric Opera, the Art Institute, the Chicago Symphony, the University of Chicago, the Chicago Boy's Club, the Rehabilitation Institute, and now the 1992 Chicago World's Fair. The firm, along with its longtime chairman, James L. Allen, maintains close ties with Northwestern University, including the J.L. Kellogg Graduate School of Management, which it helped to shape. The Management School's James L. Allen Center for Continuing Executive Education is the product of Allen's dedication to the furthering of management science and its application.

Now honorary chairman of the firm, Jim Allen recently observed, "Chicago has proved to be a lively and receptive place to start a new concept in business services. Management consulting developed and matured here; at least four of the major firms in the field can trace their roots to Chicago. We are certainly proud of our Chicago heritage."

The James L. Allen Center of the J.L. Kellogg Graduate School of Management, Northwestern University.

LEO BURNETT COMPANY, INC.

Leo Burnett Company, Inc., headquartered in Chicago, is a worldwide advertising enterprise embracing some 41 offices in 30 countries (including associates). The sixth largest agency in the United States and the seventh largest in the world, Leo Burnett is the only American agency in the top 10 that is headquartered outside New York City.

The firm is unique among the world's advertising superstar agencies. It was founded in Chicago, where it remains. It has fewer than 30 clients in the United States and most of them have been with Leo Burnett for more than a decade. Leo Burnett earns its money by creating and placing advertising. It does not own a public relations firm or a cable television system, nor does it have any of the other subsidiaries that swell the size of many competitors.

The agency operates with a board of directors and executive committee. John J. Kinsella is president and chief executive officer. C.R. (Jack) Kopp is chairman of the board. Norman L. Muse is president of Leo Burnett U.S.A. and is in charge of creative services. W.A. (Al) Wiggins is chairman and chief executive officer of Leo Burnett International.

Outside the United States, Leo Burnett agencies fall into several regional management areas: Europe and the Middle East, Australia and Asia, Latin America and Mexico, and Canada.

Leo Burnett, founder of Leo Burnett U.S.A. Advertising.

The physical appearance of the Jolly Green Giant has changed over the years, as shown in the above pictures. But, as always, he symbolizes quality products "from the valley."

The agency was founded in 1935 by Leo Burnett, who died in 1971 at the age of 79. Burnett was born in St. Johns, Michigan, in 1891. He attended the University of Michigan, where he "studied all the journalism they had in those days" and was editor of the student newspaper before landing a job as a police reporter at the *Peoria Journal.* One year later an old classmate, Owen B. (Obie) Winters, who became a well-known adman, talked the youthful Burnett into seeking—and getting—an advertising job at Cadillac Motor Company. Burnett became advertising manager in 1919 and got to know and work with the early ad great, Theodore MacManus (author of the famous "The Penalty of Leadership" ad for Cadillac).

After a stint at a similar post at LaFayette Motors Company, 10 years at the Homer McKee agency in Indianapolis, and five years as vice-president and creative head of Erwin, Wasey & Company in Chicago, he founded Leo Burnett. He had with him eight associates and three accounts—Green Giant Company (then Minnesota Valley Canning Company), Hoover Company, and Realsilk Hosiery Company. The total billing was $200,000. By 1948 billings had grown to $10 million.

The founder had some definite ideas about growth.

Among them: "The agency which expects to grow must keep in mind that the single most important service it provides is in the thrust of creative ideas. ... There's nothing with quite the marketing leverage of the brilliant copy idea. It has the power to sweep before it what may have seemed insurmountable sales problems. You can 'solve' a lot if distribution and packaging and inventory problems, at less cost, with a ground swell of consumer demand."

Burnett was midwestern to the core. He liked New York, but he thought Madison Avenue advertising tended to be flashy and superficial. He felt there was no good reason fine advertising ideas couldn't be born in Chicago. Some admen have termed the Leo Burnett approach "the Chicago school of advertising." It stressed finding the inherent drama in the product and writing the ad out of that drama, rather than using mere cleverness. "You just have to be noticed," Burnett once said. "But the art is in getting noticed naturally, without screaming and without tricks."

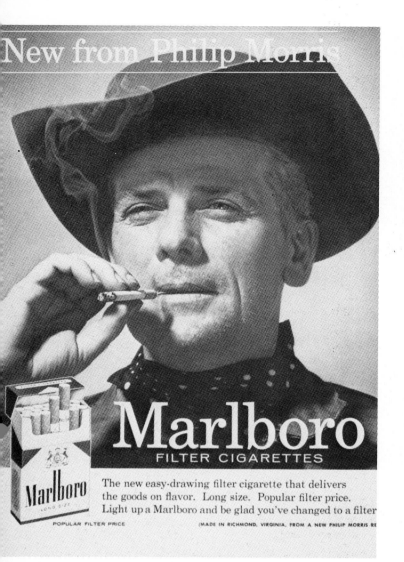

The 1955 above ad shows the original Marlboro cowboy. On the right is today's cowboy, 27 years later.

One noted example of the technique was an American Meat Institute campaign in 1945 in which red meat (such as two pork chops) was placed on a red background. The "red on red" ads ran long and successfully. Burnett commented: "This was inherent drama in its purest form, which we try to find without getting too kooky or too clever or too humorous or too anything—it's just natural." The measure of Mr. Burnett's success is that the agency's name will always be associated with symbols: Star-Kist's Charlie the Tuna, Pillsbury's Doughboy, the Jolly Green Giant, the Harris Lion, and the Marlboro Man, to name but a few.

The Marlboro campaign remains an advertising classic. It took a minor cigarette brand with a predominantly feminine image and began to turn it into the best-selling brand in the world. The campaign used close-up photos of ruggedly masculine men—with a tattoo on the forearm that became almost as well known at the time as the Hathaway eye patch.

The Pillsbury Doughboy was created one day by a Burnett creative director, when he was sitting at his desk playing with pastry dough, hitting the package against the edge "like you're supposed to do to open it." He continued, "The dough started to ooze out and looked alive. I thought, 'Why not have someone in there?' The dough led to the Doughboy."

And there are still other advertising characters that have become stars in their own right, such as Tony the Tiger for Kellogg's, Morris the Cat for 9-Lives, the Keebler Elves, and the lonely Maytag repairman. The agency created the Man from Glad for Union Carbide, a character who answered distress calls from harried homemakers in need of an airtight bag to keep leftovers from going stale. For Memorex recording tape, Leo Burnett had singer Ella Fitzgerald shatter a glass by singing and recording a high note. Some symbols such as Marlboro Country and The Friendly Skies of United are as big as all outdoors.

To ensure that its advertising creations will help sell its clients' products, the agency often tests its ads and ideas on people at its Woodfield research workshop in the city's northwest suburbs. The people who participate are representative of the buyers Leo Burnett ads are trying to reach.

Leo Burnett has experiencd ever-increasing growth and exceptional client loyalty. Green Giant has, of course, been a client since the agency's inception. Union Oil has been a client since 1938; Pillsbury, since 1944; Kellogg Company, since 1949; Harris Trust and Savings Bank and The Maytag Company, both since 1952, the year Procter & Gamble joined the agency's client roster.

Other clients include Allstate Insurance Companies, American Bankers Association, Commonwealth Edison, General Motors, H.J. Heinz, Keebler Company, Kimberly-Clark Corporation, Memorex Corporation, McDonald's Corporation, The Nestle Company, Philip Morris Incorporated, RCA Corporation, Salada Foods, Schenley Industries, Mrs. Smith's Frozen Foods Co., Star-Kist Foods, Inc., Union Carbide Corporation, United Airlines, and Wilson Sporting Goods Company.

Vital to the success of any advertising agency are its employees. "Creative talent is the name of the game," chairman Jack Kopp says, and the agency has a reputation for recruiting, training, and giving opportunity to people — and being raided by Madison Avenue. The agency pays its creative personnel higher-than-average salaries and benefits. Burnett is not a public company; the stock is owned by employees.

All this is aimed at nurturing talent and focusing on one product, advertising. "We think we have an advantage as a private company," Kopp says. "For us, earnings per share is not the be all and end all. We can invest in the future without worrying too much. In 1978, compared with the ad agencies that are public, we ranked dead last in terms of profits as a percentage of billings. In terms of a percentage of revenues paid in salaries and benefits we ranked number one. In the final analysis, the quality of your people determines the quality of the advertising you produce."

The Leo Burnett who built such a large and thriving advertising agency also deeply loved the city he was associated with for so long. He was consistent in his praise of Chicago's growth and progress. Burnett agreed with Daniel Burnham, father of the Chicago Plan, who counseled Chicago, "Let your watchword be order and your beacon, beauty." In an address of 35 pages in 1965, Burnett offered his appraisal of how well the city had lived up to that summons and that promise.

He spoke of the ever-changing Chicago skyline and physical facade, mentioning the enormous development of recent years after a drought in new construction from 1932 to 1955. He was impressed by the many plazas, malls, trees, fountains, and landscaped areas which had come to the city.

Leo Burnett was proud that Chicago had more colleges and universities than any other city; that its transportation was the best in the world, its airport the busiest; and that, as a seaway port, it handled more traffic than the Panama Canal. He found that in its cultural endowment, its commercial vitality, the spirit of its neighborhoods, Chicago was alive and pulsating. He believed that the city's progress was "powered by the initiative, the pride, and the friendly attitude of each of us who is proud to be a Chicagoan."

And finally, it was Burnett who, during an interview with *Advertising Age* in 1967, foretold the future of the agency he founded. When asked how large the agency might be in 1979 or 1975, he replied, "Look, I'm just kind of an ink-stained wretch. I don't know much about these financial matters. I do know, however, that if you make enough good ads, inevitably you grow and make some money."

And that is Leo Burnett today: creative, prosperous, and growing.

Famous symbols created by the Leo Burnett organization.

CANTEEN CORPORATION

Canteen Corporation, based in Chicago, is one of the nation's leading food-service organizations. With 18,000 employees, 82 branches, and 87 independent franchised distributors, the firm (a major subsidiary of TransWorld Corporation) operates 200,000 vending machines, and serves three million customers daily through 838 manual food operations. Its service area stretches to virtually every major market in North America, as well as selected areas in Europe and the Far East.

The venture was founded in 1929 by Nathaniel Leverone as Automatic Canteen Company of America. The name was changed in 1966 to Canteen Corporation to emphasize its diversification into fields other than vending.

The founders were convinced that the vending machine could render great service, but there were many challenges to be met in raising standards of operation, product, and equipment. In meeting them, they revolutionized a business that had been long neglected and created a major American industry.

From the outset Canteen sought to gain public confidence, selling nationally advertised brand

Nathaniel Leverone, founder of Automatic Canteen Company of America, 1929.

Patrick L. O'Malley, chief executive officer from 1961 to 1975.

merchandise of established quality, using reliable equipment that gave refunds when empty, servicing machines at frequent intervals to assure the availability of fresh product, and employing high-caliber, uniformed, bonded service personnel. In 1931 the firm moved into the Merchandise Mart, where its national and executive offices have remained ever since.

In its earliest days Canteen machines were largely confined to the sale of candy, gum, and nuts. In 1939 a soft-drink vending machine was introduced, and in 1941 the company established a bacteriological and chemical laboratory to ensure purity and uniformity of drinks sold to its customers.

Definite proof that Canteen had "arrived" was the acceptance of its service for several great expositions: Treasure Island, San Francisco Bay, The Golden Gate International Exposition in 1939; and in New York City, The World of Tomorrow in 1939 and the New York World's Fair in 1940.

During World War II production of new Canteen vendors was halted because of increasing demands for critical materials for the war. Cocoa was in short supply and products had to be allocated because of the sugar shortage. Automatic Canteen Company of America's common stock was listed on the New York Stock Exchange on August 5, 1946. Also in that year the Canteen cigarette vending machine was introduced, the company's first departure from food products.

The coffee break became a widely observed American institution, and in 1952 coffee vending machines were introduced. Production of the Canteen Hot Canned Food Vendor was started in 1956, and the Refrigerated Sandwich Merchandiser was introduced in 1958. The development of more sophisticated vending machines and wider varieties of products also contributed to the firm's growth.

Patrick L. O'Malley left the Coca-Cola Company in the early 1960s to become president of Canteen, helping to establish the firm's leadership in still another phase of the industry: manual food service. This phase reflected the astronomic growth of the away-from-home food-service market.

Canteen extended its quality concept into industrial food-service operations in 1977 with the Quality Assurance Recipe Program. Considered the most important innovation in food service since its inception, QAR is a special system of prepackaged and premixed spices, plus recipe cards in word and picture. Learning centers—another Canteen first—have been established in strategic market areas to provide training essential for maintaining the QAR program.

In 1979 president Howard C. Miller announced the introduction of Health Fare, the first continuing nutrition

James T. McGuire, chief executive officer from 1981 to the present.

Howard C. Miller, chief executive officer from 1976 to 1981.

program for adults offered on a national scale by a private-sector organization. Health Fare provides practical health tips on colorful memo sheets displayed in Canteen-managed plant cafeterias.

This is Canteen Corporation today: Its Concession Division provides tour and public food facilities at NASA's Kennedy Space Center, refreshment and restaurant operations at major sports centers, and offers food, lodging, and recreational facilities at a number of national and state parks; the Restaurant Division manages the Metropolitan Opera House restaurant at Lincoln Center in New York City; its Rowe Division supplies cigarette machines and coin-operated music and games for restaurants and other public locations. Milnot Company, a subsidiary, produces specialty food items; Dunhill Personnel System, acquired in 1977, is a specialist in middle-management placement; and Canteen of Canada provides comprehensive food service to industry north of the border.

In 1982 Canteen continues to move forward under the experienced leadership of president James T. McGuire. And as Canteen has grown, so has food service in America. In 1929 the industry grossed $2 billion. Today, combining commercial, industrial, and military operations, it will gross $105 billion, making it the largest industry in the United States.

THE CECO CORPORATION

In 70 years Ceco has matured from the innovative idea of one man and has become a major supplier of products and services for the construction industry. Ceco has enjoyed decade-by-decade growth in sales, earnings, and net worth. For calendar year 1981, the company recorded net sales of more than $450 million.

C. Louis Meyer founded the Concrete Engineering Company in Omaha in 1912 with a revolutionary idea—instead of using traditional tile forms to form and support poured-in-place reinforced concrete-joist floors, why not develop a removable and reusable steel form to supplant the forms previously left in the structure, which added to the "deadweight" of the building.

This concept brought wide versatility to concrete as a building material, helping to extend its applications to construction of every type. The business grew slowly in the early years as architects and contractors learned of the benefits.

In the 1920s the organization grew rapidly and the company became a fabricator of reinforcing bars. The firm made its mark in Chicago through its forming work for the construction of the Tribune Tower, the Merchandise Mart, and the Sheraton Towers. In 1937 the company erected a major plant and office in suburban Cicero, and adopted the name Ceco Steel Products Corporation. In 1946 corporate headquarters was moved from Omaha to the Cicero

Ceco's headquarters building in Oak Brook, Illinois, features many of the firm's products, including a poured-in-place reinforced concrete structure.

location and a new office building was erected there.

Meyer died in 1953 at age 67. His enterprise had prospered over four decades, but to secure its future and to broaden ownership, the first public issue of stock was made in 1956. New sales offices, fabricating plants, and warehouses were established in strategic locations throughout the country.

In the 1960s Ceco completed its greatest expansion program. Sales and earnings doubled and new facilities were added. Corporate acquisitions took the firm into new product areas and Ceco was listed on the New York Stock Exchange in 1961.

To indicate its wider scope of construction activities, the firm eliminated "Steel Products" from its name and became The Ceco Corporation. The company today comprises six divisions and five subsidiaries. The Concrete Forming division, using its own materials and field labor, performs as a subcontractor to install the forming work for all types of poured-in-place, reinforced concrete buildings, making ready for the placing of reinforcing steel and concrete by others. After the concrete sets, it removes the forms and their supports so that they may be reused on the same structure or other buildings.

The company also manufactures concrete pipe, concrete block, and prestressed concrete sections at its N.C. Products subsidiary, which was acquired in 1969 and now comprises six facilities in North Carolina. These forming services and concrete products account for about one-fourth of Ceco's total sales of more than $450 million annually.

Ceco's Door division manufactures steel side-hinged doors and frames, and its Windsor Door division, acquired in 1969, manufactures metal, wood, and fiberglass overhead doors for commercial, manufacturing, institutional, and residential buildings. Sales constitute

The Merchandise Mart in Chicago was the world's largest building when it was completed in 1929. Most of the floor forming in the structure was done by Ceco.

about 20 percent of total volume.

Ceco's Mitchell Engineering division, acquired in 1961, manufactures and erects complete pre-engineered metal buildings for commercial and industrial purposes. The Merchant Trade division makes metal lath and accessories, steel framing, and farm buildings. The sales of these two divisions comprise about 22 percent of Ceco's total.

A major group, Steel Mill Related Products, provides about one-third of total volume, and includes plants for fabrication of reinforcing bars and steel joists, the sale of stock-length steel to other fabricators and warehouses, and the firm's steel mill. Ceco has entered into negotiations to divest itself of steel mill operations to streamline this product group.

The corporation recently acquired four new subsidiaries: Delta Steel Buildings Co., a manufacturer of pre-engineered metal buildings; Engineered Components, Incorporated, a manufacturer of structural and architectural components for the construction industry; Tyee Lumber and Manufacturing Co., a producer of lumber and wood products; and Research Systems Group, Inc., a developer of custom software for computer-aided design, manufacturing, and drafting applications.

The year 1980 began a new decade and a new chapter in the Ceco story—after 34 years in Cicero, the headquarters was moved to a three-floor, 90,000-square-foot reinforced concrete structure in Oak Brook, showcasing many Ceco products and services. It houses 300 of some 7,000 employees working from coast to coast in hundreds of building projects.

Architectural benchmarks to which Ceco contributed include the Nebraska State Capitol in Lincoln (1922); the Golden Gate Bridge in San Francisco (1937); U.S. Air Force Academy at Colorado Springs (1959); the 70-story

High-rise condominium for which Ceco did the slab forming on 41 floors and five below-ground parking levels.

Peachtree Center Plaza in Atlanta, the world's tallest hotel (1975); Cincinnati's Riverfront Stadium (1977); and the New Orleans Superdome (1975).

The versatility of Ceco concrete forming was demonstrated in the Oral Roberts "City of Faith" medical complex in Tulsa, completed in 1980. And the company's largest contract is being executed for the Miami Center—a hotel, office, and shopping complex in Florida.

This line of Ceco doors get their share of wear and tear at a recreational center's entranceway.

CENTEL CORPORATION

Some Chicagoans think that Centel's connection to the city began when the company moved its headquarters to the Windy City in 1976, but the firm's history in Chicago actually goes back more than a half-century. In 1926 the venture's founder, Max McGraw, moved to the city to consolidate his growing electric and telephone organization, then called Central West Public Service Company. From that point the firm started to expand operations, and though Centel has evolved into one of the largest communications companies in the United States, it still retains its commitment to—and faith in—Chicago.

McGraw was an ambitious 17-year-old entrepreneur when he set up an electrical shop in the basement of a Sioux City, Iowa, drug store in 1900. He invested his life savings (about $500) for his first tools and equipment. Determined to learn all there was to know about electricity, he studied every book he could find on the rapidly expanding technology.

In 1904 the first telephone company in Des Plaines, Illinois, served 150 telephones and was located in the rear of a hardware store.

With business cards that read "Max McGraw—Electrician," the teenager made his rounds on a newspaper route he had worked since the age of 10. His first cards proudly proclaimed the slogan, "The McGraw Law is Quality."

McGraw's first year as an electrician was devoted to converting homes from gas to electric lighting. Despite the boy's persistence and hard work, the business lost $39.70—the only year (except for a small deficit in 1932) the company would ever record a loss. But 1901 saw substantial improvement: McGraw was awarded a $12,000 contract to install an electrical power system for the Sioux City stockyards.

How could such a young man, with so little experience, land such a complex, expensive contract? "I simply walked into the president's office," McGraw recalled years later, "and told him I could do the job."

McGraw's electrical contracting business grew over the next few years, and soon his company was installing telephone systems for entire towns. From there the young man logically turned to the business of supplying telephone and electrical equipment, which soon led him to the manufacture of telephone equipment. By 1907, at the age of 24, McGraw was running three businesses.

As his financial equity in these utilities increased, McGraw decided to take a stronger position in operating them, which set the stage for his move to Chicago in 1926. His consolidation of the multistate operation under the title Central West Public Service Company was the beginning of what Chicagoans know today as Centel.

During the rough Depression years of the 1930s, the firm developed innovative customer services for its natural

Max McGraw financed his first electrical shop with $500 capital earned from delivering newspapers on horseback. McGraw, age 14, seated on the horse, was photographed with boyhood friends.

gas and electric utilities by entering the home and commercial appliance business. Whenever customers visited the local Central West office to pay a bill, they were greeted by a display of the latest gas ranges or electric lighting fixtures. The firm also introduced a home service staff. Composed of women with degrees in home economics, the staff taught local homemakers the many conveniences of electric and gas appliances, particularly ranges. Annual cooking schools turned out to be the most popular consumer project undertaken by the home economists.

In 1938 the company fortified its presence in Chicago by acquiring Middle States Telephone Company (now Central Telephone Company of Illinois), which served the suburbs of Park Ridge and Des Plaines. At the time the Park Ridge-Des Plaines area was a relatively quiet, slow-growing residential neighborhood. When nearby O'Hare Airport opened in the early 1950s and a new tollway system developed, the population of both communities accelerated rapidly, as many offices, businesses, and plants were built near the new facility. And Centel's Chicago-area operations and services grew along with the community.

By the midpoint of the century the firm was concentrating almost entirely on what it knew best—gas, electric, and telephone utility systems. A series of name

Centel's first association with Chicago began in 1926, when the company's founder, Max McGraw, moved his office from Sioux City, Iowa, to Chicago "to get closer to things."

changes, culminating in the name Centel Corporation in April 1982, reflects the firm's accelerating expansion into communications-related businesses.

With the dawn of the high-technology computer era approached in the 1970s, the enterprise turned its attention to the new communications systems, selected proprietary products, and wholesale supply and distribution of telecommunications equipment and materials.

Centel acquired two proprietary product companies: Acoustics Development Corporation (ADCO) with

Max McGraw (right) with Charles Edison, son of the famed inventor, at the restored Menlo Park Edison laboratories at Greenfield Village, Dearborn, Michigan. In 1957 the McGraw and Edison companies merged to become one of the nation's largest manufacturers of electrical equipment.

headquarters in Northbrook, Illinois, and Digitech Industries, Hartford, Connecticut, were acquired in 1978 and 1979, respectively. ADCO's coin telephone enclosures now account for a major share of the national market, and foreign sales have been steadily increasing every year.

Digitech Industries has developed several unique products to provide the service engineer with powerful diagnostic tools. PACER, introduced in the mid-1970s, has the sophisticated instrumentation to monitor and identify problems in data networks. And ENCORE, a 1979 innovation, not only performs all PACER functions but can also diagnose new data-system protocols developed since PACER was introduced. In 1980 Digitech announced DATA MONITOR-200, an inexpensive, easy-to-use data communications diagnostic instrument.

Centel made its first move into cable television in 1978, when it acquired Consolidated Cable Utilities, Inc. Serving Aurora and Elgin, Illinois, the firm is now building cable systems in several nearby areas. After the acquisition of Consolidated Cable, Centel purchased a company that operates a master-antenna television system in high-rise buildings in Chicago and its suburbs. More cable acquisitions followed and today Centel offers cable service in many areas of the country: central Illinois; Lima, Ohio; many parts of Indiana, Kentucky, and Michigan; suburban Houston, Texas; and central Florida, near Orlando.

With more than 130,000 subscribers Centel is currently among the top 35 cable companies in the United States.

Just as satellite transmission spurred the present growth of cable television, Centel believes that rapid development of digital electronic-switching technology presents the company with another exceptional growth opportunity for business communications systems. The acquisitions of Livingston Communications (now Centel Business Systems-Midwest), a large Chicago marketer of telephone equipment, and Fisk Telephone Systems (now Centel Business Systems-Fisk), an interconnect firm based in Houston, Texas, give Centel a strong position from which to expand its market, and complement existing operations in the company's telephone operations. Together, this group has provided Centel with a national marketing capability and a large share of a billion-dollar market.

Centel also designs, engineers, and maintains complex communications systems for large corporations. To ensure a stable product line the firm has entered into a supply agreement with Northern Telecom, Inc., a major manufacturer of high-quality digital systems and sophisticated network software.

Centel Supply is another flourishing unit of the corporation. Originally established as a purchasing and distribution arm for Centel companies, it has expanded its customer base over the past few years. Marketing efforts have been directed toward telephone and interconnect and cable companies not affiliated with Centel.

While Centel has entered the 1980s expanding into these new communications fields, it continues to focus on its traditional areas of expertise: telephone and electric power. Today Centel is the fifth largest telephone company in the United States, servicing more than 1.1 million

In 1949 Centel built a new telephone exchange building in Park Ridge and Des Plaines, Illinois, to house new dial automatic and automatic toll ticketing equipment. By 1950 customers could directly dial over 1.6 million telephones in the greater Chicago area.

Today Centel's executive offices and headquarters for its telephone, electric, cable television, business systems, and supply operations are at O'Hare Plaza, 5725 North East River Road, Chicago.

Robert P. Reuss, chairman and chief executive officer of Centel Corporation.

William G. Mitchell, president of Centel.

customer lines in Florida, Illinois, Iowa, Minnesota, Missouri, Nevada, North Carolina, Ohio, Texas, and Virginia. The Southern Colorado Power and Western Power (Kansas) Divisions of Centel together service more than 135,500 customers.

As for the future, Centel will push ahead to convert its 365 central telephone offices to digital electronic switching, planning to have 88 percent of these offices digitally equipped by 1990. At the same time, fiber-optic cable is being introduced to reduce dependence on costly copper wires.

The company that "makes connections" also values its longtime connection to the Chicago area. Centel's commitment to Chicago is perhaps best exemplified by the community activities of its two top executives, both Chicago-area natives. Robert P. Reuss, Centel's chief executive officer since 1972, is a native of Aurora, Illinois. He graduated from the University of Illinois with a B.S. in commerce and later earned an M.B.A. from the University of Chicago. Besides his Centel responsibilities he is also a trustee of Rush-Presbyterian-St. Luke's Medical Center

and Blackburn College, a member of the University of Illinois Business Advisory Committee and Citizens Committee, and a member of the Council on the Graduate School of Business at the University of Chicago. William G. Mitchell, Centel president since 1977, is a director of Junior Achievement of Chicago, a director of Knox College, governor of Central Dupage Hospital, a member of the Chicago Association of Commerce and Industry, and serves on the advisory board of the school of management at Northwestern University. He is also a member of the executive committee of the Chicago Area Boy Scouts, and a member of the Chicago Club, Economic Club of Chicago, Commercial Club of Chicago, and the Illinois Cancer Council. Mitchell received his B.A. degree in business from the University of Oklahoma and a J.D. degree from Northwestern University.

Past, present, and future, Centel's success is built on the ability to adapt to changing times. With each transition the firm has emerged a stronger entity, acutely in tune with larger social and technological trends in Chicago and the rest of the country. Throughout its history Centel employees have performed according to the company's original motto, coined by its enterprising founder at the turn of the century: "The McGraw Law is Quality."

CHICAGO ASSOCIATION OF COMMERCE AND INDUSTRY

The Chicago Association of Commerce and Industry, one of the largest and oldest such associations in the United States, was founded in 1904 as the Chicago Commercial Association. But its predecessors existed many decades before, suggesting a strong desire for continuity in the Chicago business community.

The Association's lineage can be traced to several business organizations. There was a Chamber of Commerce (which occupied a new building at Washington and LaSalle streets in August 1865), the Board of Trade (which performed many of the functions of a chamber of commerce in the waning years of the 19th century), and a Merchants and Commercial Travelers Association (dating from 1869).

A Chicago Commercial Association was created on September 30, 1897, but the growing city needed an infusion of new leadership. So a new Chicago Commercial Association—the direct ancestor of the Chicago Association of Commerce and Industry—was established on October 9, 1904, incorporating what remained of the old Merchants and Commercial Travelers Association. Eight hundred people attended its first meeting.

In 1907 the name was changed to the Chicago Association of Commerce, and the organization was known by that title until 1947, when it became the Chicago Association of Commerce and Industry.

The Chicago Association of Commerce and Industry is an organization of business and professional leaders who work together to promote the commercial and industrial growth of metropolitan Chicago and to foster civic improvements that benefit the general welfare of all who live and work in the eight-county area.

The fledgling businessmen's association grew apace. In 1910 alone, membership increased to 3,801 from 1,094. Fifteen committees carried on the Association's work, and upwards of 600 meetings of all kinds were held each year. The Association took strong positions on almost all issues of public importance, ranging from housing, health, and the improvement of city services to immigrant education, military preparedness, and taxation.

By 1918 the Association had 5,805 members, and in 1919 it organized the Chicago Crime Commission, which has made a lasting contribution to the protection of the citizens of Chicago in the ensuing years. The Association played a leading role in the war effort in both World War I and World War II, and it helped to make a success of "A Century of Progress" in 1933 and 1934.

In recent years the Chicago Association of Commerce and Industry has involved itself in the push for more foreign trade in the Chicago region, the drive to maintain the supremacy of the Chicago region's transportation system, and continuing efforts to retain and attract business.

The Association conducts extensive economic research, takes part in public debates on governmental issues, and engages the business community in urban affairs issues such as health costs, arson, and mass transit. The Association offers more than 20 publications and maintains a large, highly skilled support staff of 60 people.

The Chicago Association of Commerce and Industry today represents 1.28 million jobs in an area that has 3.5 million jobs; 4,000 business people serve on its committees. A voluntary, not-for-profit organization, it obtains revenues from membership dues. Its membership now numbers 5,500 in the eight-county metropolitan area. Its headquarters is at 130 South Michigan Avenue.

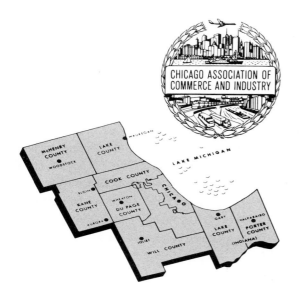

FIRST FEDERAL SAVINGS AND LOAN ASSOCIATION OF CHICAGO

Gerard M. Ungaro (seated), a founder and first general counsel of First Federal, issues the first passbook to Oscar M. Kreutz (standing), who is assisted in filling out the application by his daughter, Mary Ann.

A photograph of the 1941 board of directors taken while discussing policies to guide First Federal Savings and Loan.

The year 1930 was a disastrous one for the U. S. housing industry. Nearly one-fourth of the American labor force was out of work, jobs were needed desperately, yet an industry which historically served as a major generator of jobs—housing construction—was paralyzed by the lack of an adequate source of financing. In a terrible paradox, millions of employed and hard-working Americans were eager to buy new homes, and millions of jobless tradesmen and contractors were willing to build them, but the existing five-year renewable mortgages offered by the old-time "building-and-loan societies" were inadequate to the task of financing a nationwide housing-expansion program. By 1932 foreclosures on such mortgages had reached the point where the federal government had to set up the Home Owner's Loan Corporation to bail out $3 billion worth of short-term mortgages that had gone bad.

The real-estate and construction experts advising President-elect Franklin D. Roosevelt knew that propping up the old-style mortgages could never be more than a stopgap. Even before Roosevelt's inauguration in the spring of 1933, the New Deal's task force in housing was busy designing a new style of "conventional" home mortgage and writing legislation that would put the federal government firmly behind the idea of long-term mortgages to help ordinary Americans buy their homes.

Chicago was at the center of this new concept in home ownership, and so was First Federal Savings, whose founder was the very man who designed the new federal legislation. Morton Bodfish, a professor of real estate at Northwestern University and a member of the original Federal Home Loan Bank Board of 1932-1933 was acknowledged from the start as First Federal's founder and architect of the Federal Home Loan Act. In a modestly phrased letter of November 24, 1933, Bodfish explained his plans to former President Herbert Hoover: "A group of us are planning to launch a 'First Federal Savings and Loan Association of Chicago' as a model institution which we hope will set an example for the establishment of many others similar in character."

Bodfish did just that. First Federal of Chicago was the first savings and loan in the Midwest to receive its federal charter and the fifth in the nation. On January 26, 1934, the first meeting of share subscribers was held at 104 South Michigan, and on February 1 an office was opened at 105 West Madison. On April 17 the first mortgage loan—

$3,000—was issued to Grace B. Severance on a house at 650 Judson in Evanston. As Bodfish predicted, hundreds of other savings and loans across the nation were soon founded on the Chicago "model."

The new savings-and-loan industry did not by itself "cure" the illness the Depression had set off in the housing business. Neither did World War II, when employment boomed but much civilian economic activity, including homebuilding, had to be suspended.

But after the war pent-up demand for housing was unleashed, and so were billions of dollars in war wages that had been piling up in savings-and-loan accounts. Wartime earnings now provided a fund to finance a postwar housing boom. Again First Federal led the way, issuing the first GI loan in the Midwest and the second in the nation. By May 1947 First Federal had made its 1,000th GI loan, and the great suburban housing boom was under way.

In the five decades since its founding, First Federal has become a fixture of the Chicago scene and now is one of the largest savings and loans in the nation. Its chairman, E. Stanley Enlund, is a respected local leader who has served as president and now serves as chairman of the Chicago Association of Commerce and Industry and the DePaul University Board Trustees. Most important, First Federal and the other institutions that followed its daring "model" made it possible for millions of Chicagoans and suburbanites to live in their own homes.

CHICAGO BOARD OF TRADE

The Chicago Board of Trade has been bringing buyers and sellers of commodities together for more than 130 years. Although many commodities other than the grains are bought and sold at the Board today, the exchange was originally founded to establish order out of the chaos that existed in the grain markets prior to 1848.

At harvest time in those days, farmers traveled plank roads to bring their wagonloads of grain across the prairie to Chicago, the heart of the Grain Belt. Once in town the farmer was forced to haul his grain from merchant to merchant until he found a buyer. Because storage facilities were inadequate, the grain could not be protected and held for future sale; therefore farmers were forced to accept whatever price they could get for their crops. At the height of the season, it was not uncommon for thousands of tons of wheat and corn to be towed out into Lake Michigan and dumped. By spring, deliveries could not meet demand and prices would skyrocket. And standard grades and weights were nonexistent.

Early in April 1848, 82 businessmen crowded into the room above Gage and Haines' flour store to form an organization to meet their needs—and the Chicago Board of Trade was born.

They did not want to control prices. Rather, they wanted a single location where buyers and sellers could arrive at a fair price based on current supply and demand factors. And this is exactly how the Board of Trade works today—as a federally designated and self-regulating meeting place for buyers and sellers. The open trading activity acts like a barometer, measuring in prices the constantly changing pressures of supply and demand.

The Board set up uniform grain grades and established inspection systems. Around 1870 futures contracts (standardized, transferrable agreements enforced by the exchange) were introduced to facilitate and complement cash trade and forward contracts (tailored agreements between specific buyers and sellers).

Today the Chicago Board of Trade is the world's largest and oldest futures exchange. Trading volume at the exchange totaled almost 49.1 million futures contracts in 1981, the 12th record year in a row. The Chicago Board of Trade accounts for about half of all the futures contracts traded in the United States.

Users of futures can be classified in two ways: those who wish to minimize risk—the hedgers—and others who make it their business to assume those risks—the speculators.

One of Chicago's landmarks, the cast aluminum statue of Ceres, goddess of the harvest, stands atop the Chicago Board of Trade Building, dominating the LaSalle Street financial district.

The Chicago Board of Trade Building—141 West Jackson Boulevard.

Hedgers include the farmers, producers, grain elevators, food processors, manufacturers, and financial services who hedge in the futures markets to protect against the risk of adverse price movements. Hedging is the buying or selling of futures contracts to offset possible price changes in the cash market.

Along with hedgers, speculators have always played a crucial role in the development of futures trading. By accepting the price risks that producers and processors want to transfer, speculators perform a necessary economic stabilizing function: They allow commercial hedgers to insulate themselves from the price volatility inherent in physical commodities. Although it is a high-risk occupation, professional speculation provides the liquidity that orderly, well-run markets require.

The Board's majestic 45-story building at LaSalle and Jackson dominates LaSalle Street. It stands as a constant reminder that the histories of the Board of Trade and the city are interwoven—both rose from midwestern obscurity to international prominence.

Shortly after the end of the Civil War, the first trans-Atlantic cable revolutionized communications to and from Chicago. A cable could be sent from Chicago to London in the unheard-of time of three hours. And today the exchange is the center of one of the most intricate communications networks in the world, a system that allows price and order information to move between the trading floor and any spot on earth in seconds.

In 1893, during the Columbian Exposition, the Board opened its galleries to the public for the first time. Since then tens of thousands of people have come to its Visitor's Center each year to watch an open and free marketplace in action. In 1930 the exchange moved into its present building. A registered architectural landmark, the imposing structure is one of the finest Art Deco skyscrapers still standing anywhere and is regularly included in architectural tours of the city.

During World War II the government put price controls on grains. There was very little trading activity in the pits until after the war was over. Once the controls were lifted, the Board's worldwide influence resumed and grew steadily during the '50s and into the '60s. Today the Board, which is a nonprofit association, has more than 2,000 full members, associate members, and permit holders.

The first interest rate futures contract in GNMA certificates—mortgage-backed instruments guaranteed by the federal government—began trading in 1975. Its success led to the creation of several innovative financial instruments, including U. S. Treasury bond futures in 1977. The T-bond contract has been so successful that by

According to Alvin Meyer, sculptor for the figures adjacent to the clock on the front of the Board of Trade Building, "The idea ... is to symbolize the birth of wheat and corn. In the center appears an eagle, emblematic of the spirit of America guarding our agricultural interests."

The trading floor at the Chicago Board of Trade.

1981 it was the most active commodity on all U. S. exchanges, with more than 13.9 million contracts traded.

The Board of Trade continues to expand its product line with new investment and risk-management vehicles, including long-term Treasury notes, options on T-bond futures, stock index futures, and energy futures.

All signs indicate the exchange will continue its heritage of growth and innovation in the future. A new, 23-story addition (completed in 1982) contains a 32,000-square-foot trading floor, the largest and most up-to-date futures trading floor in the world.

CHICAGO MERCANTILE EXCHANGE

The Chicago Mercantile Exchange traces its history back to 1874, when the Chicago Produce Exchange was formed by dealers through whose terminals agricultural commodities passed from midwestern farms to eastern consumers. The CPE provided a regular and recognized market for butter, eggs, poultry, and other such agricultural products. At the same time it offered farmers a guaranteed price in advance for their products, giving them the capital to purchase seed, feed, and other necessities.

In 1919, 21 years after the butter-and-egg men had withdrawn to form their own exchange, the Chicago Butter and Egg Board, people recognized the need for futures trading in other commodities. The Chicago Mercantile Exchange was established and trading was opened December 1, 1919; the 45-minute opening session saw three cars of eggs traded.

During those early days and also during World War II, when government price controls were in effect, a CME membership sold for a paltry $100; mere poultry feed compared to November 25, 1980, when a membership was sold for $380,000, a record high for any commodity exchange.

The Chicago Mercantile Exchange trading floor, Lake and LaSalle streets—1921-1928.

Similarly, when the International Monetary Market was started by the CME in 1972, 150 seats were sold to the public at $10,000 and 500 to CME members for a nominal $100 each. The IMM membership record was broken 23 times in 1978 alone, and rose to $280,000 in 1980.

Membership prices were not the only growth areas, of course. Although no precise figures are available, it has been estimated that in the Exchange's first year there were about a dozen clerks, board markers, clearinghouse staff, and secretaries—with weekly average salaries of perhaps $20. By the end of 1981 the staff numbered more than 425 and salaries and benefits totaled $10.9 million.

In 1928 the CME moved into its own building at Franklin and Washington streets, and the occasion was marked by a banquet at which humorist Will Rogers remarked, "I'm not so much concerned about the return *on* my money as I am about the return *of* my money!"

The Merc, as it became known, after much expansion is now building twin 40-story towers flanking a 40,000-square-foot trading floor, with room for further expansion of 30,000 square feet. Occupancy of the site, at Wacker Drive, the Chicago River, and Madison and Monroe streets, is expected to occur in early 1984.

Ironically, butter and eggs, which began the Merc, have faded. No butter futures have been traded since 1976, although there is a brief weekly spot call, and eggs were down to 2,798 contracts in 1980 from their peak of 619,567 in 1973.

Humorist Will Rogers addressed the membership of the Chicago Mercantile Exchange April 25, 1928, at the dedication of the CME building at 110 North Franklin Street.

Substantially contributing to the success of the Merc since 1960 have been futures in frozen pork bellies, live cattle, and live hogs. Although many experts doubted the success of anything as inelegant as pork bellies, after a slow start the market for them increased to the point where 2.25 million contracts were traded in 1980.

Not all of the Merc's contracts have been for edibles. Such diverse commodities as copper, iron, and steel scrap have also been traded in the past, and today financial and currency futures are among the hottest items on the board. The International Monetary Market, which opened May 16, 1972, brought to the financial world the same type of hedging protection against price and yield fluctuations that agriculture and forestry had enjoyed for decades.

It was a particularly well-timed opportunity because international agreements controlling exchange rates were collapsing, replaced by a free-market floating. After a five-year germinating period, currency futures became very popular: In 1980, 4.2 million contracts were traded, with an estimated value of $288.5 billion.

Gold bullion contracts, calling for delivery of 100 troy ounces of .995 fine gold, have also achieved popularity, reaching a record 3.6 million contracts in 1979. But today the fastest-growing segment of the futures industry is financial-instrument futures, which many believe have greater potential than all the agricultural, forest products, and precious metals listings combined.

The U. S. Commodity Futures Trading Commission recently approved futures in the Standard & Poor 500 stock index, three-month certificates of deposit and three-month Eurodollars. Energy futures and futures options are awaiting approval.

The Chicago Mercantile Exchange trading floor soon after its 1928 opening.

The Chicago Mercantile Exchange has played a major role in the growth of Chicago. Along with the Board of Trade and the Mid-America Commodity Exchange, it has captured 75 percent of the nation's futures trading and an even larger percentage of financial futures trading, despite serious attempts at competition by four New York exchanges. Visitors from many other nations have studied Chicago's Mercantile Exchange, either in anticipation of using Chicago futures or to start futures exchanges in their own countries.

Hundreds of millions of dollars, and thousands of jobs, have been channeled into Chicago's economy as a result of the transactions at the Mercantile Exchange. The transactions themselves have not only enabled farmers to prosper, but also corporate treasurers, money managers, gold bullion dealers, and construction and forest products industries, among others.

Due to farsightedness and innovation, the last decade has been kind to the Mercantile Exchange—with volume rising to 24.5 million contracts in 1981, up from 3.3 million in 1970.

Chicago Mercantile Exchange, Washington and Franklin streets—1928-1972.

COMMONWEALTH EDISON COMPANY

The story of Commonwealth Edison Company is the story of electricity helping to shape the future of northern Illinois. It is a story of convincing the public that electricity had great value, of men like George Bliss and Samuel Insull and their dreams of enterprise, and of the growth of a small company into the nation's leading nuclear utility.

Today Commonwealth Edison is an investor-owned organization serving more than 2.9 million customers in 25 counties in an 11,525-square-mile service area—including Chicago and almost 400 other communities in northern Illinois.

Under the leadership of James J. O'Connor, chairman, president, and chief executive officer, in 1981 Edison had 10 fossil and three nuclear plants (with peaking units at nine sites), plans for three new nuclear stations, operating revenues of more than $3.737 billion, and sales totaling 61.2 billion kilowatt hours.

All this came from beginnings in 1868, when George H. Bliss and L.G. Tillotson opened a little electric shop on Clark Street. In the Great Fire of 1871, the shop burned and Bliss forged ahead alone. In 1882 Bliss formed Western Edison Light Company with dreams of expansion and immediate plans to prove electricity would work in

In the early 1900s Commonwealth Edison provided its customers with door-to-door light-bulb service.

downtown Chicago; if it worked there, perhaps citizens would use electricity in their homes. Setting its own example, the company wired its headquarters for 250 electrical lights and installed its own power station. The fledgling firm's determination paid off: On March 28, 1887, a Chicago ordinance gave Western Edison the right to use underground wires and conductors for the transmission of electricity in an area bounded by Lake Michigan, North Avenue, Ashland Avenue, and 39th Street.

The franchise was turned over by Western Edison to the new Chicago Edison Company, which chose as its first service district the area bounded by Harrison, Market, and Water streets and Michigan Avenue. It made its first deliveries in August 1887. The total connected load exceeded 6,000 incandescent lights and grew to 15,000 lights by 1889. To gain new customers, Edison offered the user incandescent lamps for 65 cents each—with replacements provided free of charge.

When Samuel Insull (an associate of Thomas A. Edison) became president of Edison in 1892, he began acquiring rival companies and organizations that had wiring and underground-cable franchises. Since Chicago Edison had only a 25-year franchise and a limited territory, Insull in 1897 incorporated the Commonwealth Electric Light and Power Company; the new firm obtained a 50-year franchise and a larger territory.

In 1898 several promotions were used to attract new customers; for a limited time, the company offered to install six outlets free in unwired residences if the owners would sign a one-year contract for electrical lights. This offer was widely accepted. Other promotions included selling electric fans from the backs of buggies on hot

The first electric shop was opened by the company in 1909 at Michigan Avenue and Jackson Boulevard. The principal appliances were light bulbs, portable lamps, flatirons, and electric fans—a far cry from the quantities of electrical products available today.

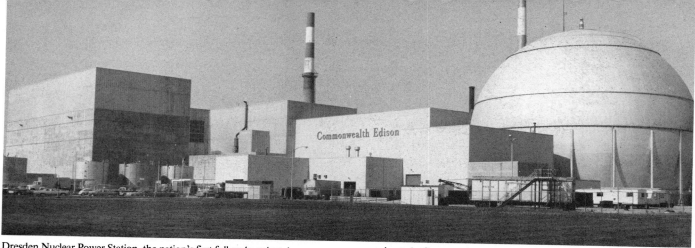

Dresden Nuclear Power Station, the nation's first full-scale, privately financed nuclear power plant, was dedicated on October 12, 1960.

summer days. As a result, electric fans were a great booster for electric light service in private residences—second only to the electric iron. Rates that year started at 10 cents for the first 30 hours, with a minimum monthly bill of one dollar per horsepower. Meters were not installed until 1900.

On September 17, 1907, Chicago Edison and Commonwealth Electric Light and Power Company were formally consolidated to form today's Commonwealth Edison Company.

The turn of the century saw new light-bulb technology with improved filaments; the opening of Fisk Station, the world's first all-steam turbine generating plant; the start of "electric shops" to sell appliances; expansion of service; acquisition of other organizations; and a move to the Edison Building at 72 West Adams Street.

In 1929 the company maximum load exceeded one million kilowatts for the first time, the millionth meter was installed, and the State Line Station was placed in service with the largest unit in the world—a title lasting 25 years.

Serving as board chairmen in the 1930s, Samuel Insull, James Simpson, and Charles Freeman shepherded years of expansion throughout northern Illinois. Consolidation with other organizations culminated in 1953 with a merger with Public Service Company of Northern Illinois. Freeman was followed as chairman by Willis Gale in 1953, J. Harris Ward in 1961, Thomas G. Ayers in 1973, and James J. O'Connor in 1980.

Through the years the company depended on coal, gas, and oil to generate electricity. In 1951 the Atomic Energy Commission invited Commonwealth Edison and other utilities to begin studies on the feasibility of atomic electricity. Edison announced plans in 1955 to build a 180,000-kilowatt-capacity unit. The Dresden Nuclear Power Station (southwest of Chicago) was dedicated on October 12, 1960, becoming the nation's first full-scale,

privately financed nuclear power plant.

Investment in a nuclear future continued in 1972 with the addition of the Quad-Cities Nuclear Power Station. Edison is the majority owner, with a quarter interest belonging to the Iowa-Illinois Gas and Electric Company of Davenport. Zion Nuclear Power Station, north of Chicago, was completed in 1974.

The three facilities give Edison the largest nuclear-generating capacity of any U.S. utility, with about 5.1 million kilowatts. In 1981 this capacity produced 27 billion kilowatt hours, or 45 percent of the company's total electrical generation. Three other nuclear stations are under construction: the LaSalle County Station, Byron in Ogle County, and Braidwood in Grundy County.

The utility's capacity not only benefits Illinois, but other states, as well. Edison is a member of the Mid-American Interpool Network, the largest power-pooling network in the nation. George Bliss and Samuel Insull could not have realized how far their dreams would go.

In 1907 a Chicago Edison Company linesman relied on horsepower to put electrical lines in place.

ESMARK, INC.

Gustavus F. Swift, founder of Swift & Company.

Gustavus F. Swift, the founder of Swift & Company, wouldn't be able to recognize its successor, Esmark, Inc., today. While both firms were associated for decades with the fresh-meats business, Esmark, a holding company formed in 1973, divested Swift Independent Packing Company in 1980. It became a corporation with concentrations in consumer-branded products and industrial and chemical products—but not meat.

The organization's roots can be traced to 1855, when Swift, then 16 years old, borrowed $20 from his father, slaughtered and dressed a heifer, and sold it to families in his Cape Cod, Massachusetts, neighborhood. Between 1855 and 1872 Swift established meat businesses in town after town in Massachusetts, finally expanding to Albany and Buffalo, New York, where cattle were beginning to move in from the West.

In 1875 he moved his cattle-buying operation to Chicago, then known primarily for its pork curing and packing; live cattle were shipped east by rail. It was clear to Swift that he would have to be able to ship dressed cattle in refrigerator cars, but it wasn't until 1880 that he had what he needed to do so—a refrigerator car.

Swift & Company, in need of capital, was incorporated in Illinois on April 1, 1885. As the firm flourished Swift kept moving plants closer to the source of his live-animal supplies: the company's second meat-packing plant was opened in Kansas City in 1887, the third in Omaha in 1891, the fourth in St. Louis in 1892.

Swift died in 1903, leaving his firm in the hands of his seven sons. Its original capital of $20 had grown to $25 million, and the company's sales had become $200 million. Swift's original little red wagon was replaced by large red wagons drawn by horses and then by refrigerated trucks. About 23,000 people worked for Swift & Company at the turn of the century.

The years immediately preceding and following World War I were extremely trying ones for Swift & Company and for the meat industry as a whole. The government was concerned about economic concentration in the industry,

Buying and selling at the busy Union Stock Yards, where live animals were shipped.

and the Packers' Consent Decree of February 27, 1920, was devised to keep meatpackers from moving into other closely aligned businesses.

Swift & Company had already diversified; it had begun processing a wide range of basic human foods, such as poultry, eggs, butter, cheese, lard, shortenings, and margarine. And the livestock operations dealt in feeds and minerals for livestock and poultry, industrial oils, glues and adhesives, wool, and leather goods.

Swift's products began to improve and to grow in number, partly because of the urging of quality by the government—which was true for all packing companies—and partly because of new developments in meat processing and packaging technology. Salty cured ham and heavily smoked bacon were replaced by a whole legion of new specialty meats, reflecting changing consumer tastes.

This meant the development of some of the most famous brand names in America. Swift's Premium meats, including Brown 'N Serve sausage, Swift's Premium Breakfast Strips, Hostess Ham, and Butterball turkeys all became well-known. So did the names of other Swift food products, such as Swiftning shortening, Pard dog food, and, later on, Peter Pan peanut butter.

All of this was reflected in the firm's prosperity. By the time of its centennial, sales had reached $2.4 billion, and the 500 plants that made up its processing, sales, and distribution network employed about 64,000 people.

In spite of this growth nothing could disguise the fact that the meat business was a cyclical one, and not particularly profitable—a packer considered himself lucky to earn a net profit of a penny or two on a sales dollar. So Swift & Company, building on some of the lines of business it had developed, began to branch out in order to earn the best return possible on its shareholders' equity.

By 1971 the organization had become a major international corporation with interests in foods, chemicals, petroleum, and insurance. In fact, domestic fresh meat sales accounted for only 42 percent of Swift's overall sales.

Swift had acquired, among other firms, Vickers Petroleum Corporation (1968), Mobil Oil Corporation's agricultural chemicals operation (1969), and a 51 percent interest in TransOcean Oil, Inc. (1970). In 1973 Esmark, Inc., was formed to be the parent holding company for these units, which included GSI, Inc., an insurance subsidiary (later sold).

Esmark continued to acquire companies in the consumer products field, adding International Playtex, Inc. (1978); and Pemcor, Inc., the maker of the Jensen brand name audio and high-fidelity equipment (1978). Esmark's

Hand weighing and packing bacon the "old-fashioned" way led to the quality reputation of Swift's Premium bacon.

Swift & Company's operation in the Chicago stockyards in 1929.

revenues reached $6.7 billion in 1979, and Swift's portion of that was $2.6 billion, but Esmark president Donald P. Kelly had devised a strategy that was again to change the face of the company.

In 1980 Esmark sold Vickers Energy for $1.1 billion to generate capital growth; Swift Fresh Meats, which is now known as Swift Independent Packing Company, was spun off in 1981. SIPCO is 40 percent owned by Esmark, and its annual sales total more than $2 billion.

What is left is a widely diversified consumer products, chemicals, and high-technology firm. Swift & Company sells processed foods; Estech, Inc., makes agricultural and consumer fertilizers; Eschem, Inc., produces adhesives, coatings, and industrial chemicals; International Playtex sells lingerie, health-care products, and Danskin apparel; STP manufactures automotive products; and International Jensen produces the Jensen line of electronic equipment.

FEDERAL SIGNAL CORPORATION

As America began to "light up," Chicago Edison was generating electrical power far in excess of demand, and it was looking for ways to sell its surplus energy. During this search two Edison employees, John F. Gilchrist and John H. Goehst, applied incandescent lamps to a painted sign, and thereby created the first electrical advertising display. Merchants accepted the idea not only for its advertising value, but also because the illuminated signs provided a measure of safety by brightening the dimly lighted streets of the cities.

Federal Signal Corporation is today a fast-growing, increasingly profitable company headquartered in Oak Brook, Illinois. The products, systems, and services of the firm are manufactured and marketed on a worldwide basis.

During 1981 sales grew to $174 million, and the company again joined Fortune's "Second 500" of publicly held American industrial companies. While Federal was ranked 346th in sales of the "Second 500," it held position 197 in income and 199 in return on equity.

Karl F. Hoenecke is the firm's chairman and president, a position he has held since 1975. Hoenecke and the board of directors of Federal have established long-range goals and objectives, which have resulted in an earnings growth of 39 cents per share in 1975 to $1.62 per share in 1981; the company anticipates good earnings growth for 1982.

The goals and objectives which have brought about this growth are: increase earnings per share by 15 percent each year; pay cash dividends of between 35 and 40 percent of net income; and earn 20 percent return on shareholders' equity (the median return on equity for the Fortune 500 industrial companies was 14.4 percent in 1981).

A strong balance sheet allows Federal Signal the flexibility to grow internally and by acquisition. Since 1975, when the current management took office, significant progress has been made through internal development of various product lines and more important, through acquisition. The major acquisitions of companies include Dayton Progress Corporation of Dayton, Ohio, a manufacturer of die components for the metal-stamping industry; Bassett Rotary Tool Company of Monticello, Indiana, a manufacturer of carbide cutting tools; Emergency One, Inc., of Ocala, Florida, a manufacturer of aluminum-bodied fire and rescue vehicles; Ace Drill Corporation of Adrian, Michigan, a manufacturer of high-speed steel and carbide twist drills; and State Sign Service of Houston, Texas. Federal Signal has also sold several operations that did not fit into the overall corporate strategy.

The firm now has three distinct business segments, which are operated as separate business units—each with its own management staff.

The Signal Group is the nation's leading supplier of warning and signal products, including vehicle lights and sirens, horns, bells, and speakers. Fifty percent of the Signal Group's sales in 1981 were for municipal applications such as police, fire, ambulances, and rescue vehicles. The rest of the market was industrial, which included warning systems for chemical plants, nuclear power plants, grain elevators, warehouses, and transportation terminals. Its Emergency One subsidiary is

This 110-foot all-aluminum aerial ladder, the tallest made in the United States, was designed and manufactured by Emergency One, Federal Signal's 1979 acquisition, and now the leading manufacturer of aluminum-bodied fire trucks. Federal Signal is proud to be a supplier of Emergency One fire trucks to the city of Chicago.

Long since replaced by a section of the Dan Ryan Expressway, this plant at 8700 South State Street was built in 1920 to house Federal's principal manufacturing operation. From this facility, Federal expanded its sign design and sign construction capabilities with neon and fluorescent tubes, as well as contributing greatly to the World War II effort by supplying air raid warning systems, signals, and sirens.

the leading manufacturer in the United States of aluminum-bodied fire trucks; the Autocall division designs, produces, and sells custom fire-alarm systems for commercial buildings, apartment complexes, schools, hotels, manufacturing plants, and hospitals; the Security Products division manufactures and markets parking control systems, safety-security systems, bridge gates, and a new microcomputer-controlled parking gate system. The Signal Group's products are marketed on a worldwide basis, with particular emphasis on Canada, Europe, the Middle East, and Latin America.

The Sign Group, the seed from which the company has flourished, is a leading manufacturer of custom-made illuminated and non-illuminated signs. Federal offers complete design, manufacture, installation, and maintenance capabilities. Products include a full range of electronic signs that show time, temperature, and changeable messages. Revenues are derived from outright sales, lease sales, and maintenance services.

The three companies comprising the Tool Group (Dayton Progress, Bassett Rotary Tool, and Ace Drill) were all acquired after 1975, and account for 22 percent of total corporate sales. Dayton's primary products are piercing punches, die matrixes, and retainers, which are sold worldwide. Bassett manufactures a variety of carbide cutting tools, including end mills, burs, drills, and countersinks. Ace Drill manufactures industrial-grade twist drills, which complement Dayton's and Bassett's product lines.

Gilchrist and Goehst founded Federal Electric in 1901; through the years, the firm grew into a corporation which has survived wars, depressions, and social changes.

A statement in the August 1, 1925, issue of the *Federalist,* the company house organ, provides a portrait of Federal Signal Corporation today, "We should aim for what is highest in service to our customers, in square dealing, in the standard of our goods, and cordial, fair relations with our competitors. No really big institution can afford to do anything else. Our business prospects at the present time are brighter than they have ever been"

That statement is as true today as when first made in 1925.

THE FIRST NATIONAL BANK OF CHICAGO

The history of The First National Bank of Chicago is bound inextricably with the growth of Chicago as a marketplace. When the doors of "The First" opened in 1863, Chicago was beginning to prosper. The population was 150,000 and economic activity had been heightened by the demands of the Civil War; but the state of Illinois was floundering for lack of capital to enhance its position on the new frontier.

The city limits were 39th Street and Fullerton and Western avenues. Railroads, not yet across the Mississippi, ran south and east from Chicago, increasing demand for wartime supplies. Public transportation facilities consisted of three systems of horse-drawn streetcar lines on unpaved streets.

In February 1863 President Lincoln signed the bill that permitted "national banks" to exist along with the familiar state-chartered institutions. That summer a group of 10 enterprising investors, led by Edmund Aiken (a 51-year-old private banker), raised $100,000 to open the bank. Included in the group were a 32-year-old distiller named Samuel Nickerson (who later led the bank for many years), a packer, a grain trader, a member of the Chicago Board of Trade, and other investors.

The bank's first location was in Edmund Aiken's office at No. 22 LaSalle Street (now, approximately 210 North LaSalle), but it quickly outgrew these quarters and moved to the southwest corner of Clark and Lake streets; the location has been changed five times in its history, as growth has exceeded space. Today First National is the oldest, largest national bank operating under its original

name and charter.

Only 18 months after opening its doors, the board of directors voted to increase the capital stock to one million dollars, the limit provided in the bank's articles of association.

With an eye toward expansion of overcrowded quarters, in 1868 the bank completed a fireproof building of iron, stone, and brick at State and Washington streets. Three years later the Great Fire swept through Chicago and destroyed the concept of an invulnerable new building, although the safes and vaults withstood the tremendous heat of the flames. (The young cashier who discovered the books and money intact was Lyman Gage, who later became president of the bank and then resigned to serve as Secretary of the Treasury in McKinley's Cabinet.) Three months later The First was able to reoccupy its quarters. As Chicago rebuilt, the bank acted in partnership with the many businesses intent upon helping the city rise from the ashes.

In 1882 The First adopted the policy of declaring quarterly dividends, and also opened the women's banking department—designed to help women entering a male bastion of daily business transactions feel more comfortable. One year later the interiors were lighted with electricity for the first time.

At the turn of the century, the rapidly expanding American economy created an unprecedented demand for credit. To meet this demand The First and The Union

The foreign exchange department of the bank is one of the oldest in the country, dating back to the 1870s.

Lyman Gage, the young cashier who found the books and papers of the company intact after the fire, later became the bank's president and then Secretary of the Treasury in the McKinley Cabinet.

National Bank, veterans in Chicago's financial world, merged. With this acquisition, the assets of The First went from $56 million to $76 million. In the spring of 1902 the bank again increased its resources by absorbing The Metropolitan National Bank, and thereby raised its assets to $100 million.

Recognizing the need for trust and savings services to the community, the bank organized The First Trust and Savings Bank, a separate corporation. In 1903 more than 1,000 savings accounts (totaling in excess of $3 million) were opened during the first seven business days. At the end of 1904 it had more than 10,000 depositors, whose balances totaled nearly $18 million.

That same year James Forgan, the bank's president, initiated a basic change in the method of conducting The First National's business—the specialization of loan activity on industry lines. The tradition of a banker who is also an expert in the interests and activities of his or her customers continues today.

When World War I broke out, American commercial banks bought Liberty Bonds and made substantial loans to customers—for purchase of government securities that financed the wartime expenditures of the United States and her allies. The bonds were selling slowly in Chicago until 1917, when The First National and The First Trust and Savings Bank turned in subscriptions aggregating more than $22 million. Some $10 million represented purchases of the banks on their own accounts, and the remainder was the result of an extensive selling campaign by Forgan.

Progress during the early and middle 1920s was steady. Early in 1928 The Union Trust Company merged with The First Trust, and everyone looked optimistically to the future. But, as the year developed, uneasiness filled the financial community. The savings department witnessed a steady succession of large withdrawals, particularly for the purchase of securities. During the Depression that followed the stock market crash in 1929, more than 11,000 banks throughout the country failed.

Fortunately for shareholders and savings depositors, The First did not suffer the disaster of others. Even in the depths of the Depression, the bank paid interest on savings deposits. When the Foreman State Banks succumbed to financial pressures early in 1931, its assets were taken over and the deposit liabilities were assumed by The First.

Franklin D. Roosevelt was inaugurated as President on March 4, 1933, using the memorable quote, "The only thing we have to fear is fear itself." The next day, a Sunday, he called a special session of Congress and proclaimed a national bank holiday. On the following Monday morning all banks were closed, a condition that

Three months after the Great Chicago Fire, The First National Bank of Chicago was able to move back into its building and act in partnership with the many businesses working to rebuild.

President James Forgan (in top hat) stood on call in the lobby of the bank to talk with customers or employees (1900s).

continued throughout that week.

The new administration's program for reopening the banks made it obvious that Federal Reserve member banks, such as The First National Bank of Chicago, would enjoy distinct advantages over non-member banks, such as The First Union Trust and Savings Bank. As a consequence, the business of The First Union Trust was transferred to The First National Bank of Chicago.

The bank's assets reached one billion dollars in 1938. Anticipating war, and recalling that costs had skyrocketed during World War I, Americans rushed to buy at the prevailing prices. Industrial production and attendant loan demand accelerated.

Business for the bank grew rapidly because of the war. It had required 75 years to amass assets of one billion dollars; that amount was duplicated in the next six years. In the beginning of the '40s, annual earnings had hovered at $5 million. They were half again as great before the war ended.

In 1944 Edward Eagle Brown, then president of The First, was invited by President Roosevelt as the only American banker to serve at the United Nations Monetary and Finance Conference at Bretton Woods, which led to the creation of the World Bank and the International Monetary Fund.

During the '50s and '60s, the corporation continued to build its reputation as a pioneer in industry specialization

Edward Eagle Brown, president of the bank from 1934 to 1959, was the American banker chosen to participate in the Bretton Woods Conference of 1944, which resulted in the creation of the International Monetary Fund and the International Bank.

The clock that kept time for thousands of passersby on the old bank building was saved and restored (1953).

loans, and experienced a period of remarkable growth and expansion. Its assets more than doubled, and loans grew almost fourfold as the bank aggressively sought to meet the expanding credit needs of the economy in general and its customers in particular.

The opening of the St. Lawrence Seaway in 1959 prompted The First to open a London office, which improved its service to foreign correspondent banks and customers engaged in international trade. A Far East office was opened in Tokyo in 1962 and overseas expansion continued in the '60s and '70s under the leadership of chairmen Homer Livingston, Gaylord Freeman, and A. Robert Abboud, culminating in 1976 with 80 branches, offices, and affiliates operating in 37 countries. Expansion of the global network was highlighted in 1979 when the bank received permission to establish a representative office in Beijing (Peking)—and thus became the first U.S. bank to open an office in the People's Republic of China. This international network incorporated five Edge Act offices operating in the United States.

First Chicago, under chairman Homer Livingston, expressed its confidence in Chicago's future in 1969 when it completed a 60-story headquarters and adjacent one-acre plaza in the center of the Loop. The commitment was made when the central business district was on the downturn, and many doomsayers were predicting that Chicago would lose its commercial life blood as suburban malls attracted affluent buyers. This same year the bank was made a wholly owned subsidiary of First Chicago Corporation, a one-bank holding company.

The new skyscraper was followed in late 1970 by a 30-story annex. By 1973 the multilevel plaza was completed,

The First National Bank of Chicago and its plaza, with the old clock from the previous building restored.

together with a personal banking pavilion, restaurant and shops, a 500-seat auditorium, and underground parking. The multimillion-dollar complex was a major factor in the subsequent and ongoing revitalization of Chicago's central business district.

Changing economic conditions in the 1970s placed a premium on professionalism and rapid response to customer needs. The First adjusted to these changes by offering new services and products to both retail and corporate customers, and by adding eight regional offices to facilitate service to customers throughout the United States. The outstanding achievement of the bank during that period was its growth in assets, as it continued to service customers around the world and maintains its position as one of the 10 largest banks in the country—with the greatest number of savings depositors in one location.

As retail business for The First continued to grow,

additional facilities were established in Chicago at Michigan and Chicago avenues and at the corner of Wabash Avenue and Monroe Street. Cash Station, a network of automated teller machines shared with other banks and savings and loans, was opened in 1979. Gold and silver passbook accounts, enabling customers to buy gold or silver without taking possession of the metal, were offered. The First Chicago VISA bank card system became one of the largest and most efficient in the country.

In the 1980s the banking industry faces the prospect of rapid changes in technology and in the laws and regulations governing the structure of the bank industry and other financial institutions. Against this challenging backdrop of innovative technology and expanding markets, the present chairman, Barry F. Sullivan, has placed a new emphasis on strategic planning and The First has reorganized itself to meet its strategic goals. Its essence statement expresses a threefold goal for the decade—to be a world-class, money-center bank with national and international reach, to be the premier bank serving the Midwest, and to be the leader in bringing banking services to the Chicago community.

GOULD INC.

Gould Inc. is well-known in the business world as an organization that has achieved outstanding growth over the past 15 years.

In 1967 it was a $100-million battery company employing 4,500 people. In 1982 it employed eight times as many people and sales had increased 2,000 percent. Today this $2-billion corporation has been transformed into a purely electronics and electrical products firm with predicted earnings growth of 15 percent per year.

Gould's transformation from battery manufacturing to electronics has been the result of aggressive asset redeployment under the direction of William T. Ylvisaker, who has served as Gould's chairman and chief executive officer since 1967. Under his leadership, Gould has pursued a strategy of corporate growth focusing on product development, new technologies, and human resources.

Gould National Batteries, Inc., the predecessor of today's Gould Inc., was established in 1910 as a distributor of electrical accessories and automobile batteries. Through a program of acquisitions over the ensuing years, the firm achieved a major position in the automobile and industrial battery market.

The year 1969 was a watershed one for Gould. It had already acquired a series of small companies in the electric heat, sub-fractional electric motors, and instrument fields.

William T. Ylvisaker, chairman of the board and chief executive officer, brought to the company a management philosophy of quality, creativity, scientific leadership, and continuing education.

In 1969 Gould acquired Clevite Corporation, then doing about $190 million in sales.

That same year, to reflect the company's growth into newer interrelated technologies—electronics, electrochemistry, electromechanics, and metallurgy—its name was changed to Gould Inc.

The acquisition of Clevite Corporation was a natural fit for Gould's strategy for growth. Clevite's bearing, brushing, and rubber-metal products were fully compatible with Gould's piston, piston ring, and sleeve business. Clevite also had growing instrument, electronic, and ordnance systems capabilities that matched well with the four interrelated technologies concept that Gould had set in motion for its growth strategy, both internal and external.

Gould's earlier acquisitions had included a small electronics operation and a sonar capability. It laid the groundwork for the corporation's subsequent growth in the test and measurement marketplace as well as in defense systems.

In 1974 Gould entered the field of transducers and quickly earned leadership positions in two areas of electronic sensing and monitoring—first in medical instrumentation and second in factory automation.

Another major step in Gould's growth came in 1976, when Gould Inc. and I-T-E Imperial Corporation agreed to merge. I-T-E was a manufacturer of equipment for the transmission, distribution, conversion, and control of electrical energy and of components to convey, connect, and control fluid energy.

Also in 1976 Gould achieved, and, in fact, surpassed the billion-dollar sales market. And that year Gould moved its corporate headquarters from Minneapolis to Rolling Meadows, a suburb northwest of Chicago.

Gould entered the programmable controller market in 1977, when it acquired what was then a small enterprise

Original art work abounds at Gould Center, the corporate headquarters of Gould Inc. A Henry Moore sculpture, "Large Two Forms," was dedicated in December 1978. (Photo courtesy of Archie Lieberman.)

named Modicon—now Gould's highly successful Modicon Programmable Control Division. Between 1977 and 1981 Modicon's revenues have grown from $12 million to $140 million.

Gould's growth strategy paid off handsomely. From 1967 to 1979 net sales increased at an average annual rate of 17.9 percent, net earnings at an average rate of 21.3 percent, and earnings per share at 12.5 percent. While that strategy was successful in terms of growth, Gould also recognized the importance of examining that strategy, testing its appropriateness for the decade of the 1980s.

At the beginning of the 1980s, Gould's business segments were electronics, electrical products, battery, and industrial.

The company moved boldly in 1980 to take advantage of the growth potential of its electronics businesses even though sales and earnings were significantly affected by inflation and recession. The timing was judged to be right to move into rapid-growth, higher-risk segments of the electronics business. This meant combining the best in technology with the most profitable opportunities in terms of margins.

The thrust of the new strategy was an aggressive deployment of assets to increase returns on investments through a series of selective acquisitions and divestitures and through internal growth. As part of this strategy, Gould decided to divest its Industrial Group and to concentrate investments in more closely related electronics businesses. Having achieved a highly profitable base of closely related electronics businesses, Gould is now focusing on six specific areas for future growth: high-performance minicomputers, factory automation, test and measurement, medical instrumentation, defense systems, and electronic components and materials.

In the electrical products areas, Gould is involved in four areas: distribution and circuit protection, industrial

Gould Center is more of a community than an office complex. Original art works, a lagoon, a private club, two 10-story towers, a management and education center, and a research and development center are nestled in a 58-acre tract in Chicago's suburban Rolling Meadows. (Photo courtesy of Archie Lieberman.)

controls, electric motors, and batteries.

Gould acquired American Microsystems, Inc. (AMI), in 1982. AMI is the world's largest commercial manufacturer of custom metal-oxide-silicon/very-large-scale integrated (MOS/VLSI) circuits used in a variety of electronics data processing telecommunications and consumer products.

The AMI merger, completed in February 1982, achieved for Gould its goal of having a strategically and technologically integrated group of core electronics businesses and products.

Gould's pattern of corporate growth—its transition from a $100-million battery company to a $2-billion electronics and electrical product developer and manufacturer with more than 100 manufacturing and research and development facilities throughout the world—took 15 years. During that period, the firm employed various strategies to achieve its growth—strategies that have been disciplined, that have made the maximum use of assets, and that have permitted maximization of profits.

Gould's strategy for the 1980s will focus on internal growth in its six electronics market areas. Each of these technology markets is witnessing rapid growth. Already Gould is a leader in most of the product areas in which it participates.

Mr. Ylvisaker has said, "Clearly, Gould is well-positioned for the 1980s. We are in the right markets with the right products and we have the best management team in Gould's history—one that is committed to the achievement of our stated goals."

W.W. GRAINGER, INC.

A graduate electrical engineer, motor designer, and motor salesman, William W. Grainger recognized the need for a wholesale electric motor distribution organization. In 1927, to serve this need, Grainger established a business at 700 West Cermak Road in Chicago. For a short time he and his sister, Margaret, worked alone, although two employees soon joined the young firm. Sales were generated principally through mail orders, using an eight-page catalog called the *MotorBook*. William and Margaret Grainger initially received, filled, and shipped the orders themselves.

When Grainger incorporated his business in 1928, his timing was impeccable. Factories, which had operated with a single motor powering entire lines of operations, were converting to individual motors for each station; and cities across the United States were converting from DC to AC current. Every change meant new motors were needed. The firm sold so many motors during this period that, at least on one occasion, it had to buy motors from a national retailer to fill customer orders.

By 1933 business had expanded to such an extent that Grainger established the first branch—a step that was to be the basic foundation of future growth. The *MotorBook,* the branches, and the territory salesmen provided the combination that has brought the company to its present leadership position.

Now a wholesale distributor of more than 9,600 products, W.W. Grainger, Inc., is headquartered in north suburban Skokie. In 1981 the company's sales exceeded $867 million, and it earned more than $56 million—both record figures. Sales that year represented approximately 7.8 million transactions, averaging $111 each, and were made to about 716,000 customers.

Grainger's operations are divided into two parts: distribution and manufacturing. The distribution group is a nationwide distributor of electric motors and motor controls, gear motors, fans, blowers, liquid pumps, air compressors, air tools and paint-spraying equipment, hydraulic equipment, and power transmission components, as well as the many other items shown in the *MotorBook*. The manufacturing group produces a substantial portion of the electric motors sold by the distribution group; it also makes other equipment, including bench grinders, sump pumps, speed reducers, gearmotors, air compressors, and fans.

The distribution group general offices and part of the central warehouse complex occupy this facility of about 900,000 square feet in Niles, 12 miles from downtown Chicago.

William W. Grainger, photographed in the late 1930s in front of company headquarters, then at 819 West Congress Street.

The *MotorBook* is published semiannually, has more than 1,000 pages, and offers nearly 10,000 products. (A 1931 *MotorBook* offered factory-rebuilt Hoover cleaners for $19.85 each, a quarter-inch General Electric-powered drill for $14.95, a gas-engine lawn mower attachment for $63.75, and electric motors including a standard 1/4-horsepower motor selling for $6.99 each in lots of 10.)

New items are added to the company's product line on the basis of product and market research as well as recommendations of employees, customers, and vendors. Before inclusion in the *MotorBook,* new products must satisfy many rigid requirements. The firm's engineering laboratory runs thousands of evaluation and quality control tests each year. The *MotorBook* lists all items offered by the company, along with extensive technical and application data. It is considered by many who rely on the publication as the "bible" of the industry.

To serve customers rapidly and efficiently, Grainger has 165 branches in 46 states, with more planned for the future. The firm has direct contact with 99 percent of its customers over the counter at its branches, by telephone, or by calls by one of Grainger's 525 salesmen at the customers' places of business. While the company has no facilities outside the United States, it sells products to customers in more than 20 other countries.

Products under the Dayton name have been important to the organization. Grainger estimates that 70 percent of its 1981 sales consisted of items bearing its registered trademarks: DAYTON (principally electric motors, fans, and heaters), DOERR (electric motors), TEEL (liquid pumps), DEMCO (v-belts), DEM-KOTE (spray paints), and SPEEDAIRE (air compressors). The remaining 30 percent is derived from sales of other well-recognized national brands.

W.W. Grainger, Inc., became a public company in 1967, and its stock was traded in the over-the-counter market until it was listed on the Midwest Stock Exchange in 1968 with the ticker symbol of GWW. In 1971 it was also listed on the American Stock Exchange, and in 1975 Grainger was listed on the New York Stock Exchange. The company's stock is now traded on the New York and Midwest stock exchanges.

The company never has had an unprofitable year, and only during three years—1932, 1938, and 1943—have sales fallen below those of the previous year. Grainger reached its first million dollars in net sales in 1937. The $100-million level was passed in 1968.

The firm is aided in its overall efficiency through a modern data-processing system. Advanced installations at the corporate and manufacturing headquarters are used extensively for inventory control, order processing, production scheduling, requirements planning, accounts receivable, and other accounting, engineering, production, and management purposes.

William W. Grainger retired from the board of directors in 1981. The firm is currently headed by his son, David W. Grainger, who is chairman of the board and president.

The company has grown because it has paid attention to its customers—distributors, dealers, contractors, service firms, industrial and commercial maintenance departments, and original-equipment manufacturers. Grainger looks forward to the future with the sense of a job well done in the past, and the knowledge that it can and will continue to serve its customers with speed, integrity, and fairness.

Since the first Grainger *MotorBook* was published in 1927, more than 56 million copies have been printed and distributed.

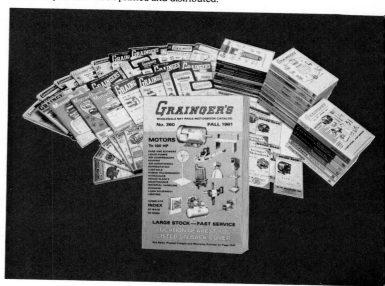

THE EDWARD GRAY CORPORATION

The Edward Gray Corporation, one of the nation's leading industrial contractors, was founded in 1926 as the Chicago Concrete Breaking Company; it assumed its current name in 1957. The organization is comprised of three divisions: construction, plant maintenance, and precision blasting.

The construction division has an outstanding record of meeting the special needs of heavy industry in new-plant construction, existing-plant expansion and renovation, and the installation of basic industrial, processing, and environmental protection equipment. Many of its projects have required performance under extremely demanding circumstances. The company regularly pours concrete foundations and sets heavy machinery or structural steel in tight physical situations—in steel plants operating at full capacity, during sub-zero weather, in pits dug 30 feet under the water table, in operating plants with minimum overhead and lateral clearances, and on rail facilities with operating schedules that cannot be interrupted. The firm prides itself on its highly successful performance record on tightly scheduled round-the-clock jobs during plant shutdown periods "when every hour counts." Its well-earned motto, "Wanted a hard job," is displayed on hard hats worn by all field personnel.

The corporation's experience in construction has allowed it to develop exceptional competence in providing a full range of plant maintenance and repair services—with crews on call around the clock. Gray's ability to provide reliable and experienced crews on short notice is built on generations of service to basic manufacturing, processing, refining, and power production industries. Well over 90 percent of its maintenance business consists of established customers.

The breaking and removal of concrete, rock, slag, and other hard materials have been part of Gray's business since its founding. It has been in the precision blasting field since the early 1930s, when the company first began to use small, precisely calculated charges of dynamite in furnace cleaning and other routine maintenance of industrial equipment. Today the firm has an international reputation in this area, having drawn assignments from as far away as India and Turkey.

Gray has long since established the utility and safety of precision blasting in situtations where multimillion-dollar installations are mere inches from the blasting site, and in hostile environments where high temperatures or inflammable gases complicate the job.

Melvin Gray, president and a son of the founder, believes The Edward Gray Corporation has flourished because, "Gray is a company that takes pride in its outstanding reputation for reliability and integrity. We believe these qualities are central to our success because, unlike many contractors that are project-oriented, Gray is customer-oriented. We see our mission as service to our customers. They are the primary source of our future business."

This special capacity for continuing customer relationships based on reliable service distinguishes The Edward Gray Corporation from others in the construction field.

Recent coke battery construction for a Chicago-area steel mill.

The Edward Gray Corporation's equipment fleet, circa 1930.

LINDBERG CORPORATION

Axel N. Lindberg, born into one of the metal-working families that had already made Sweden famous for its high-quality tool steels, emigrated to the United States in 1895 at the age of 20. Family records say he arrived at Ellis Island bearing only his train fare plus 15 cents.

His penury proved to be of little consequence. Lindberg had his skills and a determination to use them. He first went to work for a manufacturer of laundry machines in Chicago, as an apprentice machinist and odd-job man, then joined another company as a blacksmith. Here he learned the technique not only of forging tools, but of hardening them by heat. The learning process was a long one because the heat-treating specialists of that era guarded their knowledge jealously, passing it on to their successors only after subjecting them to a long and wearying apprenticeship. Twenty-seven years after his arrival here, at the age of 47, Lindberg, assisted by his son LeRoy, finally went into business for himself, paying a month's rent for the rear second floor at 413 North Carpenter Street and purchasing four furnaces, quenching tanks, benches, a desk, a typewriter, and a sign that read "Lindberg Steel Treating Company."

From that modest beginning in 1922, the company has grown to its position of prominence through a series of well-planned commercial heat-treating and manufacturing expansion programs, first in Chicago, then in other areas of the United States, and finally in Brazil and Canada.

Lindberg Corporation (the name was changed in 1967), through its 21 domestic and two international heat-treating plants, offers a broad range of essential metallurgical processes and technical services to the metal-using and metal-working industries. It is the largest commercial heat-treating firm in the world.

The firm also owns and operates Cleveland Alloy Castings and Hy-Temp Industries, which cast and fabricate high-alloy, heat-resistant consumable products used inside industrial heat-treating furnaces. Alloy Wire Belt Company of San Jose, California, was added in June 1980. This plant produces round-wire and flat-wire conveyor belts for the food-processing, building insulation, glass, and heat-treating industries. In February 1981 the company purchased Harris Metals with headquarters in Racine, Wisconsin, and additional plants in Webster City, Iowa, and Cookeville, Tennessee. They produce intricate precision aluminum and special alloy steel castings plus aluminum and zinc die castings. In addition, Harris Metals is also in the commercial heat-treating business.

Lindberg Corporation became publicly owned in 1959. Its headquarters, which is still in Chicago, contains the corporate office, finance and control center, and the technology center.

Axel N. Lindberg at the furnace, circa 1922.

IC INDUSTRIES

A widely diversified international corporation with 1981 revenues of $4.2 billion, IC Industries, Inc., had its beginning more than 130 years ago as a land-grant railroad whose purpose was to foster the growth of the fledging state of Illinois.

It was an auspicious beginning. Completion of the Illinois Central Railroad's first 705 miles of track in 1856 made it the longest railroad in the world. Such an undertaking would not have been possible without a land grant from the federal government. With support from Senator Stephen A. Douglas and Representative Abraham Lincoln, the U.S. Congress approved the grant in 1850. This land was to play an important part in the future growth of the railroad.

The Illinois General Assembly approved the ICRR charter a year later and a group of eastern businessmen began the search for capital needed to finance the new railroad. Even with considerable financing from Europe, the strain on the railroad's backers was tremendous. The route cost $25 million to build, rather than the original estimate of $17 million. It united the entire state in a large "Y" extending from Chicago and Galena in the northern corners to Cairo in the south.

Early in its history the railroad established a cooperative relationship with the young and ambitious city of Chicago. At the request of the city fathers, the line changed its plans to enter the city from the west and instead agreed to construct a mile-long trestle and enter along the lakefront.

The Illinois Central Railroad constructed a trestle in Lake Michigan for its entry into Chicago in 1852, which served as a breakwater against lakefront erosion and was the origin of involvement by IC Industries in the development of the central city.

CHICAGO: CENTER FOR ENTERPRISE

The trestle, completed in 1852, achieved an important civic goal—halting the erosion of land by the wave action of Lake Michigan. Through the years the railroad acquired land in Chicago's "front yard" that it would later develop when its freight operations were relocated outside the central city. Part of this land eventually became Illinois Center, the nation's largest downtown mixed-use development.

The Illinois Central carried both passengers and freight, and one of its goals was to assist the industrial and agricultural development of the state by providing reliable transportation. The railroad, made prosperous by the growth of Illinois and by heavy use during the Civil War, began to look westward and southward.

The Illinois Central operated on more than 400 miles of track in Iowa by 1870, and reached Council Bluffs by 1899. Its main line reached New Orleans in 1882 and the IC became the "Mainline of Mid-America."

In the 1870s and 1880s the Illinois Central's heavy freight operations in farm produce characterized it as a granger road. But by the turn of the century manufactured goods, forest products, and raw materials made up the bulk of its volume, with a consequent decline in agricultural tonnage. Intercity and suburban passenger traffic became important, though freight revenues were three times those of passenger revenues. In 1893 the IC operated 220 trains a day from downtown Chicago to the site of the Columbian Exposition in Jackson Park.

The years from 1883 to 1909 are considered to be the golden age of the Illinois Central Railroad. In this 26-year span the IC's mileage more than doubled and its annual revenues quadrupled. With more than 5,000 miles in its route system by 1900, it was one of the nation's largest railroads.

Illinois Center, the nation's largest downtown mixed-use development, is rising on land once used as Illinois Central Railroad freight yards in Chicago. The Center is providing new offices, homes, hotel accommodations, and shopping between Michigan Avenue and the lakefront south of Wacker Drive.

While the 1920s were prosperous (the IC system expanded to 6,721 miles by 1929), the trend to greater importance of freight traffic was apparent. Passenger revenues accounted for only 13.3 percent of total revenues the year the Great Depression began. The company kept up with the times, however, by electrifying its 47 miles of suburban commuter routes, starting in 1926. And in 1936 the Green Diamond, the Illinois Central's first diesel-powered passenger train, went into service covering the 294 miles from Chicago to St. Louis in 295 minutes.

At mid-century the IC was a strong and profitable link in the nation's rail system, but its directors and management foresaw only limited opportunities for growth in an atmosphere of stifling governmental regulation. Planning was initiated to create a corporate structure that could maintain ownership of the railroad while diversifying into other activities.

In May 1962 the stockholders of the Illinois Central Railroad Company approved the organization of the Illinois Central Industries, Inc., a holding company whose purpose was to seek diversification into non-rail fields. (The name formally became IC Industries in 1975.) Four years later, on the retirement of Wayne A. Johnston, who had been the railroad's president for 21 years, William B. Johnson became president. He was to be the chief architect of IC Industries' phenomenal expansion. In 1966 Johnson stated four goals for IC Industries: to modernize the Illinois Central Railroad, to complete a sound rail merger, to develop the company's valuable real estate holdings, and to diversify into business less capital and labor intensive than railroading.

In a 1972 merger with the Gulf, Mobile & Ohio Railroad, the Illinois Central became the Illinois Central Gulf with service through 12 states from Chicago to the Gulf of Mexico.

Jetway, the world's leading producer of aircraft passenger loading bridges, is a division of Abex Corporation, which became an IC Industries company in 1968.

A 1972 addition to the IC Industries family of companies, Midas International Corporation now has more than 1,500 franchised automotive service shops worldwide.

Locomotives were acquired, new track laid, piggyback service instituted, and a computer-communications system installed with $270 million invested in railroad improvements between 1965 and 1969. A merger with the Gulf, Mobile & Ohio Railroad, a 2,734-mile system running through the Midwest from Chicago to Mobile, was finalized in August 1972. The result was formation of

Pepsi-Cola General Bottlers, Inc., of Chicago, acquired by IC Industries in 1970, serves major markets in eight midwestern states.

the Illinois Central Gulf Railroad, with 20,000 employees, 1,000 locomotives, and 60,000 freight cars. It became a billion-dollar-a-year operation and today is the nation's 10th largest railroad with 7,000 route miles in 12 states.

The Illinois Central Railroad has long been a factor in the development of real estate in downtown Chicago. Because of the original downtown location of its freight yards and terminals, it acquired prime land along the lakefront south of the Chicago River. In the 1920s a plan was devised to develop "air rights" over continuing railroad uses, allowing construction of streets and other public facilities over railroad operations.

But the first structure on IC property wasn't built until 1955. It was the Prudential Building at Randolph Street near Michigan Avenue, which for a decade was Chicago's tallest building. But that was just the beginning of what became known as a mixed-use development—a combination of office, residential, hotel, and commercial development in the same area.

The result is Illinois Center, a $2-billion project on the lakefront to the east of Chicago's Loop. Rising on 83 acres of land no longer needed for railroad operations, the complex is planned to accommodate a working population of 80,000, some 15,000 residents, 16.8 million square feet of office space, and 5,500 hotel rooms. With its system of multi-level streets, covered walkways, shopping corridors, and landscaped plazas, Illinois Center has become a model of progressive urban design.

Old El Paso Mexican food is one of several market-leading brands produced by Pet Incorporated, an IC Industries company since 1978.

Hussman Corporation, which joined IC Industries as a unit of Pet Incorporated, is a world leader in food-store merchandisers and other environmental-control equipment.

IC Industries' initial acquisitions outside its original line of business were in the field of industrial products. In 1965 it purchased Chandeysson Electric Company, a rebuilder of heavy electrical equipment, and in 1968 it bought Waukesha Foundry Company, Inc.

But the landmark acquisition in this area was that of the Abex Corporation, now a billion-dollar manufacturer of automotive products, specialty castings, fluid power equipment, and railroad products. Commenting on the Abex purchase several years after its 1968 consummation, Johnson said, "The Abex merger thus transformed IC Industries overnight from essentially a midwestern railroad into a truly multinational company."

By the end of 1969 IC Industries was firmly established in transportation, real estate, and commercial products. But Johnson wanted a "fourth leg" for the company's foundation—consumer products. In February 1970 IC Industries bought Pepsi-Cola General Bottlers, Inc., of Chicago, a Pepsi bottler and distributor now serving major markets in eight midwestern states. In later years the company acquired Dad's Root Beer Company and Bubble Up Company, Inc.

Seeking to expand its activities in the consumer products field, the firm purchased Midas International Corporation, the system of franchised automotive service shops in 1972. Today Midas has more than 1,600 shops around the world.

The commercial product lines were strengthened by adding new companies under the Abex banner. Signal Stat Corporation, a maker of automotive lighting equipment and safety devices for trucks and cars, was added in 1971; A.L. Hansen Manufacturing Company, which supplies truck hardware, came aboard in 1974; and Stanray Corporation, a railroad supply and fluid power products firm, joined in 1977.

These organizations are just a few that became Abex

divisions. Others manufacture hydraulic pumps, hydraulic equipment for aircraft and space vehicles, Jetway airline passenger loading bridges, and pneumatic control valves and cylinders.

IC Industries is strong in packaged foods, the result of its acquisition of Pet Incorporated in 1978. With annual sales approaching $1.5 billion, Pet brings to consumers dairy products, Old El Paso Mexican foods, Pet-Ritz and Downyflake frozen foods, and Whitman's confections. The Wm. Underwood Co., famous for its "Red Devil" brand of meat spreads, was acquired in 1982.

The firm's consumer product lines are rounded out by the Hussmann Corporation. Hussmann is a world leader in food-store merchandisers, walk-in coolers, energy management systems, and ice storage equipment, as well as environmental-control products for industrial applications.

By 1981 IC Industries sales had grown fourteenfold and the net income had increased nearly sixfold compared to 1967, the year before the corporation launched its program of diversification.

IC Industries, with deep historic roots, is still a relatively young company. From its origin as a regional railroad, the firm has expanded to provide products and services to virtually every nation in the Free World.

And its goal remains—"Growth by design."

ILLINOIS BELL AND ITS BELL SYSTEM PARTNERS

The telephone came to Chicago in May 1877, just a year after Alexander Graham Bell made his first successful call in Boston. Gardiner Greene Hubbard came to the Windy City with six instruments he intended to promote. His demonstrations of simple telephones so much interested Chicagoans that on June 26, 1878, the first Bell office was opened there. The Chicago Telephonic Exchange published its first directory in October 1878. There were 291 listings. In December of that year the Bell Telephone company of Illinois was incorporated.

From the very beginning it was clear to the early pioneers that expanding and improving telephone service would have to be a partnership operation. One company could not do it all—research, engineer, market, install, and provide service. So other businesses were included.

Even before Bell had demonstrated the telephone, the Western Electric Company had come to Chicago. It moved from Cleveland in 1869 to be closer to the telegraphic heart of the country. By 1872 it was a thriving manufacturer of electrical equipment. In 1881 the American Bell Telephone Company (forerunner of AT&T) acquired controlling interest in Western Electric and converted it into the primary supplier of compatible telephone equipment. By 1882 it had built its first telephone for the infant system, a magneto set in an oak case, and the Bell System partnership was a functioning reality.

Long-distance calling figured importantly in telephone planning, engineering, and service goals from the start. The first "long-distance" call from Chicago was made in 1881 between downtown and Geneva, Illinois. In 1885 AT&T was formed to be the long-distance subsidiary of American Bell. Its task was to build lines which would connect telephone exchanges scattered throughout the country.

In 1892 the first major interstate line was opened— between Chicago and New York. Alexander Graham Bell himself made the first call. Thus, another of the Bell partners took its place in the growth of Chicago as a telecommunications center. In 1899 American Bell and AT&T became one company under the AT&T name. The name AT&T Long Lines was first used to designate the interstate and overseas organization in 1907.

While all this was happening, telephone service in Chicago burgeoned. Western Electric expanded its manufacturing potential when it moved into the Hawthorne Works in Cicero in 1904. There were about 30,000 telephones in the city by then.

But there was continuing need to send not just spoken but printed words over wire. By 1900 several inventors were attempting to replace the dots and dashes of Morse code with word-messages. In 1907 a Chicago mechanical engineer, Charles Krum, was financed in his efforts by Joy Morton of the Morton Salt Company and the Morkrum Company—named for Morton and Krum—to perfect such a system. By the next year an experimental model to send printed words by wire was tested over railroad wires between Chicago and Bloomington.

Illinois Bell and AT&T Long Lines people share the job of operating the Network Management Center in Chicago, which keeps long-distance traffic within the state moving smoothly.

In 1901 company wagons transported representatives to the neighborhoods and towns in which they solicited new subscribers for the Chicago Telephone Company, predecessor to Illinois Bell. Cost of telephone service was one dollar per month.

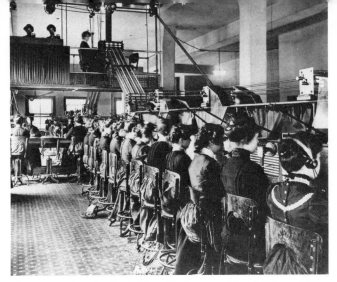

Operators at the toll-call switchboard in the main office of Chicago, 1902, where early operators were young boys.

Advanced Mobile Phone Service, a revolutionary new system tested by consumers in Chicago, allows placing and receiving calls from cars as easily as from home or business. The service should be available in many major U.S. cities by the mid-1980s.

Manufactured by Western Electric, one-half-inch lightguide cable with up to 144 glass fibers can carry 50,000 simultaneous conversations.

Within a decade the company had its own Chicago plant and in 1928 became known as the Teletype Corporation. (There were more than 600,000 telephones in the city by then.) In 1930 Teletype was purchased by AT&T to become a wholly owned subsidiary of Western Electric and later established its headquarters in suburban Skokie in the late 1950s.

Technical progress was being made on other fronts, too. In 1913 the high-vacuum tube was manufactured at Western Electric. In 1916 came the condenser microphone; the radio telephone for airplanes followed in 1917. In 1919 Western gave the desk telephone its first dial and demonstrated the first public address system at a Library Loan drive. In 1925 Bell Laboratories was formed to concentrate exclusively on research. Scientists of the Laboratories have won seven Nobel Prizes for their pure research ... three for invention of the transistor.

During World War II Western Electric produced the communications gear vital to victory and created the most advanced radar systems. The Bell System established microwave radio relay service for phone messages and network TV in 1950. In 1960 it opened the world's first electronic switching system. (Close to two million telephones were in Chicago by then.) In 1966 the Bell Labs Indian Hill facilities were established in suburban Naperville as a design and development center for electronic switching. The engineers, scientists, and technicians there apply their specialized knowledge in electrical engineering, computer science, and other high technology to building and improving the world's largest and most versatile computer, the nationwide telecommunications network. By 1980 there were 2,734,837 telephones in the portion of Illinois served by Illinois Bell.

In the 1980s the Bell Partners in Chicago face major changes in corporate structure. As a result of regulatory and judicial decisions, the Bell System will form a separate subsidiary to market all communications equipment and divest itself of all its telephone companies like Illinois Bell. This change positions both companies to participate in a new era of communications. This is now the Information Age and the Bell System and Illinois Bell are engaged in the electronic communication of a wide variety of information in a wide variety of ways. The telecommunications industry in Chicago is now the competitive business of information handling—not just voices or printed words. It has become the knowledge business. The future for the Bell System and Illinois Bell in Chicago can no more be predicted for the 1980s than it could have been for the 1880s when Gardiner Greene Hubbard arrived with his six demonstration phones.

ILLINOIS TOOL WORKS INC.

WANTED
to invest in
a growing manufacturing business
requiring additional capital

On December 9, 1911, this advertisement in a financial journal led to the creation of an innovative, quality-oriented, multinational company that registered more than $450 million in operating revenues in 1981: Illinois Tool Works Inc., known as ITW.

The advertisement was placed by Byron L. Smith on behalf of his son, whom he described as a person of "ample means, an industrious young man of high character and excellent financial connections, with business experience." The elder Smith's wish was to be the financial man behind a promising manufacturing business in or near Chicago.

The original ad now is framed and hanging on the wall of ITW's corporate headquarters at 8501 West Higgins Road, Chicago. This seven-dollar ad investment was the seed money for a company which had grown by the early 1980s to operators in 16 countries and 6,800 people, with about 4,500 of them in the United States.

Throughout its history ITW has been committed to quality and innovation in all its products, from its beginnings in precision metal-cutting tools to a company which today produces and markets specially engineered products and systems in five business segments:

Product engineering underlies the success of ITW's Hi-Cone carrier, which is the leader for multi-packaging cans in the brewery and soft drink industries.

engineered fasteners and components, packaging products, electronic products and components, precision tools and gearing, and instruments and systems.

Under the direction of Silas S. Cathcart, chairman; Harold Byron Smith, Jr., chairman of the executive committee; and John D. Nichols, president and chief executive officer, ITW today is a Fortune 500 company and has consistently scored high in other Fortune rankings. This success also is due in large part to Harold Byron Smith, an ITW director, who led the organization for 35 years, serving as president, chairman, and chief executive officer.

At the beginning of the 1980s, metal-cutting tools accounted for only some 10 percent of the firm's business, a contrast to 1911 when the need for precision metal-cutting tools spurred four Rockford plant workers to answer the ad placed in the financial journal.

Frank W. England, a tool and die maker; Carl G. Olson, a mechanic; Paul B. Goddard, a salesman; and Oscar T. Hegg, an inspector, convinced Byron Smith of their abilities and the need for hobs and milling cutters made with greater precision than ever before. In March 1912 the four Rockford men and Clyde Fiddick, a bookkeeper, each anted up $1,000 and Smith contributed $10,000 to launch the partnership.

ITW's first home was in a 40-foot by 100-foot loft in a building at Huron and Franklin streets. By 1913 the fledgling enterprise employed 30 people and had outgrown

In 1911 Byron L. Smith spent $7.14 on an ad in a financial journal that led to the creation of Illinois Tool Works Inc., known as ITW. The original ad is framed in the ITW board room.

its quarters, moving to the St. Clair Building at 154 East Erie Street, the first of several moves for the ever-growing company.

Byron L. Smith died in 1914, too soon to see the partnership become a corporation on April 29, 1915. Its first directors were Harold C. Smith, Walter B. Smith, and Bruce D. Smith, Byron's sons; Paul B. Goddard; and Frank W. England. Harold C. Smith was the firm's first president and treasurer.

In the years prior to and including World War I, there was a great need for the precision and quality offered by ITW. With the end of World War I and its military needs, ITW began a period of readjustment and searched for new products to extend the growth of the metal-cutting tool business. This new product development paid off in 1923 with a patented twisted-tooth lock washer known as a Shakeproof fastener, which moved ITW to leadership in an entirely new and promising industry: the manufacture and sale of engineered metal fasteners.

During the early 1930s the firm continued to search for new products and markets, especially as the Shakeproof products were continually improved. Harold Byron Smith, Harold C. Smith's son, joined ITW in 1931, becoming president in October 1936 upon his father's death.

Essential to a program of growth and expansion at the conclusion of World War II, the ITW business philosophy combined sound financial management with an emphasis on creative engineering and new product development. To accomplish this desired growth, ITW began to diversify product lines and decentralize the organization into relatively autonomous divisions or profit centers.

In the early 1960s ITW introduced the plastic multi-pack can carrier system which virtually revolutionized the multi-packaging industry and today still finds Hi-Cone carriers filling needs in the soft drink, food, brewing, juice, medical, and petroleum markets. The ITW of today features highly engineered fasteners, components for mass-assembly industries, lines of metal-cutting tools, computerized gear-checking instruments, specialty gears, electronic keyboards and keyswitches, adhesives and sealants, film capacitors, specialty switches, polymer thick film circuits, and disposable medical products.

ITW's products have changed since the days when the founders were searching for improved ways to make metal-cutting tools. The diversity of the company's products, technologies, and markets has extended its activities worldwide.

But one item has not changed at ITW—the belief in quality and innovation. That's as true today as it was some 70 years ago.

One of the original ITW manufacturing sites was at the corner of Erie and St. Clair streets in Chicago, modest beginnings that have led to a multinational corporation.

ITW gear-measuring equipment checks the accuracy of gears for a variety of industrial uses. Precision and quality have always been emphasized at ITW.

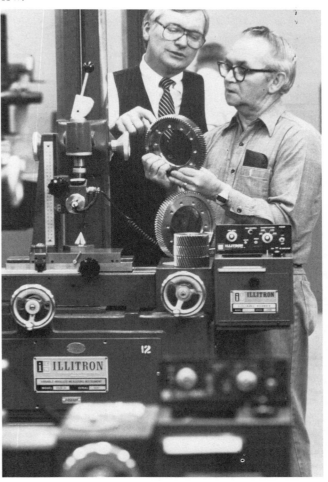

INTERNATIONAL MINERALS & CHEMICAL CORPORATION

Fertilizers to grow more grain ... animal health and nutrition products to increase poultry and livestock production ... chemicals and industrial materials for a broad range of worldwide markets. ... International Minerals & Chemical Corporation (IMC) has grown from a pick-and-shovel miner of Tennessee phosphates to a $2-billion global business serving the basic needs of millions of people every working day.

It began in 1909 as the International Agricultural Corporation (IAC), when Thomas Meadows, a pioneer in the fledgling U.S. phosphate mining business, sought to give American farmers the same inexpensive fertilizers that had helped European countries to achieve dramatic increases in food output.

Meadows and an Austrian, Waldemar Schmidtmann, started IAC with several tracts of phosphate-bearing land in Tennessee and a collection of small mines and fertilizer plants, planning to add potash to their product list as business grew.

That expansion came with the acquisition of a German potash operation but, in 1910, German government restrictions prohibited adequate exports to support the young enterprise. Faced with the cyclical problems that have confronted the fertilizer industry from time to time throughout its history, the partners struggled to expand despite low prices and meager profits.

However, in 1929, the company developed a revolutionary flotation process that achieved dramatic increases in phosphate mining efficiencies. That feat gave IAC new life during the depths of the Depression and provided the impetus for rapid and more profitable growth until 1939, when the firm became the nation's leading producer of phosphate rock and began mining potash at its new operation near Carlsbad, New Mexico.

Another equally historic engineering feat in the early 1960s would propel the company into a leadership position in potash, the second basic fertilizer raw material, when IMC overcame previously impossible underground mining problems to open the world's richest potash deposit in Saskatchewan, Canada.

Meanwhile, the company had changed its name to International Minerals & Chemical Corporation and made a number of other advances under a new leader, Louis Ware, who emphasized research and guided the growing business into new markets.

The Ware era brought new, giant mining machines to Florida; modern techniques in underground mining of potash; and development of new management techniques, utilizing computerized distribution systems and innovative marketing programs keyed to a changing business world.

Those strides were continued under subsequent administrations by Nelson C. White, who brought a mining background to the position of president and chairman of the board, and Richard A. Lenon, who has served as chief executive officer since 1971 and chairman since 1977.

The organization's expansion into new areas of business continued throughout the years following World War II. Overseas fertilizer markets were opened, and IMC's entry into major industrial and chemical markets was accelerated with the acquisition of Continental Ore Corporation in 1968, Sobin Chemicals in 1973, and Commercial Solvents Corporation in 1975.

The Canadian Prairie is the setting for International Minerals & Chemical Corporation's two Saskatchewan potash mines. IMC produces about 8 percent of the world's output of potash through its two Canadian mines and a third facility near Carlsbad, New Mexico.

Early miners of phosphate rock used picks, shovels, and wheelbarrows to remove the basic fertilizer raw material from shallow pits in Tennessee and Florida.

Today's IMC encompasses a global network of over 10,000 employees operating some 200 plants and offices, with corporate headquarters in Northbrook, Illinois, a Chicago suburb.

The $5 million in first-year sales has grown to nearly $2 billion, with earnings coming from four major business areas ... fertilizer, animal products, industry, and chemicals.

IMC continues its traditional involvement with agriculture as the world's largest private enterprise producer of two of the basic fertilizer raw materials, phosphate and potash, and as a manufacturer of the third, nitrogen.

In animal products, IMC is the nation's largest manufacturer of phosphate feed ingredients for livestock and poultry, and a leading supplier of potassium and other animal feed supplements. RALGRO®, IMC's growth-promoting implant for beef cattle and feedlot lambs, has captured the leading share of this important and growing market in the United States and overseas.

IMC also is a leading producer of certain basic and specialty chemicals. Principal products include nitroparaffins and their derivatives, industrial minerals, and a variety of other specialty products for a broad range of consumer and commercial markets.

The firm's industrial business includes nine mines and 18 plants, located principally in North America. It supplies

A giant dragline, capable of holding a one-car garage, has become a symbol of today's modern phosphate rock mining industry. IMC accounts for about 10 percent of the total world rock capacity.

20 basic industrial products for 15 major industries worldwide, ranging from steel and foundries to oil well drilling and metallurgical businesses.

IMC also continues to expand in the energy field as exploration, development, and acquisition efforts have strengthened its position in natural gas and oil. In Florida, the company extracts uranium oxide from phosphoric acid for use as nuclear fuel in electric utilities.

Together, the IMC of the 1980s retains the dedication of its founder as a reliable source of products for agriculture, but has expanded in response to new opportunities in related fields.

Built around a solid foundation from holdings of in-the-ground natural resources, the company promises to remain close to those industries which will be called upon to feed, shelter, and serve tomorrow's world.

Corporate headquarters of International Minerals & Chemical Corporation is this modern brick office complex in Northbrook, Illinois, a suburb of Chicago.

FRED. S. JAMES & CO. INC.

The precise age of Fred. S. James & Co. Inc. has been the subject of some conjecture. It can be calculated from 1858, when Alfred James established an agency on old Courthouse Square, or from 1872, when Alfred's younger brother Fred incorporated and gave the agency his name when Alfred left town for opportunities in Milwaukee. Either way, Fred. S. James & Co. Inc. emerges as one of Chicago's oldest businesses still carrying on the same basic activities under the same name—James.

Alfred James established his insurance agency after serving two years as an employee of the Home Insurance Company. His reputation for hard work and inventiveness soon brought more carriers to his agency. So did Chicago's booming business community, with its need for support services of all kinds. There were already 100,000 people in the city in 1858, with more immigrants arriving on every train to take up work in the city's mills, manufacturing plants, warehouses, stores, and railroad yards.

By 1864 Alfred James needed assistance and Fred, age 14, joined his brother in July as an office boy and immediately began learning the intricacies of the insurance business. Within a few years he was, as events shortly proved, fully capable of operating it himself.

In 1864 Fred. S. James joined the firm that would later bear his name.

One of those events was the Great Fire of 1871, which destroyed virtually every house and all business from as far north as Fullerton Avenue and as far west as Halsted Street. Among the casualties were many insurance companies. Alfred and Fred worked patiently with the policyholders to adjust their losses as best they could, gaining in the space of weeks the kind of valuable experience that would have taken years to accumulate under normal circumstances. When, in the summer of 1872, Alfred left to join the Northwestern National Insurance Company of Milwaukee (of which he ultimately became president), Fred continued the agency as Fred. S. James & Co. Inc., using a period after "Fred" to show that his full Christian name was Frederick.

By 1879 Fred. S. James & Co. Inc. was representing seven insurance carriers, and business at the firm was expanding almost geometrically as post-fire Chicago embarked on one of the most vigorous periods of expansion in its history. It would be a mistake, however, to characterize the growth as an inevitable response to Chicago's own business expansion; many insurance agencies came and went during that period, and numerous firms founded with noble intentions later came to grief during recessions or lost their identities through merger. Fred. S. James & Co. survived to become one of the giants in its field.

One reason is the continuity and competence of the company's management. In 1887 James took on George W. Blossom, a 33-year-old Iowa native, as his partner. Already known as a dynamic and original fire insurance executive, Blossom contributed his experience and his offspring as well. His son, George W. Blossom, Jr., later joined the firm and rose to become president. All together, three generations of the Blossom family have served as

Fred. S. James & Co. headquarters in the new Insurance Exchange Building, 1916.

The Alfred James establishment on the old Courthouse Square, 1865.

managing officers at James. In its more than a century of history, the firm has had only seven chief executive officers, affording clients a level of managerial continuity almost extinct in the modern business world.

The company has nevertheless shown itself to be innovative, a characteristic not always found in the conservative insurance business. As early as 1900, James pioneered the hiring of teams of engineers to furnish expert evaluations of the hazards threatening policyholders and of reducing those risks. "That seems stale now—everybody does it," said honorary chairman Arthur M. Jens, Jr., "But we were the first."

The firm's emphasis on technical talent to support its underwriters proliferated. As early as 1902 the company expanded from its specialty, fire insurance, and added suretyship to its services. In 1904 an eastern office opened in New York; in 1907 a new partner, Sam Crawford, began bringing packing-house and grain-elevator insurance to the Chicago headquarters. In 1908 the New York office offered marine insurance, and in 1913 the Chicago office followed. Each new line of service brought the need for additional support technicians, and set a strong precedent for future growth.

World War I brought expansion. A San Francisco office was opened in 1918, and other branches were added during the business boom of the 1920s. James became the first U.S. contract underwriter for Lloyds insuring automobiles. The Great Depression found the company strong, and World War II and the postwar economic boom added further growth.

But a challenge lay on the horizon. As the 1960s progressed, a technological explosion rumbled through the western democracies. Supertankers, jumbo jets, nuclear power plants, offshore drilling rigs, massive new factories, and giant merchandizing chains had to be insured against loss and liability. Demands for medical insurance, pensions, and workers' compensation followed. Such risks had to be brokered among syndicates, and to assemble such syndicates, expert brokers, backed by scientific advisors, were required. The super-insurance brokerage had to be invented.

James became such a company by sale of stock to the public, enabling it to acquire the necessary technical experts by hiring them or acquiring their firms.

The strategy proved successful. At a time when many esteemed old insurance houses disappeared, James set forth on profitable sustained growth. As 1981 ended, Arthur M. Jens, Jr., summed it up: "In 1969 our total revenues were $13.5 million, net profits $700,000, with about 400 employees. In 1981 we had revenues of $242 million, earnings of almost $20 million, and nearly 5,000 employees worldwide. We're among the top five or six insurance brokers in the world," said Jens, who retired in 1975. In the ensuing five years, Charles A. O'Malley, chairman, and William E. Burch, president, guided James through its greatest growth in the company's history.

KLEFSTAD ENGINEERING CO., INC.

A concept that changed how commercial and industrial buildings were to be constructed and financed arrived in Chicago in 1922 in the form of a Norwegian immigrant. Sivert Klefstad was 20 years old, alone, but ambitious.

Klefstad completed his education in night school while working days. In 1937 he earned his Illinois structural engineer's license and founded a company to erect steel. In spite of the Depression years and impending World War, Klefstad had a broader vision. He closed his first firm in 1939 and "paid off every dime of his $7,000 debt within six months" to establish Klefstad Engineering Company, an Illinois proprietorship.

Until that time, building services were fragmented, with a client having to deal with separate architects, engineers, and builders. Klefstad set out to establish integrated construction, with one firm accepting responsibility for all stages.

Throughout World War II the firm was kept busy with the construction of defense plants. Because of his expertise, the draft board repeatedly deferred Klefstad. By the end of the war, he was down to number 10 on the list.

The postwar years saw scarcity in raw materials, steel, and qualified men. Then came the construction boom, and the Klefstad idea came to fruition: one-stop shopping for commercial and industrial concerns.

Through his company, new or expanding businesses could gain site selection, plant layout, labor market analysis, design, engineering, construction, and even financial arrangements. As the pioneer of the comprehensive construction package, Klefstad often served as entrepreneur, providing guidance and helping to finance a fledgling business.

It is a source of continuing pride to Klefstad that several Chicago concerns began with shirt-sleeve discussions of what kind of physical plant was needed to bring an idea or product to market. And always the facility was purpose-designed. Klefstad never believed in prefabrication or set plans.

As the prime developer of industrial parks, the firm has played a major role in the growth and economic stabilization of a dozen Chicago suburbs. Upgrading farm or vacant land, Klefstad Engineering created light manufacturing and warehousing operations to increase employment and broaden the tax base. It proved that these companies could be housed in functional and cost-effective buildings that were also attractive.

The company has developed industrial parks for Bensenville, Broadview, Harwood Heights, Melrose Park, Northlake, Palatine, Schiller Park, and Wood Dale.

Klefstad is Chicago's oldest packager of commercial and industrial buildings. Since 1939 the family-owned and -operated business has built or made additions to some 600 structures which include plants, offices, warehouses, apartments, nursing homes, shopping centers, truck terminals, and water treatment facilities.

The scope of construction projects ranges from a 4,000-square-foot storage unit to an ultra-sanitary bakery which extends a quarter-mile from receiving dock to shipping doors. The facility also houses administration and a modern research laboratory.

The largest single Klefstad building, measuring 560,000 square feet, was occupied by JCPenney near Milwaukee. With some 14 acres under one roof, it was the biggest single-story building in Wisconsin. Utilizing super-automation, the plant vastly improved the warehousing operation of this major retailer.

Sivert Klefstad, founder and chairman of the board of Klefstad Companies, Inc.

While a Klefstad building has never been "cheap," the construction has always been quality and the designers have planned for future expansion. As the business grows, so does the plant. These two factors have led to a great deal of repeat business; one Chicago-area firm has specified Klefstad a dozen times for its building needs.

Klefstad provides a "turnkey building" with the exception of furniture. And through the concept of total responsibility for the construction, clients realize great cost savings and are also able to take possession of a factory or warehouse as quickly as possible. In response to demand for its comprehensive services, Klefstad has grown from the founder working in his home to three operating subsidiary corporations under Klefstad Companies, Inc. This parent organization also serves as the holding company for income-producing real estate and vacant land held for future development.

Klefstad Engineering Co., Inc., incorporated in 1957, continues to design, engineer, and build under the leadership of Stanley Klefstad, a son of the founder. The firm has a separate operating division, Herlehy Excavating, which fulfills excavating contracts for Klefstad and some outside business projects.

Kent Klefstad, another son of the founder, has established Klefstad Arizona Builders as a general contractor and developer in Phoenix.

Byness, Inc., the third Illinois firm, designs, builds, and maintains heating and air conditioning systems for Klefstad projects and several independent customers.

The son of Stanley and the grandson of Sivert, Steven Klefstad serves as property manager, helping to oversee three million square feet which is rented to 80 commercial and industrial tenants in Illinois and Wisconsin.

From the Chicago office of Klefstad, the fourth since its founding, some 50 full-time employees and field crews plan, build, and operate a variety of commercial and industrial ventures. In the future, Klefstad anticipates more office and warehouse projects and some renovation of existing buildings.

Since its inception, the Klefstad Engineering Co., Inc., has earned a name for quality workmanship, personal dependability, and value for the construction dollar. Three generations of the Klefstad family look forward to extending that reputation.

Stanley Klefstad, president and chief executive officer of Klefstad Companies, Inc.

KRAFT, INC.

National Dairy Products Corporation was founded in 1923 by pharmacist Thomas H. McInnerney to meld independent dairy operations through financial, production, and marketing management. Until his vision helped create a national industry, milk had been bought from local dealers—often ladled from farm cans brought to the front door by horse-drawn wagons.

In 1923 McInnerney had acquired Hydrox Corporation of Chicago and Rieck-McJunkin Dairy of Pittsburgh, then added major dairies in New York and Philadelphia in 1925. Operating companies in Milwaukee, Cleveland, and on the East Coast were purchased over the next few years. In 1930 National Dairy acquired its most famous operating entity, the Kraft-Phenix Cheese Corporation. Annual net sales were boosted to $375 million with the merger.

James L. Kraft, born in 1874 near Fort Erie, Ontario, began his reputation for quality food products as a cheese wholesaler in Chicago. With total assets of $65, which he used to rent a wagon and a horse named Paddy, Kraft began business in 1903. He bought a load of cheese each morning at the South Water Street Market, which he then sold to retail grocers in the city.

James L. Kraft, founder of Kraft Foods Company.

After adding the full-time help of his four brothers, Kraft incorporated in 1909. A line of 31 cheese varieties packaged by Kraft was available in American cities by 1914. A technological breakthrough, which was patented in 1916, was the pasteurization, blending, and packaging of cheese in tins. The process assured uniform taste and quality that could be preserved without refrigeration. Six million pounds were consumed by World War I soldiers.

As the firm was expanding through growth and acquisitions, it made an early commitment to the individual consumer. Kraft Kitchens were established and the first home economist was hired in 1924. The Kitchens have developed numerous products and have generated thousands of recipes for "good food and good food ideas."

Perfection of the five-pound loaf of foil-wrapped cheese was so successful that within one month of introduction, 15,000 of the now-classic rectangular wooden boxes were being produced each day.

The year 1929 marked the beginning of hard times for many; it proved to be the start of a new era for Kraft. With more than 50 subsidiaries and operations including Canada, Australia, England, and Holland, the "Kraft" brand name was established throughout the world. And it was the largest cheese company in this country.

Following National Dairy's acquisition of Kraft in 1930, the introduction of products bearing the "Kraft" trademark continued. The milk/ice cream portion of the business was strengthened with the 1935 introduction of the Sealtest System of Laboratory Protection, which ensured quality control with uniformity of all fluid milk and dairy products.

Continued growth was assured through the development of new products and their introduction to the

Kraft's former nine-story general office in downtown Chicago overlooking Lake Michigan. It was completed in 1938 and sold in 1982.

A variety of Kraft's retail products.

consumer through innovative advertising. James L. Kraft
pioneered the use of various media from the start of his
business. As early as 1911 he had utilized outdoor
billboards, mailed circulars to retail grocers, and advertised
on Chicago elevated trains.

The firm underwrote the first food advertisement in a
consumer magazine and helped create the mechanism of
color magazine ads that appeared nationally. It sponsored
the ''Kraft Musical Revue,'' later changed to the ''Kraft
Music Hall,'' beginning in 1933, and helped make names
such as Jolson, Whiteman, Crosby, and Dorsey household
celebrities. The caliber of entertainment reflected the
quality of new generations of Kraft products: Miracle Whip
salad dressing, Kraft French dressing, Velveeta pasteurized
process cheese spread, Kraft macaroni and cheese dinner,
Parkay margarine, and Kraft caramels.

During World War II Kraft products went G.I.—
government issue. In 1943 half of all its cheese production
was purchased for military troops. Following the war, Kraft
made substantial investments in a new medium—
television—to introduce sliced process cheese and Cheez
Whiz process cheese spread, as families enjoyed ''Kraft
Television Theatre.'' The series set audience and studio
production records that still stand.

Kraft has been recognized by the National Academy of
Television Arts and Sciences for promoting child health
and disseminating nutrition information. The company
won the Gold Leaf Award from the Food Marketing
Institute and *Family Circle* magazine for excellence in
communicating health-related information.

And today Kraft continues its long-standing policy that
its commercials do not appear on television shows labeled
with ''mature audience, parental discretion advised,'' or
whose story line involves excessive shock, sex, or
violence.

The two-pound Parkay light spread is one of Kraft's newer products.

In 1952 Thomas H. McInnerney, president and
chairman emeritus, died at age 85. The business he
founded, National Dairy, had annual sales of more than
one billion dollars that year. James L. Kraft died the
following year, after observing the 50th anniversary of the
company he had founded in Chicago.

Kraft merged into National Dairy in 1957 as the Kraft
Foods Division. In 1969 the name was changed to Kraftco
Corporation and, then in 1976, to Kraft, Inc. The
modification of the corporate title was intended to
emphasize food processing as the firm's primary business
and to identify the whole organization with one of the best
known and most widely respected trademarks in the world.
Within a year it was on its way to becoming the only major
food organization serving as both a manufacturer and
distributor to the food-service industry.

The corporation now offers thousands of processed,
packaged food products for individual consumers, retail
grocers, food-service, and industrial customers—with
annual sales of more than seven billion dollars in 1981.

From corporate headquarters in suburban Glenview,
Kraft (a wholly owned subsidiary of Dart & Kraft, Inc.,
since 1980) continues to fulfill consumer expectations for
quality with the best value possible.

CHICAGO'S
CORPORATE HISTORIES
CONTINUE ON PAGE 489 OF
VOLUME II